*The Decolonized Eye*

# THE DECOLONIZED EYE

*Filipino American Art and Performance*

SARITA ECHAVEZ SEE

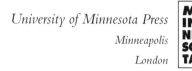

*University of Minnesota Press*
*Minneapolis*
*London*

The University of Minnesota Press gratefully acknowledges financial assistance provided for the publication of this book from the Office of the Vice President for Research at the University of Michigan.

All royalties earned from the sale of this book will be donated to the Filipino American Coalition for Environmental Solidarity, http://www.facessolidarity.org. FACES works in solidarity with communities in the United States and in the Philippines for transnational environmental justice through advocacy, education, service, and organizing.

In chapter 3, material from the DVDs *Hella Pinoy* and *Badass Madapaka* and from the CDs *Badly Browned* and *Husky Boy* is used with permission from Rex Navarrete. In chapter 4, material from the play *House/Boy* is used with permission from Nicky Paraiso.

Lyrics in chapter 4 from "Something Wonderful" by Richard Rodgers and Oscar Hammerstein II copyright 1951 by Richard Rodgers and Oscar Hammerstein II. Copyright renewed. Williamson Music, owner of publication and allied rights throughout the world. International copyright secured. All rights reserved. Reprinted with permission.

Published by the University of Minnesota Press
111 Third Avenue South, Suite 290
Minneapolis, MN 55401-2520
http://www.upress.umn.edu

Library of Congress Cataloging-in-Publication Data

See, Sarita Echavez.
   The decolonized eye : Filipino American art and performance / Sarita Echavez See.
       p.    cm.
   Includes bibliographical references and index.
   ISBN 978-0-8166-5318-8 (hc : alk. paper) — ISBN 978-0-8166-5319-5 (pb : alk. paper)
   1. Filipino American arts.   2. Postcolonialism and the arts—United States.   I. Title.
   II. Title: Filipino American art and performance.
   NX512.3.F55S44 2009
   700.9'045—dc22

                                                                                                    2009028218

Printed in the United States of America on acid-free paper

The University of Minnesota is an equal-opportunity educator and employer.

16 15 14 13 12 11 10 09                                        10 9 8 7 6 5 4 3 2 1

*Dedicated to the memory and recovery of*
*Mescalito José Echavez,*
*who went missing on October 16, 2003,*
*in the East Village in New York City*

# Contents

# Acknowledgments

I WISH TO THANK THE ARTISTS who so generously allowed me to reproduce and critique their work in this book. For providing time and funding during a crucial stage in the writing process, I am grateful to the American Association of University Women.

# Foreign in a Domestic Sense

I
T IS A BEAUTIFUL, BAFFLING IMAGE. Blond wigs form the contours of the floor plan of a basilica in Paul Pfeiffer's *Leviathan,* a
1998 print that exemplifies the digital and installation artist's signature use of strangely modified images of the body (see Plate 6). Yet
the wigs disrupt the very architecture they want to approximate. They
lavishly spill out of the Christian frame they themselves construct, satu-
rating and filling the entire print. All too (un)fittingly, the Christian
basilica is formed by and overlaid onto iconic American blondness,
signifying what might be called the bicoloniality of the Philippines.[1]
*Three hundred and fifty years in a convent, fifty years in Hollywood:* So goes
the popular refrain summing up the Philippines' history of colonial
encounter with Spain and the United States. The sumptuous blondness of the wigs in *Leviathan* signifies an intense desire to be *very* blond,
to ape the Western shape, and to assimilate. But the blonder the subject,
it seems, the more tattered and permeable the borders of the form. In
other words, the imperial frame does not succeed, and the artist successfully frames the failure of the imperial frame.

Pfeiffer's carefully arranged wigs embody the contradictions of a political entity like Filipino America that is a simultaneously inassimilable
and assimilable vestige of American imperialism. *Leviathan* captures and
ironizes the contradictions of a subjectivity that is "foreign in a domestic sense." Filipino America owes its existence to the monumentally violent and monumentally forgotten inclusion of the Philippines

into the United States more than a century ago when the Philippine-American War broke out in 1899. While statistics deliberately are not tallied by the United States after the decentralization of the war, which precipitated a move to the southern Philippines and the emergence of "banditry" and *lladrones,* estimates of the number of Filipino deaths range from one hundred thousand to one million, up to about one-sixth of the population. The U.S. military deployed a total of one hundred twenty-six thousand soldiers, while the U.S. Treasury spent $600 million (as opposed to $50 million on the Spanish-American War) and $8 billion on veteran pensions. Ever since, the United States has attempted to define and contain the Philippines and Filipino America, but these entities have caused no end of confusion for America, which has generated a succession of contradictory ways of categorizing colonized subjects ("nationals" or "noncitizen nonaliens") and colonized land ("unincorporated territory"). In 1901 the U.S. Supreme Court declared that the Philippines and other colonies are "foreign to the United States in a domestic sense."[2] Organized by an account of simultaneous interiority and exteriority, the U.S. empire wants to contain its colonies and colonized peoples, and yet by its very nature it cannot. Images like *Leviathan* and convoluted legal phrases like "foreign in a domestic sense" expose the innately contradictory nature of U.S. imperialist desires to incorporate, define, and contain colonized peoples and lands.

If Edward Said declared in 1993 that the task of the critic is "to inventory the interpellation of culture by empire," this book demonstrates how Filipino America contributes to the process and products of an American post/colonial cultural archive. From the late 1980s to the present, a coterie of affiliated artists of Filipino descent has generated a sense of cultural momentum emanating from the two American metropolises where they are or have been based, New York City and the San Francisco Bay Area, forming a "cultural moment" that evidences all the creativity and anomalies of a minority, post/colonial entity like Filipino America. The texts and artists I gather here make for a motley genre- and medium-crossing study, featuring a range of styles, mediums, venues, and audiences. In addition to a chapter on Pfeiffer's digital and installation art, this book describes and analyzes Angel Velasco Shaw's experimental videodocumentary *Nailed,* which records the voluntary crucifixion of a female faith healer in the Philippines; the artist Manuel

Ocampo's stunning oil paintings of damaged, ravaged Asian bodies; the stand-up comedian Rex Navarrete's astonishing mimicry and punning abilities; the campiness of playwright Nicky Paraiso's combination of cabaret and solo autobiographical drama; and Reanne Estrada's intricate sculpture. Though some are much better known than others—Paul Pfeiffer and Manuel Ocampo are the most famous of the group—all are key agents in the generation of what the Philippinist ethnographer Albert Alejo calls "cultural energies." With their overlapping artistic practices and shared aesthetic ideologies, these artists point to a culture of *presence* and strategies of *indirection* that counter the invisibility surrounding Filipino America's history of racial subjugation and colonization.

Their aesthetic and political affinities emerge out of a network of informal and formal affiliations. These artists all know each other socially, professionally, and politically. For example, Nicky Paraiso and Angel Shaw are part of an informal group of Filipino artists in New York City, including the writers Luis Francia and Jessica Hagedorn and the actor Ching Valdez-Aran, who began gathering for food and company in the 1980s and who call their meetings group sessions in "Filipino therapy." Paraiso first met Paul Pfeiffer when the queer Filipino American organization Kambal sa Lusog formed in New York City in the early 1990s. Manuel Ocampo and Shaw began a series of informal conversations about art and aesthetics when Ocampo lived in New York City in the 1990s. Currently the curator for performance at La MaMa Experimental Theatre Club in New York City, Paraiso used video footage shot by Shaw for his 1994 full-length solo performance *Asian Boys,* which includes interviews of several gay male Filipino American artists, including Pfeiffer and the novelist-playwright Han Ong, who, in the same year, collaboratively wrote and performed the play *Airport Music* with Hagedorn. Paraiso's solo play *House/Boy* was staged at La MaMa in 2004 and directed by Ralph Peña, one of the founders of Ma-Yi Theater Company in New York City, which is a Pan-Asian American theatrical laboratory and cultural hub. Also an actor, Peña was a member of the ensemble of Hagedorn's staged version of *Dogeaters,* which had a run in New York's Public Theater in 2001. Among the many events organized in 1999 by Filipino Americans marking the centennial of the outbreak of the Philippine-American War, a two-week-long conference at New York University primarily organized by Shaw eventually culminated in the 2002 publication of the multigenre, interdisciplinary volume *Vestiges of War: The Philippine American War and the Aftermath of an Imperial Dream, 1899–1999,* which features the work of about two dozen scholars and artists, including art by Pfeiffer and Ocampo. All of these New York–based artists are familiar with, if not personal affiliates of, the stand-up comedy of Rex Navarrete, who until recently was based in the San Francisco Bay Area but now lives in Hawai'i and travels more and more frequently to the Philippines. Save for Paraiso, all of the artists featured in this study travel regularly to the Philippines, and they circulate quite easily among the influential, privileged Manileño cultural intelligentsia who have significant ties to American cities like New York, Los Angeles, Chicago, and San Francisco.[3] The list of collaborations and crossings in this economy of cultural energies goes on and on.

I would emphasize that my principle of selection is *formal, not cumulative.* The artists and writer-performers that I have chosen are exemplary, and the politics of the aesthetic they so powerfully forward can indeed be extended to an analysis of others. Fiction writers and poets like Jessica Hagedorn, Han Ong, Peter Bacho, Eric Gamalinda, Luis Francia, Brian Roley, Noel Alumit, Bino Realuyo, Michelle Cruz Skinner, Zack Linmark, and Catalina Cariaga are but a few of the rapidly increasing number of published contemporary Filipino Americans whose work very much resonates with the claims of *The Decolonized Eye.* But I have deliberately chosen to follow the visual, performative impulses of the coterie of artists and writer-performers that is at the heart of the book. Such impulses, to my mind, have to do with a fundamental critique of history. Subject to a history of invisibility and thoroughgoing excision from American history, writer-performers like Rex Navarrete and Nicky Paraiso have refused fiction, certainly forms of fiction that have lent themselves to the linear, developmental writing of history. They instead have embraced the performative and the theatrical, ephemeral forms that rely on both repeated presence and regular disappearance. In other words, the performative allows them to record *and yet not record* experience. Such aesthetic, formal strategies are deeply linked to the colonial cultural context of the Philippines and Filipino America in which I have striven to ground my readings.

Together these artists make three crucial interventions in contemporary American culture and scholarship. First, these artists work against the disavowal of imperialism and what Oscar Campomanes has called the "*conspicuous* invisibilization in academic and public culture conversations" of America's first Asian colony (Tiongson 33). Second, these artists reveal how American imperialism needs to be studied in terms substantively different from those set out by postcolonial studies, which, primarily rooted in the histories of former European and especially British colonies, relies on the spatial and political distinction between the imperial metropolis "over here" and the colony "over there." The images, language, and performances created by these artists instead respond to the positioning of Filipino America as "foreign in a domestic sense." Third, these artists unexpectedly reverse dominant American narratives of immigrant assimilation. According to the "immigration mythography" of assimilation, racialized subjects undergo a transformative process of adjustment and accommodation proper to successful absorption into the body politic, a process that reinforces the nation-empire (Tiongson 40). In contrast, the Filipino American integrationist desire for America paradoxically leads to the disintegration of the empire. America's imperial act of acquisition has produced subversive assimilation or what Allan Isaac has called "acts of assimilation gone awry" (xviii). In short, the Filipino American cultural moment calls for a fundamental rethinking of the workings of empire and the workings of the nation.

## The Disarticulation of the Empire

If *The Decolonized Eye* describes the practices, ideologies, and products of these artists, it also explains the reasons for their strangely shadowy existence in American culture and scholarship. If one heeds what is happening in the shadows of the American empire, one starts to see the profound impact and unexpected consequences of colonialism, the history of which irrupts in ordinary and extraordinary ways. For example, asked for my and my parents' place of birth while I was filling out a form at a Californian Department of Motor Vehicles, I balked when I saw that the section titled "Birthplace" had space enough for only two initials. I was born in New York. The clerk tapped the letters "N" and "Y." When I told her that my father was born in Singapore, to my surprise she did not flinch and instead breezily typed up the entire word "S-i-n-g-a-p-o-r-e" in a smaller font and neatly squeezed it into the blank space. But when I told her that my mother was born in the Philippines, she shocked me by entering the letters "P" and "I." The Philippines *still is* part of America, I mused to myself. In St. Louis, Missouri, the site of the 1904 World's Fair, one of the local middle schools until only recently used the "Igorot" as its mascot, a reminder of the more than one thousand Filipinos exhibited at the fair. At the University of Michigan, where I teach, the anthropology and natural history museum displays Visayan burial items and late-nineteenth-century photographs of gun-toting white anthropology professors and students. America's heartland is riven by its transoceanic empire, and the most interior states can be mapped, it seems, by the Philippines.

Generally, however, Filipino America is strangely and structurally invisible, and its position at the crossroads of race and empire has everything to do with that invisibility. Indeed, questions about the historical record of imperial disavowal dominate debates—from Puerto Rico to Hawai'i—in the otherwise heterogeneous study of U.S. colonial and post/colonial discourses, histories, and cultures. In Philippine and Filipino American studies, historians and cultural critics like Vicente Rafael, Oscar Campomanes, E. San Juan Jr., Dorothy Fujita-Rony, Catherine Ceniza Choy, Allan Isaac, Augusto Espiritu, Mae Ngai, and others have described Filipino America's positioning in American culture as that which must be categorically erased or misrecognized in order for America to deny its imperial history and presence. Thus, Choy has asked: "Can we imagine the United States as an extension of the Philippines?" (135). What might be learned from a sustained study of Filipinos' similarly uncanny and paradoxical location both inside and outside the American empire?

By the "disarticulation" of the empire, I refer to three aspects of the imperial and post/colonial cultures of the United States. First, the compulsive, organized nature of imperial forgetting has rendered inarticulate and incoherent the history of colonialism. Unlike other Western colonial projects, American imperialism traditionally does not recognize itself as such. To the extent that it has entered the national imagination, the transoceanic empire is perceived as a scattered, diffuse, almost nonterritorial entity, especially after continental consolidation. The empire appears disembodied, simply expansive swaths of the Pacific Ocean littered with barely discernible bodies of islands. Moreover, because the American empire constitutively forgets that it is an empire, it offers neither space nor speech for the exploration of its post/colonial cultures. For more than a century now, America's official policy of benevolent assimilation and its dominant culture of imperial forgetting have made it nearly impossible for Filipino America to articulate its history of multiple colonialisms and racial subjugation. The attempt to create the space for such an intervention is very much an ongoing project, hence my decision to use the solidus in "post/colonial" to indicate the unfinished business of American colonialism.

Second, I argue that the Filipino American cultural moment participates in what a range of critics have called, drawing upon Antonio Gramsci, a "politics of articulation." Riffing on Stuart Hall's work in Black British cultural studies so that he can describe the "creation of political or religious ensembles . . . in moments of colonial stress" in Oceania, James Clifford notes:

> Something that's articulated or hooked together (like a truck's cab and trailer, or a sentence's constituent's parts) can also be unhooked and recombined. When you understand a social or cultural formation as an articulated ensemble it does not allow you to prefigure it as an organic model, as a living, persistent, "growing" body, continuous and developing through time. An articulated ensemble is more like a political coalition or, in its ability to conjoin disparate elements, a cyborg. While the possible elements and positions of a sociocultural ensemble are historically imposed constraints that can be quite persistent over time, there is no eternal or natural shape to their configuration. (478)

The small yet influential "sociocultural ensemble" of artists that is the subject of this book draws upon its own scattered history, archipelagic sensibility, and diasporic imagination and produces a range of responses to its predicament of unintelligibility and invisibility. To register the cost of American imperial disavowal, Filipino America turns to language and lingual forms of multivalence like the pun, while simultaneously turning to the body and its fragmentation as the ironic site for re/membering history. If, as Terry Eagleton has put it, literature is a kind of organized violence committed against language, Filipino

American expressive culture has organized its own semiotics and aesthetic of violence. In particular, these artists' response to textual and lingual disarticulation—the imperial project of obliterating or degrading vernacular languages, erasing history, and suppressing literatures—involves recurrent depictions of bodily injury and degradation, acts of aggressive joking and teasing, sophisticated forms of camp, and cross-cultural and translingual punning. These are images and acts of subversive disarticulation, which brings me to the third part of my thesis about the disarticulation of the empire. To "disarticulate" means both to "separate (bones) at the joints" and to "break up and disrupt the logic of (an argument or opinion): *novels disarticulate theories" (New Oxford American Dictionary)*. In short, "disarticulation" refers to the act of breaking up or eviscerating something whole. Referencing the body in a rich variety of ways, Filipino American artists and cultural producers respond to a matrix of historical, psychic, and cultural dispossession by producing a visual and rhetorical grammar of violence that in turn "disarticulates" the empire. That which is incorporated or ingested shall disarticulate the empire. According to the politics of this aesthetic, the empire falls apart—it is in fact cannibalized by its radical interior.

But even as the artists and texts featured in this study can be said to call for a literal reading of colonial violence, their semiotic playfulness disallows the literal reading of their literalness. While the artistic and cultural practices serve as complex and powerful recording devices—acts of memory that index and counter the power dynamics of imperialism—the emergence of a Filipino American cultural moment cannot be described simply as an essentialist project of recovery. The subjectivities produced by these texts are marked by playfulness and slipperiness: a relentless, ingrained kind of punning. Born of plural colonial histories of warfare and massive upheaval, this ability to survive through the rapid switching of identities, languages, and epistemologies accounts for the ephemeral yet remarkably persistent nature of Filipino American post/colonial cultural forms and production.

## Imperial Citizenship

These aesthetic acts of subversive assimilation have their legal counterpart, calling attention to the shuttling between legal incorporation (word) and cultural cannibalism (flesh) that defines Filipino subjectivity. In deportation cases throughout the twentieth century, Filipino Americans have tried to expose imperialism through the legal system. These cases involve longtime illegal residents in the United States who never converted their status as colonial subjects to that of immigrants after 1934, when the United States' conferral of semiautonomy on the Philippine Islands ended the threat of Filipino migration to the continent. In the more recent iterations of the 1980s and 1990s, litigants have sued for American citizenship and have argued that they or their ancestors were born in the Philippines during the territorial period, 1898–1946, when it was part of the American empire, sometimes citing British citizenship clauses from America's colonial era.[4] Beginning with the 1901–1922 *Insular Cases* and especially after World War II, a series of deportation cases have involved "illegal" U.S. Filipino residents suing for U.S. residency and citizenship.[5] The creation and concept of "unincorporated" territories continue to shape immigrant and imperial discourse in today's courts. For example, in the 1994 case *Rabang v. INS,* a Filipino American plaintiff tried to appropriate the logic and discourse of revolutionary postcoloniality of the early American republic to make the case against exclusion from the U.S. body politic. Traversing the limbo of both exclusion and colonization, Filipino Americans have used postcoloniality to become "American." In so doing, the assimilationist act of suing for American citizenship—if pushed to its logical end—spells the undoing of America's boundaries. Reminding America of its own (British) post/colonial status while invoking the idea of imperial citizenship, their claims turn on a fundamental recognition of empire that the courts, not surprisingly, are unwilling to enact, given that automatic American citizenship then would have to be extended to any number of formerly or currently occupied countries and U.S. territories. For if these "illegal" residents gained recognition from the courts, much of rest of the world would qualify for American imperial citizenship.

The colonization of the Philippines and other lands necessitated the modification of the U.S. Constitution so as to allow a form of taxation without representation, which was achieved in the *Insular Cases.* To the U.S. Supreme Court the direct colonization of the Philippines was troubling, not so much because it involved the devastation of a heterogeneous society and economy but because "the Philippine question" threatened the integrity of one of the basic principles of the U.S. Constitution: no taxation without representation, which was a point of contention between the United States and its former colonial master, Great Britain. The colonization of the Philippines and the external acquisition of colonized subjects became transformed into an internal debate about representation and taxation. The (foreign) colonization of the Philippines became in the *Insular Cases* a (domestic) debate about taxation. Yet because the *Insular Cases* contained a few references to the legal status of colonized peoples—Filipinos were deemed "wards" or "nationals" subject to the authority of the United States—commentators even at the time speculated on the impact of the incorporation of former Spanish colonies on the Constitution and on citizenship. In an 1899 *Harvard Law Review* article "The Constitutional Questions Incident to the Acquisition and Government by the United States of Island Territory," Simeon Baldwin, president of the American Historical Association in 1906, writes: "Their children, born after the ratification of the Spanish Treaty, if it should be ratified, will all be citizens of the United States. They must, therefore, by the XV. Amendment have the same right of suffrage which may be conceded in those territories to white men of civilized races. One generation of men is soon replaced by another, and in the tropics more rapidly than with us. In fifty years, the bulk of the adult population of Puerto Rico, Hawai'i, and the Philippines, should these then form part of the United States, will be claiming of the XV. Amendment" (407). Baldwin thus concludes: "The XIV. Amendment would seem to make every child, of whatever race, born in any of our new territorial possessions after they become part of the United States, of parents who are among its inhabitants and subject to our jurisdiction, a citizen of the United States from the moment of birth" (406).[6]

As distant in time and space as such debates seem, the 1994 case *Rabang v. INS,* which was handed down by the U.S. Court of Appeals, Ninth Circuit, is an example of one of several recent attempts by Filipinos to make the case for citizenship or legal residence based upon the recognition of imperialism. Typically, persons born in the Philippines and residing in the United States have tried to establish that they are not "aliens" with respect to the United States, usually to counter deportation proceedings back to the Philippines, in some cases after having lived in the United States for two decades. While earlier plaintiffs and courts assumed that Filipinos acquired the status only of "nationals" at birth, what makes *Rabang v. INS* particularly interesting is its novel claim for citizenship based upon the plaintiffs' or their parents' birth in the Philippines during the territorial period. According to Avelino Halagao Jr., the estimated Philippine population in 1946 exceeded eighteen million, and of those Filipino inhabitants approximately seven million were alive in the 1990s. While the Court of Appeals rather curtly upheld the district court's ruling that such a claim is invalid, the vigorousness of the dissent—and its turn to seventeenth-century English common law to hold that the plaintiffs are, indeed, U.S. citizens—delineated the overlapping nature of white settler post/colonial, American revolutionary, and Filipino American post/colonial legal identities, even as they compete for legitimacy in the courts.

By refusing to accord U.S. citizenship to Filipinos born during the territorial period, the majority opinon in *Rabang v. INS* endorsed a colonial reading of U.S. colonialism, using the language of "cession" and "acquisition" to elide the long and devastating war that broke out between the Philippines and the United States. The war did not happen; rather, the United States "acquired" the Philippines. As one scholar of U.S. expansionist rhetoric points out, the term "cession" is striking because it effects the concealment of agency: "The term suggests a mode of consensual, non-conflictual expansion and, like the term 'acquisition,' it conceals agency. In its ideal form, cession is tautological, a transaction between two parties on the same side: settlers who occupy and willingly 'cede' territories and the United States that then 'admits' them as states, as in the case of the Northwest Ordinance or the annexation of Texas" (Dallal 23). Moreover, while the court recognized citizenship by birth, a legacy of English common law, it refused to apply the Fourteenth Amendment's citizenship clause to what it called "outlying lands subject to the jurisdiction of this country." In doing so, it relied on a revenue clause in one of the *Insular Cases (Downes)* to define the phrase "in the United States," instead of turning to other landmark citizenship cases, such as the 1898 case *U.S. v. Wong Kim Ark*. Thus, the court restricted the definition of "natural-born citizen" to those persons born in the states of the Union.

In contrast, the dissent in *Rabang* held that persons born in the

Philippines during the territorial period are U.S. citizens. Justice Pregerson argued that the principles of common law were recognized by both the framers of the Constitution and the authors of the Fourteenth Amendment and that the court's decision violated these principles: "What is significant about these earlier cases is that the courts, without considering the Citizenship Clause, assumed that the United States was free to grant or withhold citizenship to the people of the Philippines while the Islands were under the complete dominion and control of the United States" (1455). Pregerson turned to *Wong Kim Ark,* which upheld the citizenship of a U.S.-born person of Chinese parents during the Exclusion era for a definition of the phrase "in the United States" and for a general discussion of the common law rule of citizenship by birth. Pregerson also pointed out that *Wong Kim Ark* cited the 1608 *Calvin's Case,* which established that "a person's status as a natural-born subject requires that (1) the person's birth occur within the bounds of the King's dominion and (2) that the parents owe obedience to the King at the time of the child's birth" (1457).[7] Directly contradicting the majority decision in *Rabang v. INS,* the *Wong Kim Ark* court argued that the category "'natural-born British subject' means a British subject who has become a British subject at the moment of birth" and that it "was adopted by the English Colonies and was implicitly incorporated by the framers into the original Constitution" (1458). Thus, the case for Filipino American citizenship contains a post/colonial claim that demands the United States' self-recognition of its double position as anticolonial and imperial, and it hinges on America's recognition of its history of imperialism and racial exclusion. Just as the borders of the colonial architectural form are constituted yet also disrupted and exceeded by the hyper-blond wigs in Pfeiffer's *Leviathan,* the boundaries of the United States are consolidated, disrupted, and exceeded by these plaintiffs' arguments for imperial citizenship. In the realms of the aesthetic and the law, Filipino Americans' oscillation between hypervisible and barely visible corporeality indexes the relationship between minority invisibility and imperial amnesia. At the same time, a similar logic links these legal cases to cultural texts like *Leviathan:* in both instances, the assimilationist desire for American belonging paradoxically leads to the disarticulation of the empire.

An example of the combination of minority invisibility and imperial amnesia that produces Filipino America, deportation cases like *Rabang v. INS* provide the context for contemporary artists' oscillation between hypervisible and barely visible corporeality. In the two chapters that form Part I, "Staging the Sublime," I analyze visual representations of bodily injury in the work of the filmmaker Angel Shaw and the painter Manuel Ocampo and bodily erasure in the work of digital and installation artist Paul Pfeiffer. In chapter 1, "An Open Wound: Angel Shaw and Manuel Ocampo," I make sense of these patterns of physical mutilation by juxtaposing my close readings of Shaw's experimental film *Nailed* and Ocampo's paintings with Sigmund Freud's writings on melancholia. I foreground Freud's theorizing of the coincidence of the psychic and somatic and the melancholic's potential for social protest and Reynaldo Ileto's examination of the *"pasyon"* narrative in anticolonial mass movements in the Philippines. In chapter 2, "A Queer Horizon: Paul Pfeiffer's Disintegrating Figure Studies," I turn from the theme of excessive embodiment to its opposite: Pfeiffer's conception of the human figure as it gradually disintegrates in deferral to the space that surrounds it. Digitally modifying video and photographic images of iconic bodies, Pfeiffer deploys formalism and abstraction in ways that signal the emergence of a queer decolonizing aesthetic. From these renderings of the aggressed body, I turn to the use of aggressive language and ambivalent wordplay—teasing, jokes, and puns—in Part II "Pilipinos Are Punny, Freud Is Filipino." This second pair of chapters focuses on the performativity of language and the theatrical staging of the body. In chapter 3, "Why Filipinos Make Pun(s) of One Another: The *Sikolohiya*/Psychology of Rex Navarrete's Stand-up Comedy," I analyze the translingual puns and bicultural joke structures of stand-up comic Rex Navarrete. In my reading Navarrete's comedy becomes the basis for a diasporic version of *sikolohiyang Pilipino,* the indigenous psychology movement that revolutionized the humanities and social sciences beginning in the 1970s among Manila academics. In *sikolohiyang Pilipino,* everyday Filipino phrases and sayings—rather than the unconscious—are the foundation for psychological concepts and worldviews, and I combine this radically intersocial approach to psychology with Freud's language of the unconscious so as to offer an alternative methodology for analyzing bicultural languages like Taglish (a combination of Tagalog and English) and the translingual production of meaning in Navarrete's puns and jokes. Chapter 4, "'He will not always say what you would have him say': Loss and Aural (Be)Longing in Nicky Paraiso's *House/Boy*," describes writer-performer Nicky Paraiso's signature combination of cabaret and performance art in his solo play *House/Boy*. Drawing on camp sensibility, the sentimentality of Hollywood musicals and Visayan love ballads, and autobiographical drama, Paraiso mournfully portrays the impossibility of communicating with his father by interweaving various portraits of the Filipino "houseboy," including autobiographical accounts of his father's life as a male nurse, Hollywood caricatures of gay Filipino domestic servants, and other allegories of America's configuration of the Philippines as "foreign in a domestic sense." The conclusion, "Reanne Estrada, Identity, and the Politics of Abstraction," focuses on the visual artist Reanne Estrada because her minimalist shapes and use of degradable materials propose counterintuitive ways to think about identity as a politics of evading rather than securing visibility and legibility. Retreating from the gaze, Estrada exemplifies the work undertaken by artists of color to *turn away* from illusion and the representation of external, recognizable reality—especially the figural representation of the racialized body—as the basis for producing and evaluating racial art. Instead, Estrada uses abstract, nonmimetic shape such that form rather than content becomes the mode in which race gets represented.

This sense of the abstract is not to be confused with its common usage in art historical parlance. According to the influential mid-twentieth-century American critic Clement Greenberg, abstraction in art historical terms refers to the culmination of a historical process that leads from Cubism's "destruction of realistic pictorial space" to abstraction strictly speaking, especially the abstract expressionist art championed by Greenberg wherein the "flat picture plane's denial of . . . realistic perspectival space" produces a consistent emphasis on the two-dimensional flatness of the canvas itself in painting (Greenberg 567, 566). According to Eugene Lunn, cubism effected a "revolutionary assault on the seeming stability of objects, which are taken apart, brought into collision, and reassembled on the picture surface" so as to produce "contingent syntheses by which human activity and perception remake the world" (quoted in Singhal 13).[8] If the development of modernism in art turns on such achievements in painting, then it is a development that is "governed by *self*-critical procedures addressed to the medium itself" (Harrison 191). Debates about abstraction within this particular usage of modernism focus on developments that are internal to the evolution of a medium, e.g., in the movement in painting from perspectival depth to the fragmentation of the object and the emphasis of the two-dimensionality of the canvas. Within the parameters established by such definitions of modernism, wherein modernism "implies a property that must be principally internal to the practice or medium in question," abstraction generally emerges as the litmus test for *modernity* (Harrison 191).[9] In the case of artists of color, those who produce representational work as a means of exploring issues of race and colonialism are considered aesthetically backward or naive. In contrast, artists like Estrada and Pfeiffer, whose work is perceived as abstract or antirepresentational, are embraced as modern or postmodern—they are praised for transcending race—at the expense of critics paying any attention to the ways in which their work engages with the legacies of colonialism and racial formation.[10] Thus, for example, one reviewer can praise Pfeiffer's works because they "possess an internal logic and are self-sufficient and modernist" (Ho 125).

In contrast, I argue that, by turning to more abstract rather than representational or illusionist works, these Filipino American artists have forestalled critics' raced tendency to evaluate their work purely on the basis of content, i.e., the figural representation of brown bodies. Demanding more formalist interpretation, these artists moreover draw our attention to the persistently raced ways in which their work is judged on the basis as to whether they lack or demonstrate modernist achievement. In necessarily circuitous ways, they lead us to an understanding of the relation between race and the aesthetic that ironically and powerfully leads us back (and forward) to the positioning of modernism "*in face of* (though emphatically *not* in disregard of) the pervasive condition of modernity," especially the social realities and conditions that produce and are produced by the American empire (Harrison 192).

Filipino American artists have understood the historical relation of abstraction to the *real*. That is to say, it is through abstraction that the American empire emerges. As I elaborate in chapter 2, the idea of empire is abstracted from the materiality of conquest and then reduced to concepts that can be debated rhetorically in nineteenth-century continental expansionism and early-twentieth-century transoceanic expansionism, a process that Jenine Dallal calls "unmanifest destiny."[11] William James described this process succinctly in 1899 even as the conquest of the Philippines was under way:

> The worst vice that an oration or any other expression of human nature can have is abstractness. Abstractness means empty simplicity, non-reference to features essential to the case. Of all the carnivals of emptiness and abstractness that the world has seen, our national discussions over the Philippine policy probably bear away the palm. The arch abstractionists have been the promoters of expansion; and of them all Governor Roosevelt now writes himself down as the very chief. The empty abstractions had unrestricted right of way—unfitness, anarchy, clean sweep, no entanglement, no parley, unconditional surrender, supremacy of the flag; then indeed good government, Christian civilization, freedom, brotherly protection, kind offices, all that the heart of man or people can desire. The crime of which we accuse Governor Roosevelt's party is that of treating an intensely living and concrete situation by a set of bald and hollow abstractions.[12]

I argue that formal, aesthetic abstraction emerges as a practice in Estrada's art, a practice that calls attention to modes of rhetorical abstraction underpinning the legacy of American colonialism. Like Estrada, the artists and writer–performers discussed in this book collectively suggest that identity is a decolonizing practice, one that ironically comes most alive when identity is under erasure. This book investigates the resulting (identity) politics of (abstract) form.

Broadly speaking, how does *The Decolonized Eye* contribute to and differ from recent, comparable scholarship, especially in the fields of Philippine and Filipino American studies, postcolonial studies, American studies, ethnic studies, and Asian American studies? In addition to the scholars whom I already have referenced, this book is indebted to a thriving circle of published Philippinist and Filipino Americanist cultural critics like Martin Manalansan, Neferti Tadiar, Enrique Bonus, Fatimah Tobing, Paul Kramer, and Eleanor Ty; *sikolohiyang Pilipino* scholars Virgilio Enriquez and S. Lily Mendoza; and more recent and forthcoming scholarship by cultural critics like Sharon Delmendo, Theodore Gonzalves, Lucy Burns, Victor Bascara, Celine

Parreñas Shimizu, Benito Vergara, Nerissa Balce-Cortes, Jody Blanco, Dylan Rodriguez, Christi-Ann Castro, Dawn Mabalon, and Elizabeth Pisares; and historians like Kimberly Alidio and Arleen de Vera. I also am influenced by Reynaldo Ileto's signature combination of historical and literary analysis, a methodological style that clearly inspires the scholarship of Vicente Rafael and Augusto Espiritu; and the politics of style forwarded by Vicente Diaz in native Pacific Islander studies. Yet *The Decolonized Eye* differs from the extant scholarship in Philippine and Filipino American studies in several ways. I delineate the significance of a group of affiliated artists that no other scholar has recognized as a coherent social, political, and cultural formation. I insist on the cultural valence of Filipino America in a field that tends to be Philippine-centric. Since most of these artists are based in New York City, I geographically shift the focus from the usual Filipino American loci of California, Washington, and Hawai'i to the East Coast. Finally, as I explain in greater detail below, I methodologically depart from the historicist and Marxian approaches that shape the field's dominant mode of cultural analysis, and I instead deploy a unique, hybrid methodology that combines the techniques and insights of psychoanalysis, Filipino indigenous psychology, narrative theory, art history, museum studies, performance studies, and queer studies.

Not surprisingly, literary and cultural scholarship on the colonization of the Philippines and its aftermath has been dominated by photography and the technologies of colonial surveillance. What Benito Vergara has called the "kodak zone"—a phrase first coined by an American *Harper's Weekly* journalist in 1899—refers to the tight conjunction between vision and colonial mastery, especially early on in the relationship between the United States and its new colony.[13] While the contemporary Filipino American cultural moment continues to interrogate vision as colonial apparatus and regime, I am interested in its striking turn to a more kinetic, embodied, and theatrical ethos and praxis, overtaking and displacing that earlier emphasis on the visual. These texts are highly performative. These texts want to be acted, filmed, danced, and sung; they "seek the theater," as Joseph Roach has put it. Kinetic memories sink the deepest and endure the longest. These texts are products of a culture of presence, wherein performance is the main vehicle and site of collective belonging and fracturing and of unofficial historical inquiry. Accordingly, notions of the collective are defined in theatrical ways. In the arenas of cultural representation, academic scholarship, and everyday practices, this theoretical "staging" of the community significantly renovates existing notions of community formation and maintenance. While in Asian American studies the idea of community often is conceptualized either as an ethnic enclave within the immigration paradigm or as a dispersed global community in transnational paradigms, in Filipino America "community" is better conceptualized as an "audience." The repeated images and rhetoric of violence that have emerged as a disturbing yet powerful pattern are replayed before this community–audience in ways that underscore the stakes, costs, and power of nationalism and post/colonial nostalgia.

In the study of postcolonial literatures, a wide range of scholars like Jenny Sharp, Anne McClintock, Gauri Viswanathan, Homi Bhabha, Simon Gikandi, and Rey Chow, along with those associated with sub-altern studies like Rajagopalan Radhakrishnan, Dipesh Chakrabarty, and Gayatri Spivak have made crucial yet sporadic attempts at analyzing the specific mechanics of American imperialism. The field remains dominated by accounts of British colonialism and the Commonwealth and thus elides accounts of U.S. imperialism. Americanist studies of empire and literature such as John Carlos Rowe's *Literary Culture and U.S. Imperialism: From the Revolution to World War II,* Malini Schueller's *U.S. Orientalisms: Race, Nation, and Gender in Literature, 1790–1890,* and Amy Kaplan's *The Anarchy of Empire in the Making of U.S. Culture* powerfully capture the paradoxes inherent in America's relationship to its own imperial history. However, these scholars' emphasis on American Orientalism—their elaborate descriptions of the construction of the fetishized Other—ultimately begins to *stand in* for an account of the actual effects of imperialism on contemporary communities that are "foreign in a domestic sense." Scholars have but only recently begun to seriously tackle the phenomenon of minority American cultures undergoing a process of decolonization. Edited volumes like Amy Kaplan and Donald Pease's *Cultures of United States Imperialism,* Vicente Rafael's *Discrepant Histories: Translocal Essays on Filipino Cultures,* Lisa Lowe and David Lloyd's *The Politics of Culture in the Shadow of Capital,* and Ella Shohat and Robert Stam's *Unthinking Eurocentrism: Multiculturalism and the Media* have opened the way for studying the complex, dynamic interaction between hegemonic and minority cultures. Departing from this wide range of scholarship on empire, postcolonialism, and minority discourse, *The Decolonized Eye* offers a sustained account of the various ways in which a culture survives the violence particular to the American empire. As such, this book finds itself more in the company of scholars in Chicano/a and Latino/a studies, Arab American studies, Native American studies, and Native Pacific Islander studies because they are highly attuned to the specific workings of U.S. empire, they investigate the intersections between the logics of race and empire, and they prioritize the perspectives and creativity of simultaneously minoritized and colonized cultures. Moreover, by showing what the interpellation of Filipino American culture by empire looks like, this book addresses the gaps in the extant scholarship by insisting on the theoretical and scholarly "thickness" that can emerge from specificity. Only then can queer, decolonizing strategies of indirection like camp, mimesis, joking, and punning be appreciated as articulations of the conditions of possibility that constitute this contemporary post/colonial archive.

In Asian American literary and cultural criticism by groundbreaking scholars such as Elaine Kim, Sau-ling Wong, Lisa Lowe, and David Palumbo-Liu, and more recently published critics like Rachel Lee, David Eng, Susan Koshy, Viet Nguyen, Eleanor Ty, Donald Goellnicht, Tina Chen, Laura Kang, Rajini Srikanth, Karen Shimakawa, Kandice Chuh, Grace Hong, and James Kyung-Jin Lee, a general commitment to a pan-Asian American politics of "coalitional reading" has emerged even as these scholars have made elegant, passionate calls for the preservation of difference (Wong). For the past two decades now, Asian American studies has been wrestling with the ethics and politics of teaching and reading Asian American texts in a university classroom. In so doing, this body of scholarship has implicitly formed a canon of Asian American texts that prioritizes the analysis of literature, especially novels, short stories, and autobiography in an important effort to claim space for the academic study of Asian America. However, this marked emphasis on the canon and the institution comes at some cost: It presumes and effects an objectification of the text as a finite, finished product, cut off from the artistic communities and cultural moment from whence it came. Departing from the politics of the canon, I track the emergence of a specific community of artists and their "cultural energies." As an a-disciplinary, multimedium study that merges formalist strategies of close reading with broader cultural claims, this book documents the dialectical relationship between artists, texts, and contexts and the aesthetic ideologies that emerge from that interaction.

While Filipino American cultural production has found something of an institutional and intellectual home in ethnic studies and American studies, fissures within Asian American studies—Lois-Ann Yamanaka's fiction has served as a catalyst for the eruption of intense disputes and feuds in the field, some of which revolve around anti-Filipino racism within Asian America—require scholars of Filipino American studies to rethink anew and productively its relation to Asian America.[14] *The Decolonized Eye* is an attempt to describe the difference of Filipino American difference, whose "wild heterogeneity," as I think of it, often is at odds with the deraced coalitional politics of Asian American studies, which has its own brand of color blindness to the detriment of racially heterogeneous Asian American communities like Filipino America with its explicit in-group vocabulary and coding for race mixture. Filipino and U.S. Filipino theorists return repeatedly to the metaphor of the archipelago as a way of inscribing and at other times undermining nationalist aspirations. The Philippine archipelago and its diaspora generate a wild heterogeneity—of region, religion, language, class, sexuality, and race—that intersects unevenly with a history of plural colonialisms and migration patterns.[15] There is a keen awareness of the smallness and specificity that necessarily and ironically accompanies this proliferation of difference, an order of particularity often illegible to outsiders or perceived as too narrow and hence valueless. Just as Caribbean and native Pacific cultural studies scholarship has sought to demonstrate, however, I argue that the so-called specificity of Filipino America can become the powerful basis for an altogether other kind of worldliness. Thus, while I see this study as a rejoinder to the indifference or bemusement of those who would find scholarship on contemporary Filipino America too limited in value or scope, I also see this book reaching out to a differently worldly readership.[16]

The specificity of *The Decolonized Eye* yields insights about decolonizing cultures that challenge three basic assumptions in postcolonial studies, Asian American studies, and American studies. First, I offer a new reading of racial assimilation that undoes the powerful linkage between modernity and assimilation, which overdetermines the interpretation of American narratives of migration, cultural adjustment, and psychic accommodation, and I propose instead that Filipino American desires for belonging and home surprisingly lead to the disintegration rather than the consolidation of the American empire. Second, I offer a new reading of empire that challenges the validity of the metropole-colony binary still governing postcolonial studies and, to a large extent, diaspora studies, and I propose an alternative framework—"foreign in a domestic sense"—for thinking about the contradictions of a colonized Other. Third, my description of the Filipino American cultural moment reveals a peculiar temporality that has not been satisfactorily explained by any of these fields. Born of America's persistently forgotten imperial past, this contemporary cultural moment is both vestigial and incipient. A remainder from the past that nonetheless reads as new and alien, the Filipino American cultural moment poses a temporal paradox that throws into crisis the "post"—the pastness—of postcolonialism.

That the Filipino American cultural moment constitutes simultaneously new and unfinished business indicates the need for alternative analytic frameworks for Filipino American art and expressive culture. Filipino American experience and expression baffle disciplinarity. After all, colonization itself "goes beyond academic compartments" while, paradoxically and ironically, disciplinarity guarantees colonial regimes of knowledge.[17] Fundamentally a-disciplinary and methodologically hybrid, *The Decolonized Eye* draws upon a wide variety of overlapping theoretical and analytic approaches to conduct Filipino American cultural critique, including psychoanalysis, Filipino psychology, critical race theory, and feminist narratology. Moreover, I draw upon the cultural analysis developed in visual and museum studies, especially the work of Hal Foster and Mieke Bal, to attempt formalist textual readings that are at once rhetorically compelling, theoretically informed, and politically engaged. I privilege the interpretive techniques of Freudian psychoanalysis, especially those developed by scholars like Hortense Spillers and Saidiya Hartman, who work at the intersection of psychoanalysis, race, and gender because it presumes that the act of reading leads to blind spots as much as it yields insights and meaning. Hence, chapter 1 opens with a reading of Sigmund Freud's "Mourning and Melancholia," which in literary and cultural studies has become the basis for a much-discussed, much-circulated conceptual and theoretical model for the subject. Indeed, I would argue that in the last decade and a half or so, postcolonial and minority literary studies have been fixated on melancholia in ways that by now have become somewhat mechanical. By contrast, in my analysis of the paintings of Manuel Ocampo, I not only reverse the direction of the interpretation by eventually using Ocampo to read Freud, but I do so to call greater attention to the kind of playfulness, humor, and even pleasure that can emerge in such (re)encounters with Freud, all the more conspicuously and ironically so in an account of melancholia. These kinds of insights and moves have been strikingly absent in the scholarship of literary and cultural critics engaged with psychoanalysis. As my turn to fetishism in the latter half of the book indicates, however, it is my hope that postcolonial and minority studies would move on from its fixation on melancholia to other conceptual and theoretical models that Freud offers for the analysis of the posture of the subject. In my rereading of fetishism, I show that, with the particular lens of Filipino America's cultural moment, Freud's texts reveal awareness of lateral movement in and across languages. Such translingual, transnational acts of meaning-making sort very well with Filipino indigenous psychology's highly intersocial emphasis on the importance of everyday idioms and sayings for the investigation and theorization of the subject. It is in the dialectical encounter between Filipino America and Freud and between (artistic) text and (psychoanalytic) theory that such insights emerge. There is a special pattern to the blind spots in dominant American culture that produces the structural invisibility of Filipino America, and contemporary Filipino American art and expressive culture consequently have generated wily strategies of misdirection and indirection that demand an especially heightened awareness of acts of coding, masking, and mimicry. Hence, I turn to queer and performance studies for theories of camp, drag, gender play, and racial transgression, exemplified by the work of José Muñoz, Martin Manalansan, Judith Halberstam, and Judith Butler.

The wiliness, campiness, and subversiveness of these texts demand a certain flexibility from the reader and critics, however, and there are marked shifts in my voice and style from chapter to chapter. In other words, even as these artists and texts perform subversive acts of assimilation, they require the critic–subject to assimilate to the object of analysis. For example, I offer plural readings of Manuel Ocampo's paintings and Angel Shaw's videodocumentary to account for the incongruity and grotesque humor of their work, whereas in Paul Pfeiffer's chapter I find myself adopting his deliberately parasitical, citational style and his method of serial references to classical or canonical artists. Rex Navarrete's comic voice of the everyday calls for an appropriately informal voice on my part, and his constant punning allows me to theorize conceptual puns that illuminate, for example, Nicky Paraiso's subtle parallelism between paternal colonialism and domestic servitude. Paraiso's combination of sophisticated, achieved camp and intimate autobiographical anecdote compels me to simply follow the narrative arc, aurality, and affect of his play *House/Boy.* Finally, Reanne Estrada's art calls attention to the physical labor and materiality of the artist of color's process; and if the artist creates labor and value where there was none, perhaps so too does the critic.

An intense hunger exists among Filipinos and Filipino Americans to know more about Filipino American history, art, and expressive culture. The urge to learn more about the past and presence of Filipino American history and culture has been fueled by the series of centennial events since 1998 marking America's conquest and colonization of the Philippines. The "unofficial" Philippine-American War lasted for more than a decade after the 1902 official declaration of war's end. But I wrote this book in response to an even deeper set of problems and needs in Filipino America. If, as I hope this book shows, Filipino America has developed sophisticated, wily forms of expressive culture that have survived and countered the onslaught of American imperial violence, that particular combination of psychic and material violence also created colonial mentalities that are very much alive today. Historically configured as the object of Western anthropological study, Filipinos cannot "have" culture. Filipinos instead "are" culture, displayed as dehumanized objects in past World's Fairs and present-day natural history museums in the United States. Of course, this drastically uneven allocation of culture—who gets to have culture and who gets to be culture—is an intrinsic part of the workings of Western

modernity and racism. However, Filipinos have internalized this colonial idiom and uncritically accepted the idea that Filipinos "have
no culture." The Philippine archipelago has produced no counterpart
for the monumental Buddhist architecture and Javanese epics typically
associated with Southeast Asia. Filipinos are at best superb mimics of
Hollywood actors and Motown musicians. Such are the maxims of
Filipino common sense. There is precious little recognition of the variety and sophistication of the cultural forms that have withstood the
violence of American forgetting and that continue to proliferate in the
twenty-first century. This book is for Filipino Americans, so that we
can cherish both what has been bequeathed us and what we persist in
inventing and envisioning.

I

STAGING THE SUBLIME

# An Open Wound

## Angel Shaw and Manuel Ocampo

Because when you see the scars on her hands and you feel them,
you feel where the skin has healed over a wound like that,
you just get this sensation of nothing can hurt you.
I mean, it's not even that—but that you can bear the pain . . .
—ANGEL SHAW, *Nailed*

All we have to open the past are the five senses . . . and memory.
—LOUISE BOURGEOIS

IMAGES OF BODILY INJURY suffuse contemporary Filipino/American art and cultural production, graphic depictions often attended by hurtful humor and a rhetoric of pain.[1] Consider the work of artist Manuel Ocampo and videomaker Angel Velasco Shaw. Ocampo's oil and acrylic paintings trade on a gorgeous, grotesque corporeality—torn bellies, spilling hearts, and headless, defecating corpses. In the experimental video *Nailed,* Shaw documents the self-inflicted crucifixion of Lucy Reyes, a faith healer in the Philippines who for more than twenty years annually donned a buttercup yellow wig and crown of thorns before having her hands and feet partially nailed to a cross. Binding these otherwise wildly divergent texts is a dramatic pattern of wounds that is rooted in a history of colonial violence and loss. These visual representations of injury form a belligerent response to the numbing effects of organized imperial forgetting.[2] Shaw and Ocampo sa(l)vage

For the past 13 years, I have been one with God!

FIGURE 1. Scenes from *Nailed*, by Angel Velasco Shaw.

the body. They insist on the somatic and the sensual as a means of opening the Filipino American past, which turns out to be a history of lost histories. Theirs is a passional aesthetic of remembering through dismembering. Ironically, however, the violence depicted by these artists inevitably turns inward. These are portraits of self-mutilation, yet the representation and rhetoric of pain are oddly stubborn, defiant, and even celebratory. Here, the representation of the body is inextricably linked to the desecration of that same body.

To make sense of this pattern of self-injury and injury, I juxtapose these texts first with Sigmund Freud's writings on melancholia and then with Reynaldo Ileto's examination of the *pasyon* narrative in mass movements in the Philippines. In his 1917 essay "Mourning and Melancholia," Freud offers a fascinating, if open-ended, explanation for the phenomenon of melancholia, a prolonged and severe form of depression. Freud offers a theorization of loss, especially the inability to name the lost object, that illuminates the devastating impact of imperial forgetting on Filipino America, what the historian Mae Ngai has called a "problem of nonrecognition [that is] tantamount to nonmembership in the national community" (125). What happens, psychoanalysis helps us to ask, when "nonrecognition" is internalized by the post/colonial subject? How does one *represent* that historical and identitarian predicament? I then take up Freud's intriguing claim that the "complex of melancholia behaves like an open wound" (174).[3] Freud's analogy links physical trauma with psychic trauma and, along with the unnaming of loss, forms the basis for the theorization of what I call post/colonial melancholia.[4] By analogizing melancholic loss with physical injury, post/colonial melancholia offers a psychosomatic way to interpret these recurrent images of violence and, more generally, to theorize the positioning of a strangely anomalous entity like Filipino America.

To complement and complicate this negative, rather reactive portrait of post/colonial subjectivity, I turn to Reynaldo Ileto's writings on the cultural and political significance of Christ's crucifixion in late-nineteenth-century and early-twentieth century Philippines. In his groundbreaking 1979 study *Pasyon and Revolution: Popular Movements in the Philippines, 1840–1910,* Ileto focuses on the shifting meanings of Christ's crucifixion and underscores the potentially revolutionary significance of the *pasyon*—Filipino vernacular versions of the passion narrative of suffering—as a complex source of inspiration for anticolonial, anticlerical mass movements. A century later in the U.S. Filipino diaspora, the *pasyon* has irrupted again as a sign and site of cultural contestation. As a theatrical performance of self-injury, the *pasyon* has continued to evolve as a powerful source of cultural expression and political engagement. Ground-clearing agents in the Filipino American cultural moment, Shaw and Ocampo invoke this earlier tradition of semiotic reappropriation and, in doing so, create a space of visibility for a culturally coherent movement that mobilizes yet again what I call the "infinitival," rather than infinite, politics of the *pasyon*.[5]

## Post/colonial Melancholia: A History of Lost Histories

In "Mourning and Melancholia," Freud compares the common experience of mourning with the pathological condition of melancholia. Both mourner and melancholic have suffered from a profound loss. But melancholia differs from mourning in two important ways: first, the unconscious nature of melancholic loss, and second, the drastic drop in the melancholic's self-esteem.

According to Freud, while a grieving person can name the lost object, it is not clear what exactly the melancholic has lost. The melancholic does not know—cannot consciously perceive—what has been lost, even though he or she experiences the loss. How can one mourn properly if one cannot even name what has been lost? As it turns out, the ability to mourn is inextricably bound with language. Successful mourning entails naming the lost object, thereby processing and recovering from bereavement. In a colonial regime, though, language itself constitutes the lost object. The attempted destruction of native languages and the imposition of a singular, dominant language mark the catastrophic foundation of a colony—what Ocampo calls *Heridas de la Lengua* ("Wounds of the Tongue"). Deprived of the ability to speak, the colonized subject cannot name loss and therefore cannot mourn. The colonized subject attempts to mourn the loss of language but necessarily fails. In other words, the post/colonial subject paradoxically mourns the loss of the ability to mourn. The history of the colonized turns out to be structurally melancholic, a history of lost histories.

Bereft of language, the colonized subject has nothing left but the body to articulate loss, hence the prevalence of fragmented, damaged bodies in Filipino/American art. So while a great number and range of critics have used Freudian melancholia as a way to theorize subjectivity, especially in relation to sexual, racial, and gendered subordination,[6] or as a metaphor for national, transnational, and diasporic imaginings,[7] what has remained underexplored is the role of the body in melancholia. More typically, the model of hysteria, i.e., Freud's 1905 analysis of Dora, is invoked to theorize the repression of language and the reversion to the body as a means of voicing intensely repressed desire. The difference between hysteria and melancholia is subtle but significant. Whereas hysterical symptoms indicate the workings of repression, melancholia is about foreclosure. In other words, if hysteria is about the silencing of nonnormative subjects, melancholia is about the utter loss of language. Thus, in melancholia the body not so much speaks as falls apart.

Part of this distinction between hysteria and melancholia may depend upon the *kind* of power relation that exists between the subject and what Kaja Silverman calls the "dominant fiction."[8] For example, the hysterical Dora is treated as a perverted subject (a lesbian), a retarded subject (a child), and an imperfect subject (a woman, hence, a man without a penis). Dora's inclusion within the dominant fiction depends upon her ability to follow the script of heterosexual femininity. Logically, then, her marginalization (she is hysterical, bisexual, et cetera) indicates her refusal to follow the script. If we cast her cough as a symbol of this refusal to be a good girl, Dora's hysteria becomes social protest.

In post/colonial melancholia, the stakes and consequences change. According to Freud, his hysterical patients—white lesbians, gay white men, and straight white women—have either strayed from or refused their proper, normative roles *within* a civilized society. In contrast, the racially marked, colonized subject completely exceeds the bounds of humanity. Inhuman and bestial, Freud's "primitive" is frozen in time.[9] Culturally deprived and depraved, the "primitive" is considered almost incapable of language. From the colonizer's perspective, the colonized subject can never have lost language since s/he is inherently incapable of language. If any communication occurs, it is only through the sheer physicality and painful presence of the dismembered, colonized body. Indeed, from the perspective of the colonized, the pain is often so overwhelming that the best that one can muster is an incoherent scream.[10]

If the vocalization of pain occurs at all—as in the slaughtering of a pig in Shaw's *Nailed*—it is through inarticulate sounds, such as screaming, that take the place of language. Significantly, in his painting *Heridas de la Lengua* (see Plate 1), Ocampo pointedly uses Spanish, the language of the colonizer, in the title, which also appears in capital letters within the painting. Ocampo puns on the linguistic and bodily wounds to the *lengua,* which means both "language" and "tongue." Ironically, the Spanish language provides the double entendre that enables the representation of lingua-somatic violence committed against the colonized. Ocampo's use of Spanish symbolizes a kind of double violence: not only does his use of Spanish symbolize the attempted suppression of native languages, it underscores the desperate position of the colonized subject who must articulate his or her pain in the language of the colonizer.[11] Because such articulation must occur in Spanish, the attempt at expressing pain reinscribes the power of the colonizer and repeats the violence done to the native *lengua.* Thus, Ocampo's use of a Spanish title symbolizes the vicious circle in which the very articulation of post/colonial loss repeats the scene of colonial violence.[12] Ocampo's painting does not merely repeat the violence, however. In *Heridas,* this violence is amplified to the point of absurdity. The bodily injuries are not limited to the excision of the tongue but extend to the amputation of the head and limbs. The violence of colonization deprives the colonized subject of both head and tongue, of both subjectivity and language.

Melancholia departs from mourning in a second, significant way. There is a drastic drop in the subject's self-esteem, a drop that is absent in mourning: "In grief the world becomes poor and empty; in melancholia it is the ego itself." Indeed, melancholics are known for their constant, public self-berating and "delusional belittling" (Freud 167). In short, the ego learns to treat itself as an object. All the former ambivalence toward the lost object is redirected at the ego itself. No longer the lost object but the ego is the target of extreme hostility, what Judith Butler has called "unowned aggression." There is "something profoundly unchosen" about this destructive rage, which inhabits within yet does not belong to the colonized subject (Butler 162). Not surprisingly, what makes melancholia so dangerous is this self-destructive impulse. Fundamentally, melancholia describes the management—or mismanagement—of unowned aggression.

This radical not-belonging also may be called "disenfranchised grief," inextricable from the dispossession of land, language, and autonomy at the core of the colonial enterprise.[13] In post/colonial melancholia, the original dispossession of land and autonomy translates into dispossessed rage and grief. Thus, the tragedy of post/colonial melancholia arises not merely from the loss of an object but from the *theft* of an object. This is a layered theft: not merely losing an object or losing the right to own that object, but losing the right to own that loss.

## A Culture of Com/Plaint

And yet what Freud calls the melancholic's "delusional belittling" exhibits traces of social protest. All of the melancholic's hostile attention to the self radically diminishes the ego, but oddly enough melancholics tend to display this routine self-abasement in rather public ways: "The patient represents his ego to us as worthless, incapable of any effort and morally despicable; he reproaches himself, vilifies himself and expects to be cast out and chastised. He abases himself before everyone and commiserates his own relatives for being connected with someone so unworthy" (Freud 167). If melancholics are so ashamed of their failures and deficiencies, the constant exhibition of these faults doesn't make sense at first. What motivates this theatrical self-exposure? Freud further notes that these incessant "complaints" about the self are really "plaints in the legal sense of the word" (169). Grief turns into grievance, as Anne Cheng has argued.[14] All the complaints about oneself actually apply to someone else. The self-reproach is indexical: it points at something or someone else. As Freud puts it, this is an "attitude of revolt" (170). Ironically, of course, the plaint consistently misses its target. The colonized subject's legitimate plaint and "attitude of revolt" against the colonizer miss the target (the colonizer) and are redirected and transformed into complaints about the self. In other words, instead of aiming at the injustices of the external world, the melancholic diverts this rage against the self. The melancholic does not hide but rather displays this unceasing self-flagellation because the "complaints" are fundamentally accusatory, not self-accusatory. Melancholia is a way of replaying, remembering, and representing loss but at an extraordinary cost, that of unceasing self-punishment and self-torture.

This volatile combination of protest and public mutilation recalls the *pasyon,* the story of Jesus Christ's life, bloody death, and resurrection.

In *Pasyon and Revolution,* Reynaldo Ileto has stressed the power of this most vernacular of national narratives in the Philippines, emerging as it did in a wide range of forms: "poems, songs, scattered autobiographies, confessions, prayers and folk sayings" (10). Narrowly interpreted, the *pasyon* functioned as a tool of colonial Spanish oppression, a way to control and discipline native populations by emphasizing the values of obedience and submission and by analogizing the relationship between believer and God with that of servant and master. But narratives are notoriously unstable things. As Ileto argues, religiopolitical organizations and mass movements in the Philippines have focused on particular aspects of the *pasyon* text, insistently interpreting and identifying with Christ as a victim of political oppression. For example, Apolinario de La Cruz founded the *Cofradía de San José* in 1832. This small religious organization in Tayabas, a Tagalog province, developed into a revolutionary, peasant-based movement against the Spanish. Ileto calls Apolinario a "Tagalog Christ," one who embodied the contradictory features of humility and authority associated with Jesus Christ and who both drew upon and diverged from Christian teachings in ways that the Spanish interpreted as politically threatening. By 1841, the Spanish had killed and imprisoned hundreds of *Cofradía* followers. According to Ileto, following a mock trial, Apolinario was executed, "his body cut up into pieces, his head put in a cage and displayed atop a pole stuck along the roadside" (62).

Within the Spanish colonial regime, the ritualized self-sacrifice is officially sanctioned, readily accessible, yet potentially revolutionary. The *pasyon*'s revolutionary potential inheres in the instability of a powerful sign, that of the martyr. Such a figure draws upon and converts the symbolic value of a suffering Christ from the acceptance of hierarchical relationships, e.g., between God and man and between colonizer and colonized, to the acceptance of the pain that necessarily accompanies an anticolonial struggle for a greater, communal good. In vernacular versions of the dialogues between Christ and Mary, the son's rejection of filial duty and his turn to a higher cause and community reveal how the closest of kinship bonds can be severed and transformed. Ileto stresses the importance of concepts like *damay,* which is translated as "participation, involvement, or empathy":

Death at the hands of the "establishment" was, after all, an event familiar to them through the story of Christ; it would have been one more act of *damay* for them to die for their cause. Apolinario taught the cofrades to accept suffering, even death, for the sake of their union. Perhaps he was right; perhaps those hundreds of deaths contributed to the survival of an ideal. . . . But even more than the memory of a specific man and a specific movement, it was the vitality of the pasyon tradition that made it possible for ordinary folk to recognize the appearance of other Christ-like figures, each bringing the same message of hope that Apolinario brought. In this way did he live on in those that came after him. (62–63)

The significance of Apolinario's and his followers' deaths thus lies not so much in their nearly suicidal failure but rather in the recapturing of an established iconographic and rhetorical symbology like that of the *pasyon,* which oscillates so crucially between modes of passive acceptance and active insurrection.

Previously dismissed as irrational, instinctual, and fragmented by nationalist historians in the Philippines, these mystical and millennial movements have now come to be viewed as the larger context for the emergence of famed revolutionary heroes like Emilio Aguinaldo and Andrés Bonifacio. Radically rewriting the history of events familiar to Philippine scholars, Ileto privileged the unfamiliar worldview of such "cults" and, for the first time, allowed Filipinos to view Bonifacio and the rise of the Katipunan as far from unique phenomena. According to a *Philippine Daily Inquirer* review, Ileto's rereading of the *pasyon's* significance "demonstrated the plausibility of the absurd in Philippine history: that it was the ritual reading of the *Pasyon*—this colonial, Catholic instrument for thought control in that era—that really gave 'the grammar of dissent' for the revolutionaries" (Molina-Azurin). Ileto offers a powerful critique of a number of scholarly and academic blind spots:

Social scientists unable to view society in other than equilibrium terms are bound to conclude that these movements are aberrations or the handiwork of crazed minds, alienated individuals, or external agitators. On the other hand, many scholars sympathetic to these movements tend to fit them into a tight, evolutionary framework

that leads to a disparagement altogether of cultural values and traditions as just a lot of baggage from our feudal and colonial past.
The present study points out precisely the possibility that folk religious traditions and such cultural values as *utang na loób* and *hiya,*
which usually promote passivity and reconciliation rather than conflict, have latent meanings that can be revolutionary. This possibility
emerges only by regarding popular movements not as aberrations,
but occasions in which hidden or unarticulated features of society
reveal themselves to the contemporary inquirer. (10)

Writing history "from below," as he puts it, Ileto also offers a new *interpretive* strategy of reading history. Much of his work is devoted to thick,
close readings of various vernacular texts, and he is highly attuned to
rhetorical experimentation and semiotic slippages. Often resembling
literary analysis, *Pasyon and Revolution* implicitly advocates a literary approach to history and culture. An understated yet important innovation,
Ileto's methodological experiment is unsurprising given his larger
argument that inventive and deliberate misreadings of the *pasyon* text
generated political energies that converted into mass movements.

Emerging during Spanish colonization, the amalgamation of self-
degradation and protest that defines "passional culture"—a term used
by a scholar of southern Spanish penitential rites—has survived both
the violent transition to American rule and the rapid onset of imperial
forgetting in the colony and the metropole.[15] In Filipino America, the
presence of "passional culture" is all too evident: the sheer physicality and theatricality of contemporary artists and writers are inescap-
able. Post/colonial melancholia is played out literally through the body,
through violent images of bodily fragmentation. Here, the melancholic's failure to hit the target—the confusion of (anticolonial) plaint with
(self-injurious) complaint—has a cultural, political significance that is
tied to the colonial relationship between the Philippines and Spain. In
the Filipino/American context, however, the struggle for cultural and
political expression is additionally shaped by the burden of massive
forgetting: the almost complete erasure of the Philippine-American
War and America's imperial legacy from the United States' national
imaginary. In other words, imperial forgetting enacts a kind of psychic
violence. Not surprisingly, in Ocampo's and Shaw's work psychic in-

jury coincides with physical injury. These artists attempt to represent post/colonial loss and imperial violence in their work and, more significantly, to engage with the very terms of cultural representation in the United States that continue to reinscribe a politics of imperial forgetting. Filipino/American art insists on an intimate connection between psyche and soma or, more specifically, between psychic trauma and physical injury. Thus, in the most literal sense, there is something psychosomatic about the violence and contestation that define post/colonial melancholia.

If the death of the "Tagalog Christ" tenaciously lives on as part of the symbology of the Filipino diaspora, its continued existence has to do with form (the colonial dissemination and mass recognizability of the narrative), content (Apolinario's "message" of a higher spiritual or protonationalist calling), and a third element that I provisionally call "incarnated style." With the phrase "incarnated style," I want to invoke Christian and animist cultures of embodied presence and devotional praxis, i.e., beliefs in the material manifestation of the ineffable or the divine. But I also refer, rather loosely, to Arjun Appadurai's work on the "social life of things" and, in particular, his discussion of luxury goods "not so much in contrast to necessities (a contrast filled with problems), but as goods whose principal use is *rhetorical* and *social,* goods that are simply *incarnated signs*" (38). Appadurai uses incarnation as a way to theorize consumption and an economics of desire such that the exclusivity of luxuries can be marked and acknowledged but without falling into a crude opposition between extravagance and necessity. However, I am more interested in the thick materiality and utter malleability of such signs: "The necessity to which *they* [luxury goods] respond is fundamentally political" (38). (In historiography studies, Hayden White has called this the "content of the form of history"; and in African American cultural studies, a number of critics have commented on the politics and materiality of style, e.g., hair politics.)[16] While the ephemeral, malleable, yet durable nature of incarnated signs like the *pasyon* accounts for its survival through time and across space, e.g., the Filipino diaspora, the embodied theatricality of the *pasyon* accounts for the viability of kinetic memories and performance as a method of cultural transmission.

## Passional Potentiality and Infinitival Subjectivity

For incarnated style to work, a distinctive community of readers or viewers must exist. It is the volatile nature of the *kind* of subjectivity proposed by Apolinario and his *cofrades* that explains the power and survival of the *pasyon*. For nineteenth-century *campesinos* interpreting vernacular versions of the *pasyon,* did the Tagalog Christ actively or passively suffer? Why were the Spanish and then American regimes always trying to determine whether Filipinos were assimilated friends or belligerent foes? Why do "Filipinos today seem to be so adept at handling tricky situations that demand shifting or multiple identifications and commitments" (Ileto, "The Philippine-American War" 7)? In Angel Shaw's *Nailed,* Lucy Reyes claims she is possessed by the spirit of Holy Infant. What theory or conception of agency could begin to account for Shaw's representation of Reyes's crucifixion?

Separated by enormous gulfs in time, the diverse political and cultural conditions that I cluster together in this book nonetheless produce a conception of the self primarily defined by potentiality rather than agency, what I call "infinitival subjectivity."[17] With the grammatically inflected phrase "infinitival subjectivity," I simply mean that Filipinos are, at any given moment, potentially active or potentially passive. This suspension between action and inaction is not surprising given the ambivalence of the *pasyon* subject. The definition of the Latin word *passio* contains, by the fourteenth century, both *passivus* ("passive, being acted on") and *passum* ("subject of action") (Latham 334–35). Conventionally referred to as a grammatical "mood," the "infinitive" is defined by the *Oxford English Dictionary* as "the name of that form of a verb which expresses simply the notion of the verb without predicating it of any subject." Unattached to any particular subject, the infinitive expresses the potential for various kinds of actions, which can be rather haphazard and unpredictable precisely because they are not connected to a subject. I am especially interested in the disconnect between event ("the notion of the verb"; something *happens*) and agent (the idea of a "subject" that makes something happen).

But I want to stress once more that the *pasyon* disallows the theorization of endless or unlimited possibility. First, the *pasyon* owes its origins and circulation to colonial structures, which necessarily delimit agential event. Second, for an event (change) to occur, there must be some kind of connection between the subject and the verb.[18] Ever dependent on the act of interpretation, collective action here is not unlimited but infinitive.[19] Hence, the very idea and grammar of the passion are structured by a paradoxical combination of insurrection and willing acquiescence that explains the cultural survival of these spectacular rites and aesthetic in the contemporary moment.

## Wounds of the Tongue

Manuel Ocampo's paintings are explicit variations on the *pasyon,* which is used repeatedly as a symbol of colonial violence.[20] Ocampo's use of Spanish text illustrates the primacy of language as a site of traumatic violence and melancholic loss. In the following close readings of Ocampo's *Heridas de la Lengua,* though, I address the physicality of these portraits of decapitated, amputated figures and the physicality of colonial violence even as some of the paintings are "deliberately scraped and peeled to create a sense of mock-historical time" (Laurence 143).[21] Significantly, the figure in *Heridas, Senakulo, Regalo de Sacrificio,* and other *pasyon* portraits is male (see Plate 1 and Figures 2–3). As such, *Heridas* lends itself to the model of castration as the primary, if problematic, way to theorize colonized subjectivities. Below, I first outline the uses and limitations of employing castration as an interpretive model. I then turn to melancholia as an alternative model that more fully accounts for Ocampo's disturbing combination of violence and self-mutilation and that allows more fluid delineations of colonized subjectivities.

It is almost banal but still necessary to address the castration anxiety that pervades the depiction of beheading in *Heridas. Heridas* works as a powerful portrayal of colonial castration, yet it simultaneously resonates with and appeals to a male chauvinist nationalism. How so? Recall Freud's classic scene of castration, which underwrites his conception of fetishism. Once upon a time, the little boy is horrified by the sight of his naked mother's—not breast, not pubic hair, but—vagina, otherwise known as the missing penis. In this clearly misogynist formulation, the boy (never a girl) learns his first, rather traumatic lesson about sexual difference. Happily, of course, his penis assures him that he is on the right

FIGURE 2. Manuel Ocampo, *Senakulo,* 1989. Acrylic on canvas and wood, 177.8 x 121.92 cm.

side of difference. Unhappily ever after, however, he is haunted by the threat of castration. In other words, the boy's castration anxiety derives from a visual threat to his sense of bodily integrity. As the feminist narratologist Mieke Bal puts it, "One gender's wholeness must be safeguarded by the other's fragmentation" (*Double Exposures* 300).

In the colonial context, one nation's integrity is safeguarded through the dismemberment of another nation. In *Heridas* a beheaded male figure represents the scene of colonial castration. Oblivious or defiant, the

FIGURE 3. Manuel Ocampo, *Regalo de Sacrificio,* 1990. Acrylic on canvas, 182.88 x 121.92 cm. Collection of Georganne Deen, Los Angeles.

figure sits upright and stubbornly clutches a knife. Someone else, let us say the colonizer, beheaded and amputated the man. The centered, bleeding heart turns and faces us, a frontal attitude that discomfits us even as it fascinates us. Like it or not, the viewer is forced to participate in the colonizing gaze. In other words, we are compelled to gaze at the castration that secures our own sense of wholeness. Viewed as a scene of castration, *Heridas* offers a powerful representation of colonial subjugation that engages and troubles the colonizing gaze.

Yet the interpretive model of colonial castration reveals some of the limitations of Ocampo's representations of colonial violence. The power of *Heridas* relies on a particular (straight, male) subjectivity that passes itself off as normative, even universal. Within the framework of colonial castration, Ocampo's selection of male figures has disturbing repercussions for the theorization of colonized subjectivities because the problematic representation of woman as lack in Freudian castration parallels the absence of woman as focal colonized subject in Ocampo's paintings.[22] The Philippine nation is figured as masculine, a conflation between man and humanity (see Figure 4). According to the fetish-

FIGURE 4. Manuel Ocampo, untitled, 1988. Oil on canvas, 46 5/16 x 40 inches.

ism model, women count as incomplete subjects at best. In Ocampo's paintings, women are not present as central subjects and so anticolonial nationalism seems to be a male prerogative. Instead, the representation of the colony as female seems to stand in for the actual representation of female colonized subjects. In her essay "The Pasyon Pilapil: An-'other' Reading," Priscelina Patajo Legasto emphasizes gender in her analysis of the *Pasyon Pilapil,* the traditional religious text widely disseminated during Spanish rule that Ileto examines in greater detail in *Pasyon and Revolution.* Legasto suggests that the two "archetypal and contradictory" roles of Eve as the source of innate evil and corruption and of the Virgin Mary as the representative of goodness and purity were an important tool of Spanish colonization in the realm of signifying practices (85). Legasto then extends this analysis to the way in which imperialists and nationalists rely on very different but equally passive representations of the Philippines as female: "The Philippine colony was imaged as woman prostituted by imperialists but held sacred by nationalists. In both valuations, however, the country, like woman, was represented as passive, immobile territory contested over by males" (87).

The conclusion that Ocampo's work is misogynistic is a bit too hasty, though, and the dismissal of Ocampo's work as chauvinist is peremptory. What happens if one reverses the relationship between (Freudian) theory and (Ocampo) text? Instead of assuming that the castration model reveals the limitations of Ocampo's paintings, how might one read *Heridas* such that it begins to reveal the inadequacies— no pun intended—of the castration model? How might *Heridas* mark the limits of Freudian castration?

Consider a melancholic reading of *Heridas.* Glance again at the decapitated head and severed limb. If a painting can be taken as a composite of visual signs, the head, hands, and feet are two obvious indications of pointing and looking.[23] They direct our attention to things within or without the painting. But in *Heridas* both head and leg have been lopped off. Hence, the eyes that would gaze back at us— that would accuse the colonizer—are missing in this grotesque, visual narration of violence committed against the colonized. Similarly, the finger that would accuse is missing in the painting *Regalo de Sacrificio* ("Gift of Sacrifice," Figure 3). In this scene of self-amputation, the left hand is missing while the right hand grips a knife, angled precisely at the point of amputation. Symbolized by the missing left hand, the plaint—the legitimate protest against colonialism—is markedly, violently absent. Instead of posing a threat against an external enemy, the right hand clutching the knife turns inward as the direction and target of rage change. Thus, the plaint against the colonizer becomes an act of self-injury.

Take a second look at the bleeding heart in *Heridas*. At first glance, the arced strokes resemble blood spraying out of the chest. But upon closer inspection, one notices that the brushstrokes move in the opposite direction of what one would expect from blood.[24] They begin outside, in the margins of the painting, and move in toward the chest. Instead of spurting blood, the curved lines look like the blurred, frozen movements of something stabbing at the torso. Moreover, the curving streaks are gray, not red. The wound to the chest simply is not as literal and as gory as the bright red amputated limbs. The chest injuries occur at another level altogether, daubed onto the seated figure as a second layer of paint and meaning. Supposing that *Heridas* is a self-portrait, the artist's brush itself becomes a self-mutilating dagger. *Heridas* contains a layered representation of post/colonial melancholia wherein the distinction between self-injury, subject-formation, and political expression is difficult to detect.

## Melancholic Laughter

Should we always take Ocampo's paintings so seriously? What happens when we allow the interjection of humor in our third reading of the Christlike figure in *Heridas*? Though disturbingly pathetic, the beheaded figure's stubbornness may also strike us as absurd, ludicrous, and even funny. His head and leg are sliced off and still he clutches a knife. What, we may muse, does this fellow think he is doing? Does he not know when to give up? The figure resembles a chicken running around with its head cut off, and the spouting blood looks like it belongs to a cartoon. It is horrifying to watch, yet we want to laugh a little, even though we know it is tragic.

The open wounds of *Heridas* turn out to be jokes in which Ocampo is poking fun at himself. This self-mocking, perhaps melancholic laughter is a powerful, if extremely unpredictable, source of pleasure. While such laughter risks trivializing the violence that underpins post/colonial rage, the laughter clearly functions as a defense mechanism, a way to survive the ravages of grief. Moreover, in poking fun at himself, Ocampo calls upon a community to do something other than tear others and self apart, instead to explode in laughter, to fall apart laughing. However ephemerally, the communal act heals even as it causes pain to both the group and the individual. Melancholic laughter functions as aural evidence within a community that daily contends with a history of post/colonial loss and the forces of imperial amnesia. *Heridas* exploits the melancholic tension between individual complaint and collective plaint, shifting and converting the symbolic value of images of injury from that of martyrdom and suffering to that of communal laughter and healing. Ocampo's *pasyon* paintings are prototypical examples of post/colonial melancholia in Filipino/American art, wherein the representation of bodily injury is simultaneously an expression of social protest, self-denigration, self-mockery, and communal regeneration.

In the preceding series of readings of Ocampo's *Heridas de la Lengua,* I have argued that the melancholic's unnaming of loss—this monumental absence of appellation—serves as an interpretive point of departure for a reading of Ocampo's inclusion of text, i.e., Spanish, English, and Filipino. For Freud, pathological, prolonged reactions to loss are precipitated by the subject's failure to name the lost object. For Ocampo and the post/colonial context, however, language itself is a site of loss, a form of captation through decapitation. I also offered the concept of post/colonial melancholia as an alternative to heteronormative, masculinist approaches to the intersection between colonialism and psychoanalysis, like those modeled on fetishism and castration. Though its association with grief and loss comes with risks, i.e., the reactionary mobilization of crude nostalgia for an impossibly pure homeland, precolonial community or "whole" subject, post/colonial melancholia also opens moments of political possibility and futurity by envisioning the potential conversion of individual grief into societal grievance: melancholic complaint gets transformed into anticolonial plaint. Finally, Ocampo's portraits offer themselves as jokes, objects of ridicule that provoke the formation of communal bonds of laughter.

However, if *Heridas de la Lengua* is a portrait of the psychosomatic violence and loss that constitute Filipino post/colonial melancholia, I thus far have managed to sidestep a discussion of its depiction of whole bodies, e.g., the portrait of the Virgin and infant floating next to the central figure. Titled *At Pilipinas,* the framed picture of an incongruously serene mother and child counterbalances both the gore of the central figure and the floating scroll inscribed with the painting's main title. What does this embedded text "do" to the primary text?

The family portrait can be interpreted several ways. First, the pair's tranquil domesticity sets up a binary between the (female) home and the (male) nation that, once again, casts the colonized subject as heteronormatively male, separate from and protective of the familial domestic space. Indeed, in the previously mentioned *Pasyon Pilapil* text studied by Ileto, Legasto, and other Philippinist critics, the dialogue between Mary and Jesus depends upon a similar binary. Pleading with her son to stay with her, Mary symbolizes the familial and filial obligations that are the final obstacle in Jesus's (and the protonationalist's) path toward an alternative community and a higher calling. Ileto elaborates upon the significance of these scenes of home-leaving:

> The pasyon text also contains specific themes which, far from encouraging docility and acceptance of the status quo, actually probe the limits of prevailing social values and relationships. Take the extensive treatment of Jesus Christ's preparation to depart fom home. This is a classic exposition—found in common soap operas and novels of the role of *utang na loób* in defining an adult's response to his mother's care in the past. For all the comfort and love *(layaw)* that she gave her son, Mary asks, why must she lose him? Jesus, despite his attachment to his mother, can only reply that he has a higher mission to fulfill—to suffer and die in order to save mankind:

> | *Ngayon po ay naganap na* | The longed-for hour |
> | *ang arao ng aquing pita* | when I shall save mankind |
> | *nang pagsacop co sa sala,* | has now arrived, |
> | *Ina, i, ito ang mula na* | Mother, from this day on |
> | *nang di nating pagquiquita.* | each other we shall not see (78: 7) |

There comes a time in a man's life when he has to heed a call "from above." In the pasyon it is God's wish that is carried out; but what was to prevent the Indio from actualizing this "myth" by joining a rebel leader who was often a religious figure himself? To pave the way for this experience, the *pasyon* posits the possibility of separation from one's family under certain conditions. In a society that regards the family as its basic unit even in the economic and political spheres, this certainly goes "against the grain." (Ileto 14–15)

Women are powerful obstructions to the kind of "separation" from the home and family required by these mass movements.

Returning to our reading of the family portrait in *Heridas:* adjacent to and slightly behind the decapitated Christ figure, the positioning of the pair indicates their separate, marginal, yet necessary presence. This indispensable subordination to the central figure recalls some of the ongoing debates about the role of women in depictions of Christ's sexuality, especially in Western medieval and Renaissance studies. For example, Caroline Walker Bynum has countered the prevailing argument among scholars of the late Middle Ages and early Renaissance, first articulated by Leo Steinberg, that the explicit representation of Christ's sexuality was intended as a display of (male) power: theologically speaking, Christ's vulnerability to both death and the temptations of the body ultimately underscores how impervious he is to the body.[25] Instead, Bynum argues that not only should we be careful of assuming that medieval viewers of these portraits of Christ eroticized genitalia and other body parts that modern viewers automatically associate with sexuality and desire,[26] but that there are important alternative ways of reading Christ's body that depend much more thoroughly on female presence and/or feminine, especially maternal and nurturing, qualities. Bynum reminds us that "many medieval assumptions linked woman and flesh and the body of God. Not only was Christ enfleshed with flesh from a woman; his own flesh did womanly things: it bled, it bled food and it gave birth" (101). Perhaps more flexible when it came to the possibility of gender reversals, medieval people "sometimes saw a breast (or a womb) when they saw Christ's side" (Bynum 87). Though women still occupy marginal roles and spaces in these representations of Christ, Bynum reminds us of the interdependence between marginal and central figures.[27] Similarly, I think, Ocampo sets up a subordinate yet interdependent relation between the decapitated Christ figure and the floating painting of Madonna and child, a colonial dynamic that is amplified by the interplay between the Filipino text *At Pilipinas* and the Spanish text *Heridas de la Lengua*. (*Pilipinas* refers both to the country, named after a Spanish monarch, and to the women of the Philippines.)

Finally, however, *Heridas* indicates the limits of female marginality in anticolonial texts. The second half of this chapter is thus devoted to the question, What happens when the subject of the *pasyon* is a woman? In Angel Shaw's *Nailed*, Lucy Reyes's gender and racial reversal makes a difference. Moreover, Shaw's complex transnational identification with the native female penitent opens complicated questions about the political feasibility of a feminist diaspora. For if in Ocampo's work the textual ambivalence of puns in the colonial language (*lengua* means both "tongue" and "language") facilitates cultural continuity for the Filipino diaspora, in Shaw's video the ambivalent aurality of her narrating voice produces a fascinating oscillation between connection and disconnection with the homeland. Shaw's identification with Reyes is shot through with both *heimweh*, a painful longing for the homeland, and *fernweh*, the "opposite of homesick" (Johnson).[28]

### The "Wide Open" Eye and the Cutting Style of Nailed

Like Ocampo, Filipino/American videomaker Angel Velasco Shaw engages and critiques the colonizing gaze in her 1992 experimental documentary *Nailed*. *Nailed* is a remarkably dense onslaught of sound and scene, in which Shaw weaves performance art and personal narration with live footage from her yearlong stay in the Philippines.[29] Here too the act of self-affirmation is invariably, paradoxically self-injurious while the act of self-injury turns out to be self-affirmative. After all, the fifty-minute video centers on a woman's reenactment of Christ's crucifixion. But while Ocampo's paintings offer melancholic laughter as a source of communal healing, Shaw's intense identification with Lucy Reyes's suffering posits a substantially different kind of post/colonial melancholia that mobilizes a complex politics of nostalgia and foregrounds the gendering of colonized subjectivity. Out of the mélange of images and events that make up *Nailed*, I analyze three distinct sections that precede or interrupt the depiction of Lucy Reyes's crucifixion: the opening dream montage; the juxtaposition of an infant's baptism with the slaying of a pig; and, finally, a performance piece by the writer Jessica Hagedorn.

Belying the title's promise of pain, *Nailed* opens with a tranquil montage of Philippine sky and beach imagery. Over these stereotypical images of a tropical Eden, Shaw narrates a disquieting dream about battling angels, one of which falls to Earth and explodes into fragments: "When he hit the ground, his body shattered into a lot of different parts, but one portion of his face remained intact. It quickly solidified into the ground. His eye was wide open. And a golden tear formed. . . . That was a dream I had one night." Shaw's narration transforms landscape into dreamscape. The images of sun-drenched beaches and tumbling blue waves lose some of their tourist, escapist appeal and instead become highly personal and somehow numbing. Shaw's tone is personal, intimate, and yet detached, befitting the word image of the fallen angel's cracked head, staring eye, and single tear.

From the very beginning of *Nailed,* Filipina/American subject formation is associated with deformity and fragmentation.[30] What keeps this partial subject "intact"? The golden tear symptomatizes the presence of nostalgia, a special kind of post/colonial melancholia that vacillates between wistful longing and tempered rage. The *Oxford Encyclopedic Dictionary* defines nostalgia as a "form of melancholia caused by prolonged absence from one's home or country." It is derived from the Greek words for "return home" and "pain." Literally a form of homesickness, nostalgia commonly denotes a wistful longing, a backward glance across time. In Shaw's case, this glance travels across space toward something that figures as home or a lost home. But Shaw does not travel back in time, a crucial difference between her project and those of anthropologists and ethnographers who freeze the object of study in space (as exotic Other) and time (as primitive and backward). Shaw is sick for home, but the sickness is also about longing for a home that is not there. Again, in melancholic terms, the post/colonial subject mourns not the loss of an object that she once "had" but the loss of a stolen object that she never had and has no right to have. The post/colonial nostalgic glance at "home" is perhaps about reappropriation, about mapping memories on a landscape that has been stolen. Moreover, the "wide open" eye potentially registers the horrors of colonization or perhaps gazes longingly at the landscape impossibly designated as home.

In the form of a video camera, of course, this "wide open" eye functions as a recording device of past and present injuries.

After this opening dream montage, two interwoven events frame the pending appearance of Reyes: an infant's christening and the slaughtering of a pig. Like much of *Nailed,* this twelve-minute section is filled with jarring jump cuts and unlikely couplings of images. A series of jump cuts begins with benign portraits of Shaw's baby god-daughter at her baptism. Her still floppy head nestled in her mother's arms, the newborn yawns at the camera documenting the communal affirmation of her identity. Abruptly, her christening is relentlessly inter-cut with much too close, lingering shots of a live pig being staked and gutted in preparation for a feast presumably to be held after the naming ceremony. Its life and horrifying death are recorded and res-urrected on screen. One of the last images of the pig is implicitly Christlike, its decapitated head hanging on the side of a tree. Basically, Shaw chronicles a pig's *pasyon.*

According to *Nailed*'s editing logic, the tortured animal's awful shrieks mark the child's naming and inclusion within a community. From several angles and at close range, we witness the first cutting of the pig as a wooden stake is driven through its abdomen. The pig's shrill death scream holds at a single sustained pitch, pausing only for quick, sharp gasps before continuing to cry. Head shots of the baby and then of the pig form tightly paired edits, spliced together by the intolerable scream. In one of these paired edits, the baby's blurry, limp head floats sideways in the foreground, her body cut off by the edge of the screen. In the next frame, the pig writhes in pain, the camera focused on its moving mouth and unblinking eyes. The pig is stabbed, drained of its blood, disemboweled, roasted, carved, and then methodi-cally chopped up into neat little squares (see Figure 5). The animal gradually disintegrates while the oblivious infant is gently rocked and cradled in her relatives' arms.

On the one hand, the child's baptism provides the occasion for the affirmation of the communal self, and the celebratory feast reinforces kinship ties and strengthens group identity. On the other hand, Shaw's attention to the pig's pain foregrounds the cost of such communion and foreshadows *Nailed*'s main event, Reyes's crucifixion. According to this sequence of images, self-affirmation coincides with extreme pain

FIGURE 5. Angel Velasco Shaw, "Reverence," from *Nailed*.

and physical mutilation. In other words, Filipina/American subject-formation is here associated with a paradoxically self-affirming desire for disjointedness and fragmentation that cannot be accounted for by colonial castration.

But while the central event of *Nailed* remains the exhibition of a woman's pain, the video is emphatically "autoethnographic," a combination of ethnography and autobiography.[31] *Nailed* is an explicitly autobiographical video that contains elegiac elements. As the closing credits roll, we read that the documentary is dedicated to the "spirit" of Shaw's dead father. At the same time, *Nailed* identifies itself both with and against traditional ethnography by foregrounding questions of authority and spectacle. The narrator's perspective is plainly subjective, unlike ethnography's tradition of neutral objectivity (which, of course, usually turns out be a veiled subjectivity). If *Nailed* functions as a portrait of another woman, it is simultaneously a self-portrait, constantly shifting and playing with the subject and object of observation. The videomaker herself appears in several scenes, accentuating the fictitiousness of documentary objectivity and explicitly inscribing herself into a text that foregrounds the ambivalence of post/colonial identity. For example, Shaw strolls down a bustling Manila sidewalk dressed in a traditional Spanish Filipino *saya* and reading excerpts from a Mark Twain essay on American imperialism—an incongruous melding of past and present that typifies the post/colonial aesthetics of *Nailed*. The Twain essay is an embedded text that explicitly alerts the viewer to the presence of post/coloniality and the videomaker's concern with decolonization. Importantly, Shaw's use of Twain enacts an ironic reversal of the marginalization of Filipino/American history. In *Nailed,* the work of a canonical American writer and thinker becomes a footnote in a Filipino/American experimental documentary.

Later in the video, of course, the visual references to American neo/colonization and mass culture are much more frequent. One particular scene is chilling perhaps because it contains no overt violence or injury. An assembly of rural schoolchildren sing and act out an American school rhyme—"The neck bone is connected to the shoulder bone. The shoulder bone is connected to the arm bone," et cetera—with distinctly American twangs. This aural sign functions as a kind of echoing mirror for the video's American audience, of which Shaw is both a member (looking at the schoolchildren) and a performer (looked at by the video's audience). The exoticization of the Philippines as a backward culture and nation begins to fail as a primary mode of spectatorship. Instead, the video begins to work as a mirror that reflects images and sounds of America, not just the Philippines, creating an eerie proximity that displaces and interpellates an American audience.[32] Thus, the video fulfills and extends Mary Louise Pratt's definition of autoethnography, wherein "people undertake to describe themselves in ways that engage with representations others have made of them."[33]

In another example of autoethnographic technique, an actor (Jessica Hagedorn) sits with her back to the camera as she watches *Nailed* on a small television. Effectively, we look over her shoulder as we watch her watching a penitent flagellate himself. In *Nailed,* looking at someone else entails looking at oneself. Or, more accurately, looking at someone else always entails looking at oneself looking at someone else. *Nailed* affords the viewer a space for critical self-reflection. It offers a mode of looking that keeps the masterful, colonizing gaze in check. Indeed, the act of flagellation is very hard to look at, so Shaw's distancing technique affords some relief from the sight of the blood. Interestingly, we see no faces, only torsos and the backs of heads. The penitent sports a wide ribbon of blood across his back while Hagedorn's torso is swathed in red cloth, a reenactment of physical injury that recalls Ocampo's paintings.

Perhaps this dramatic representation of flagellation explains why the first images of Reyes are rather ordinary, almost easy to miss. The faith healer is plainly dressed, calmly talking among her followers, quiet images that the viewer almost misses since they are intercut with the more dramatic splicing of the pig's *pasyon* and the infant's baptism. Narrating her first meeting with Reyes, Shaw recalls Reyes's explanation of her motives for the annual crucifixion, that she had had a vision of the Santo Niño when she was eighteen years old. According to Reyes, the Santo Niño told her that she had a "calling" that involved annual crucifixion. Shaw says, "And that was kind of a hard story to hear, even if it was in translation, from this woman who was so sweet. I mean, she had the face of a cherub." Of course, *Nailed* is a visual narration of what is a "hard story to hear." Using another technique typically found in autoethnographic film and video, the narrator speaks in first-person voice-over throughout the video. Shaw's tone is personal, intimate, and at times self-enclosed, making us feel as if we were eavesdropping on an internal conversation as she repeats phrases like, "I'm not part of this trance" and "routines that are rituals." Already, we feel anxious or even guilty about hearing and seeing something to which we are not usually privy.

Despite what she claims, the narrator *does* sound like she is in a trance. Shaw's first-person voice-over is an aural reenactment of Reyes's performance on the cross. Because Reyes is figured as a messenger of God, apparently possessed by the Santo Niño, Catherine Russell's study of ethnographic films of possession rituals seems relevant. Russell notes: "The actual experience of possession remains outside the limits of visual knowledge and constitutes a subtle form of ethnographic resistance: films of possession cannot, in the end, represent the 'other reality' of the other's subjectivity. Possession is itself a form of representation to which the filmmaker might aspire, but it is also a *mise en abyme* of representation, with its final signified content always beyond reach. I would like to argue that the end point of the possession semiosis is the subjectivity of the Other, which thus resists cinematic representation along with its ideology of visibility" (194). Shaw's trancelike narration is a simulation of Reyes's interiority, which "remains outside the limits of visual knowledge." While Shaw's video recording of Reyes naturally constitutes an attempt at visual representation, the aural content of *Nailed* nonetheless underscores the impossibility of representing the faith healer's experience on the screen. I would even argue that the aural re-enactment represents the videomaker's acknowledgment of the complicity and representational problematics that necessarily attend any representation of the Other.[34]

Indeed, this sense of complicity extends to the viewer of *Nailed*. Both the content and the form of *Nailed* configure the viewer's position as a kind of vacillating tension between witness and spectator. Here, it is important to distinguish between witness and spectator, the latter of which implies greater distance from the ethnographic subject and is more closely associated with the colonizing gaze. Russell distinguishes between the two terms in her analysis of the filming of possession rituals, which, like the crucifixion, are "community events intended to be witnessed, but they are not addressed to a spectator" (235). Reyes's crucifixion clearly takes place within a communal, public space, filled by an organized chaos that renders long, stable camera shots impossible and that requires Shaw to change positions and angles hurriedly and frequently. Thus, what Russell calls the "automatic or fixed point of view" associated with the spectator becomes technically impossible for Shaw (235). On the other hand, Shaw's camera equipment and autoethnographic sensibility necessarily prevent her and the viewer of *Nailed* from becoming witnesses.

But confronted with the visual confusion of *Nailed,* what retains the viewer's attention? If *Nailed* is a "hard story to hear," it is often very hard to watch, but there is something that makes us try to witness. As painful as it is to watch and hear the act of injury, there is something compelling about the representation of violence. According to *Nailed*'s editing sequence, the pig's slaughter prepares us for the documentary's central event. In a sense, the pig's *pasyon* compels us to watch further in anticipation of Reyes's crucifixion. *Nailed* capitalizes on the viewer's anticipation of the public crucifixion as much as possible, a use of suspense that propels and motivates the entire documentary. Suspense motivates the viewer; it keeps the curious viewer waiting and watching.

With a mixture of guilt and desire, Shaw narrates her own impatience to see Reyes: "I was in such a hurry to get to the stage, this half built stage where Lucy was going to be crucified, because I wanted to see whether or not she was going to suffer. I felt horrible about that because I think the majority of the people who were there also came for the same reason, partially—I mean, I think they believed in her. They believed in this re-enactment. They believed that she had a calling and that she was special and that somehow she was a messenger from God. And I wanted to see signs of that." Like the viewer, Shaw knows that Lucy will be crucified. Since we know *what* will happen, the suspense comes from not knowing exactly *how* it will happen, i.e., whether Reyes will suffer. Shaw seeks visible evidence of Reyes's suffering: "And I wanted to see signs of *that*" (emphasis added). But the ambiguity of the pronoun "that" raises another possibility: "that" may also refer to the other people in the crowd. In other words, Shaw's attraction to the stage reveals a desire to see evidence of the crowd's faith in Reyes as much as a desire to see Reyes's *pasyon*. In this way, Shaw's editing and narrating styles produce intensely personalized effects that nevertheless engage with a community of witnesses and viewers.

Moreover, Shaw's use of suspense affords her the space in which to experiment with an antilinear and fragmentary style of editing and mixing without ever losing the viewer. That is, the overriding narrative or *telos* of Reyes's crucifixion allows the production of something antinarrative. *Nailed* both refuses and relies on the power of linear narrative. Shaw's fragmentary editing style can be viewed as a series of wounds to the traditional, linear narrative. At the same time, this fragmented documentary feels so seamless and smoothly knitted together. While the juxtaposition of myriad images is relentless, spanning election campaigns, fiestas, church services, rice farms, and urban nightlife, Shaw's fragmentary editing style never lapses into incoherence. It is as if the "wide open eye" and cutting style of Shaw's camera work and editing are bound together by the visual promise of yet another open wound, that represented by Lucy Reyes. Though it certainly risks bombarding the viewer, the constant shuffling of disparate images is bound together by Shaw's first-person narration and by the promise of a woman's voluntary crucifixion.

*Nailed* is a melancholic production both in the sense that it represents Filipina/American subject-formation as melancholic and that it produces an aesthetics of melancholia. As an experimental videomaker, Shaw makes explicit the connections between vision and violence in her critique of the colonizing gaze. But her identification with Reyes ("I want to embrace the 'Lucy' in me") indicates that there is another significant dimension to this representation of the relationship between vision and injury that cannot be reduced to an oppositional stance against the colonizing gaze. Rather, Shaw's identification with Reyes's wounds suggests that Filipina/American subjectivity is impelled by a desire for parts, shards, and fragments, a gendered process that diverges radically from the search for unity and wholeness that drives colonial castration.

### *Heimweh/Fernweh:* The Sound of Distance

As complex as its attitude toward the spectacle of Lucy Reyes's crucifixion is, *Nailed* does more than disrupt the colonizing gaze and its male-privileging economy of castration. Despite its emphasis on the body, *Nailed* dramatizes not the creation of presence, but rather the aurally marked, transnational dialectic of distance and proximity. Shaw's narratorial voice reenacts and closes in on—gets proximate to—Reyes's trance. By drawing our attention to the aural elements of Reyes's *pasyon,* *Nailed* proposes an alternative mode of proximity that recognizes the limits of connection between such radically differently placed subjects and yet keeps alive the possibility of intimacy. In fact, Shaw ultimately *must* switch from the visual to the aural because she is trying to do the impossible. In the attempt to document on video the phenomenon of possession, she wants to make material not only what is invisible but what is immaterial. So the documentary finally turns away from the nostalgic lure of authentic, "indigenous" presence. But in doing so, Shaw still is proposing a potentially problematic homosocial and transnational bond with Reyes, who is figured in the video as emblematic of the maternal homeland, the stereotypical bearer of female, indigenous secrets. Shaw thereby risks the crudest form of diasporic *balikbayan* nostalgia.[35] Shaw is filled with homesickness, or *Heimweh,* conflating her psychic pangs—*Weh* means "pain" in German—for the homeland with Reyes's performance of somatic pain.

But as I already have noted, the filmmaker's tone remains curiously remote and detached. Subtending Shaw's longing for proximity is its opposite: *Fernweh* (literally "distance pain" in German). My switch to German is opportunistic but, I hope, compelling: In English, "wanderlust" is offered as the antonym for nostalgia, but it does not quite capture the politics of feeling suggested by the German antonym. Hence, *Nailed* offers a mixture of *Heimweh* and *Fernweh* both visually and aurally. This mixture makes possible a critical and paradoxical return to a homeland that is ever lost. In so doing, *Nailed* disrupts the economy of organized forgetting in the United States and the internalization of that imperial imperative both in the homeland and in Filipino America.

## Conclusion: Loss in American Culture

If Gayl Jones's question posed at the beginning of her novel *Corregidora*— "How could she bear witness to what she's never lived?"—continues to haunt the United States, it is because Jones's answer is so troubling. In Arlene Keizer's reading of African American slave narratives and their generic descendants, there exists a "space of postmemory" (6). But enjoined across generations to remember over and over the trauma of slavery, the women of *Corregidora* obtain no freedom from the repetition of history. They are enslaved yet again as matrilineal reproducers— psychic breeders—of a kind of somatic memory that not only refuses to go away but fully inhabits their bodies.

The question for Filipino America is in some ways the opposite: how can one remember what has been so ruthlessly forgotten? How does Filipino America represent the twinned regimes of organized imperial forgetting and internalized post/colonial forgetting in American culture? How might Filipino American texts offer a space of "postforgetting"? How has Filipino America come to mark and *transform* the space of imperial forgetting and absence? The answer here involves the spectacle of physical trauma. Clustering radically differing texts, this chapter deliberately overreaches itself so as to underscore the wider, cross-media significance of a particular pattern of injury. In identifying an aesthetics of post/colonial melancholia in Filipino/American art, I of course do not claim that this is representative of all Filipino/American art. Indeed, at first glance, the two artists' works are almost incomparably different. Yet I juxtapose their work in this cross-media study because these texts share a distinct pattern of mutilation and injury that I call post/colonial melancholia.

The Filipino American cultural moment is marked by excessive embodiment, which constitutes an aesthetic response to the relegation of Filipino America to invisibility and absence in an imperial culture of forgetting. These artists' insistence on the body is a way of remembering through dismembering. But these acts of memory are primarily *aesthetic* and *stylistic*—rather than historical—interventions. Perhaps registering the problems of creating presence through history, they instead turn to the terrain of style, form, and the aesthetic. Invoking the *pasyon* narrative and its vernacular iterations in Philippine anticolonial history, these artists create an aesthetic of embodiment that contains a theory of potential subjectivity defined not by (authenticating, immanent) presence or by (obliterative, assimilative) absence, but by a simultaneity of absence and presence. Here, absence and presence do not discount each other. Characterized by the oscillation between the agential and the assimilative that is at the heart of the *pasyon* narrative, this infinitival subject of potentiality *can be* the agent of insurrection or it *can be* the passive recipient of violence. Indeed, its very potentiality and flexibility have secured its cultural survival through time and around the globe. The *pasyon* is eminently local *and* global. Recognizable throughout the archipelago and the diaspora, the power and appeal of its local irruptions (and the contemporary Filipino American cultural moment is one such instance) has to do both with the plasticity of the sign and the hybridized incarnational-animist interpretive tendencies of the community of readers within which it circulates.

Post/colonial melancholia is a significant phenomenon in these texts, in Filipino/American art, and arguably in the lives of Filipino/ Americans. These artists point toward constructive ways to represent and to theorize both the continuities and rifts among Filipino/ Americans. These texts proffer definitions of community that, rather than based on affinity and the often-homogenizing pressures of co-alitionist alliances or on what Kandice Chuh most recently proposes as "subjectlessness," are predicated on performative acts of injury. For both in these texts and in the everyday joking and banter that define Filipino/American communities, moments of healing, mourning, and resistance emerge during the performance of pain. This phenomenon suggests that Filipino/American art is embedded in a culture of presence, a "passional culture" that insists on the body as a vehicle for artistic, political, and religious expression. This cultural argument may sound reductive or dangerously essentialist to some, but the fairly stable status of Filipino/American history, art, and cultural production *as* absence (or, at best, as an irksome anomaly) in the United States speaks to the need for critical approaches that understand this insistence on the body as part of a combative engagement with imperial forgetting. Filipino/American art and cultural production reappropriate both the violence of Spanish and American colonization and the violence of American amnesia. In short, the process of Filipino/American decolo-nization is far from over. That the body is persistently represented as fragmented and mutilated attests to the vestiges of colonial trauma—post/colonial melancholia.

Emerging through a peculiar intersection between the psychic and the material, the historical and psychic trauma of the past is recon-structed and represented through physical trauma. Simply put, Ocampo and Shaw make loss visible. Such a mournful attitude toward the lack of presence and visibility may sound all too familiar, much too aligned with essentialist fictions of a whole or authentic precolonial subject or the prescriptions of cultural nationalism. Here is where the recent "emergence" of Asian Canadian cultural studies and its impressive criti-cal self-reflexivity can be particularly informative for Filipino American cultural studies as it struggles with the intragroup problems of nation-alism and essentialism and with the larger context of political "non-recognition." It seems to me that recent iterations of Asian Canadian cultural criticism—perhaps in response to Canada's official racial policy of distinguishing between "visible" and nonvisible minorities—have been much more careful and inventive about the mobilization of identity politics. For example, in her essay "At the Edge of a Shattered Mirror, Community?" on Asian Canadian (especially Chinese Canadian) art and cultural production, Karlyn Koh issues a powerful warning about the assumptions and consequences of cultural projects or movements primarily animated by the promise of a "revelation of a self made whole by a successful search for her roots" or a "mourning in pathos for a loss of identity or authenticity" (164). Koh methodically dismantles the fictions of essentialism to theorize an alternative kind of intersociality, a radical vulnerability and exposure to the other: "Lying at the edge of the mirror, the pool of origins, a 'self not whole' risks being enclosed in the reflection it searches for and sees as self-knowledge. Or, facing outward, toward an unknown other, 'we Chinese Canadians' does not invent its self, but lets itself be invented, beyond the 'we' that we say we are" (162).

But by *enfleshing* loss, artists like Shaw and Ocampo emphasize the pain and costliness of the representation of loss. As I demonstrate in my close readings, their passional aesthetic of theatrical violence ultimately forgoes easy elegy. The overwhelming insistence on bodily injury and fragmentation suggests that this coming into visibility does not result in the restoration of wholeness and presence. Thus, though I would heed Koh's eloquent warnings, I want to argue that, before we conduct a poststructuralist or anti-identitarian critique of that kind of nationalist essentialism, there must still be a space for mourning and for loss, especially because, as I have argued in more detail elsewhere, there is no space for (minority) loss in American culture. Constitutively defined by the disavowal of empire, American dominant culture is instead obsessed with white loss. For example, the rifts in white fraternity produced by the Civil War as well as the continuing ideological valence of the Lost Cause tradition are monumental, formative phenomena in the making of a modern United States.[36] As such, the tragedy for Filipino America is not simply the utterly fragile fiction of an achieved self in an archipelagic-imagined community, but that there is no space for mourning any kind of loss.

On the other hand, Asian American literary studies recently has proffered the possibility of "subjectlessness." For example, Kandice Chuh suggests "conceptualizing Asian American studies as subjectless, as motivated by critique of subjectification rather than desire for subjectivity" (151). But the Filipino American cultural moment clearly refuses to cede such desire. Instead, artists like Shaw and Ocampo invoke a passional aesthetic that mobilizes an old yet new tradition of infinitival subjectivity and that plays with *Heimweh/Fernweh* notions of distance and proximity. Shaw and Ocampo repopulate the space of imperial forgetting with bodies and voices. They bring the floating, murdered bodies of Jessica Hagedorn's novel *Dogeaters* back down to the ground:

> It is then that the bullet hits him, and he falls. Stunned, Romeo is not sure why he has fallen. He tries to get up but can't, and the look of astonishment on his face is suddenly replaced by fear. He thinks he hears Trinidad calling his name. Then the world goes momentarily silent and falls away from him. He is floating on a slab of concrete, suspended above the wide avenue strewn with broken umbrellas, smashed cars, and bodies trampled by a panicked crowd. (168)

But as we see in the next chapter, the digital artist Paul Pfeiffer takes up where Shaw and Ocampo leave off. In Pfeiffer's world of computer-modified images, the relationship between figure and ground goes even more awry as the horizon itself begins to wander the American landscape.

# 2

## A Queer Horizon

### Paul Pfeiffer's Disintegrating Figure Studies

In the middle, there's the sun. Behind the sun, there's the sky,
a golden orange. Wisps of cloud are tinged brown. Sometimes
there's the flapping silhouette of a passing bird. And near the top,
there's some kind of black band that runs across the width of
the projection. As it scrolls slowly, ever so slowly, downward,
moving in front of the sun, reaching the very bottom of
the image, then reappearing at the top, it ripples. It's water.
It's rather a neat trick.
—REVIEWER'S DESCRIPTION OF PAUL PFEIFFER'S
*Morning after the Deluge* (2003)

EXCESSIVE EMBODIMENT, I have argued thus far, is a feature of
Filipino America's cultural moment. The borders of Manuel
Ocampo's canvas and Angel Shaw's screen just barely contain
the somatic violence and drama of colonial melancholia; the human
body is filled by simply too much presence. In contrast, Paul Pfeiffer's
digital and installation art features the erosion of the body and the
threatening expansiveness of space. Undeniably dazzling, if deeply un-
settling, the heaven and wavering horizon of Pfeiffer's twenty-minute
video loop *Morning after the Deluge* reveal no trace of human presence
(see Plates 2 and 3). An occasional insect, bird, or jet trail may wing
its way across the enskied canvas, but the projection screen otherwise
is filled solely by the colored void of fused dusk and dawn breaking

over the Atlantic Ocean. According to one critic, Pfeiffer thus pulls off "rather a neat trick": "Two films of the sky over Cape Cod—one of a sunrise, the other of a sunset—have been combined. The midpoint of the video projection—when the ribbon of sea is halfway down the screen, passing right through the middle of the blazing red sun—is actually made up of an image of a half-risen sun, and upside-down, that of a half-set sun" (Coxhead). Why then does the artist call *Morning* a figure study?[1] Seeking an answer to this simple question, this chapter tracks Pfeiffer's evolving conception of the human figure as it gradually disintegrates in deferral to the space that surrounds it. Drawing our attention in his earlier work to the Western colonial and neocolonial topographies that produce the human figure, Pfeiffer eventually banishes the figure altogether from the scenic landscape and, crucially, from the scene of representation itself. In other words, the backdrop emerges triumphant as the central figure recedes, and the viewer is left to sort out the political implications of the shifting epistemological and perspectivist "ground" upon which the figure usually depends. In Pfeiffer's kind of cosmos, it is no wonder that the horizon is so queer.

However, to understand that both the technological wizardry of *Morning* and its rhetorical description as a figure study are much more than a "neat trick," several nomadic detours from the close analysis of Pfeiffer's work are necessary. Starting with an account of Pfeiffer's critical reception in the West and the Philippines, this chapter moves from a discussion of classic perspectivism to feminist and psychoanalytic debates about Medusa's sublime sexuality, followed by accounts of camp sensibility, queer Filipino notions of *biyuti* (beauty) and hybrid devotional praxis, and Renaissance artists' depictions of Christ's sexuality. The haphazard trajectory of my argument mimics that of Pfeiffer's oeuvre with its diverse and quickly spiraling cultural references. Nonetheless, I detect in his work a methodical and intensely thought-out response to major shifts in dominant American aesthetic ideologies from the expansionist era of the nineteenth century to our current moment of globalizing neocolonialism. It may seem a pity to spoil the sheer loveliness of Pfeiffer's *Morning* with awful questions about sexual politics, colonial discourse, and the ideology of the aesthetic, but I hope to show that beauty itself constitutes the crime. The disquieting effect of all of

Pfeiffer's oeuvre insistently, if obliquely, indexes the brutality of the beautiful world made over by the American empire.

## Reception: *A Star Is Born*

Celebrity looms much too large in Filipino culture. Of no small significance are the detailed descriptions of classic Hollywood sex icons in Jessica Hagedorn's novel *Dogeaters*. From Elizabeth Taylor's "one violet eye, one arched black eyebrow" and Montgomery Clift's "shoulder in giant close-up," Hagedorn's ten-year-old narrator learns that the couple is "drunk with their own beauty and love, that much [she] understand[s]" (16). As a fictionalized topography of the colonized mind, Hagedorn's intoxicated, star-fixated Manila is flawless. So it is fitting that Pfeiffer has become something of a celebrity in the American and European art world and that celebrity and image are the topic of his most lauded work.[2] In scores of art journals and newspapers critics have praised his digitally modified video loops or stills of Black celebrity athletes like Michael Jordan and Larry Johnson, whose moments of ecstatic triumph on the basketball court are transformed into scenes of pain that allude to the traumatic spectacle of tortured or lynched Black men (see Figures 6–7).[3] Two books solely devoted to Pfeiffer have been published, and the serene yet naggingly familiar vista of California's seashore adorns one of their covers (see Figure 8). The photograph turns out to be one of George Barris's famous portraits of Marilyn Monroe taken in the year of her death, her iconic body now digitally expunged from the rocky beach. With perfect and ironic asymmetry, Pfeiffer's sudden fame in the art world depends upon Monroe's famously premature death.

Like his contemporaries Hagedorn and Shaw—the three are close friends—Pfeiffer is based in New York City, where he obtained a master of fine arts degree in printmaking from Hunter College, taught at Pratt, and participated in the Whitney Museum's Independent Study Program. Ever since a splashy entry in the 2000 Whitney Biennial, his has become one of the more prominent names in queer and Asian American arts, education, and activism in New York. But his critical reception reveals some troubling divisions and contradictions that generally have to do with the vexed intersection between identity politics, high-art venues, and the flexibility of American apolitical formalism.[4]

FIGURE 6. Paul Pfeiffer, three stills from *Fragment of a Crucifixion (after Francis Bacon)*, 1999. CD-ROM, projector and mounting arm, dimensions variable. Collection of Martin and Rebecca Eisenberg.

FIGURE 7. Paul Pfeiffer, *Four Horsemen of the Apocalypse (8)*, 2003. Digital duraflex print, 16.5 x 20.5 inches (41.9 x 52.1 cm). Courtesy of the artist and The Project, New York.

On the one hand, a handful of critics attentive to the dynamics of the Filipino and Filipino diasporic art world tend to embrace him a little too cursorily as a "diasporic" Filipino artist, whose sacrilegious use of Catholic symbology attracts their attention only to be fitted awkwardly into a sweeping generational and often nationalist survey of artistic progress in the Philippines.[5] In this account, Pfeiffer's art and racial background are part of, and subsumed by, a linear history of anticolonial struggle in the

Philippines, which reaches its apotheosis in the art world with the emergence of an "indigenous cosmological imagination" (Guillermo).

In contrast, most reviewers in the West have ignored the possibilities of reading the intersections of sexuality, race, and colonialism in his work, though Pfeiffer has exhibited in venues explicitly associated with Asian, Filipino, and queer America, especially earlier in his career.[6] Usually, American and European critics and curators hastily narrate biographical details: A gay and mixed-race Filipino, Pfeiffer was born in Hawai'i and attended Christian missionary schools in the Philippines and on a Native American reservation.[7] They then move on to purely formalist readings of his work.[8] Unlike Manuel Ocampo, whose surge in popularity coincided with the peak of American multiculturalism and the anti-apartheid campus movement in the late 1980s, Pfeiffer generally has not been identified as an "ethnic" artist, and his apparent transcendence of race and ethnicity has made him a target of negative criticism, especially outside of the West. For example, *Morning* was a prize-winning entry in the 2003 Cairo Biennial, and its conspicuously expensive and elegant installation was perceived as symbolic and material evidence of American hegemony in the art world. Unfortunately, the legitimate indictment of first-world budgets and arrogance eclipsed any possibility of taking seriously Pfeiffer's location at the racial and sexual margins of America.[9] Curiously enough, this racial transparency—Pfeiffer has become an artist whose racial identity is not so much invisible as *seen through*—extends even to the work that blatantly addresses the politics of race, masculinity, and representation, such as his video stills and loops of Black celebrity athletes. Hardly a single reviewer has commented substantively on the hypervisible Blackness or whiteness of his subjects.[10] While both sets of reviewers, Filipino and Western, reference America as a general source of powerful cultural influence, America completely drops out of even the most sustained, sophisticated discussions of the aesthetic implications of Pfeiffer's work, distracted as they often are by his harnessing of new, especially video-loop techniques or by the sensationalism of his religious allusions.[11] Thus, neither the West's selective indifference nor the Philippines' insular nationalism does full justice to the politics of Pfeiffer's aesthetic. But the gaps in Pfeiffer's critical reception are symptomatic of a much larger problem in the cultures of U.S. imperialism. This chapter ultimately argues that America's imperial aesthetic is doubly self-effacing. The empire not only forgets imperialism, producing the historiographical amnesia constitutive of Filipino American invisibility. In the realm of the aesthetic, the American empire also forgets that it forgets imperialism. Given this predicament of double disavowal, it comes as no surprise that Pfeiffer's politics of aesthetics eludes nearly all his critics. As I argue in the next section, no one really seems able to get the tragic and campy joke of Pfeiffer's *24 Landscapes,* the title of the aforementioned Marilyn Monroe series (see Figure 8). Even though *the* body—the most recognizable American icon of excessive embodiment[12]—has been wiped from the terrain, Monroe's blond corporeality never absolutely

FIGURE 8. Paul Pfeiffer, *24 Landscapes,* 2000. Digital cibachrome prints, twenty-four photographs, dimensions variable. Collection A & J Gordts-Vanthournout, Belgium.

disappears. Two important questions are presented to Pfeiffer's viewer: exactly what of Monroe's hyperwhiteness and hyperfemininity lingers behind, and what has happened to the land that now seems to advance upon us and glare back at us? None of Pfeiffer's critics entertain, let alone respond to, these basic questions. As it turns out, Monroe's monumental disappearance is key to understanding imperial America's own peculiar fading from the scene of aesthetics.

### Gridding the Body: From Albrecht Dürer to Marilyn Monroe

When Pfeiffer claims of his work that "they're all figure studies, in a sense," he is referring to his overt preoccupation with the spatial epistemology of classic Western perspectivism. Pfeiffer's oeuvre thus can be said to narrate a supplementary and parasitical yet deviant art history of the West.[13] Beginning with the use of body parts to re-create classic architectural forms (see Plates 4 and 6), Pfeiffer has progressed to the manipulation of whole, typically Black bodies displaying extreme affect; to the near extinction of bodies, whose ghostly motions draw attention both to them and to their setting; and to the total erasure of the body from its backdrop.[14] Finally, as I have noted, *Morning* offers the paradox of a figure study that is aboriginally absent of bodies. Though his tools consist of software programs like Adobe Photoshop, which, incidentally, he likens to oil painting, Pfeiffer might be one of the socially responsive painters whom Michael Baxandall describes in his study of Italian Renaissance culture and perception:

> Some of the mental equipment a man orders his visual experience with is variable, and much of this variable equipment is culturally relative, in the sense of being determined by the society which has influenced his experience. Among these variables are categories with which he classifies his visual stimuli, the knowledge he will use to supplement what his immediate vision gives him, and the attitude he will adopt to the kind of artificial object seen. *The beholder must use on the painting such visual skills as he has, very few of which are normally special to painting, and he is likely to use those skills his society esteems highly. The painter responds to this; his public's visual capacity must be his medium.* Whatever his own specialized professional skills, he is himself a member of the society he works for and shares its visual experience and habit. (40; italics added)

As absurdly achronic as this comparison between Pfeiffer and Quattrocento painters may seem, Pfeiffer similarly "works for and shares [the]
visual experience and habit" of our current moment. Pfeiffer responds
especially to what Jonathan Crary calls the "relentless abstraction of the
visual" (2).[15] However, by situating Pfeiffer in the Filipino American
cultural moment, I also am arguing that he participates in "marginal
and local forms by which dominant practices of vision [are] resisted,
deflected, or imperfectly constituted" (Crary 7).[16] Persistently in a citational mode that feeds on canonical works of art and literature, Pfeiffer
is writing, with all the attendant risks, a history of oppositional *and*
appositional moments that "only becomes legible against the more hegemonic set of discourses and practices in which vision [takes] shape"
(Crary 7).

In interviews and his own writing, a quirky pastiche of autobiography, critical theory, and high and popular cultural references,
Pfeiffer explicitly cites and interrogates basic drawing tenets. He exerts,
for example, all kinds of pressure on the vanishing point in his essay
"*Quod Nomen Mihi Est?* Excerpts from a Conversation with Satan,"
in which he amasses different psychic and cultural manifestations of
terror.[17] Among the sampling of images from his own portfolio, he
includes Albrecht Dürer's sixteenth-century woodcut of a man drawing a reclining woman, a high misogynist moment in the development of one-point perspective and "geometrical optics" (Crary 16; see
Figure 9).[18] A conspicuous depiction of scientific progress by the most
famous member of the German Renaissance, Dürer's woodcut participates in what Donna Haraway calls the "social relations of domination
[that] are frozen into the hardware and logics of technology" (277).[19]
Recall the simple formula for linear perspective: "Vision follows straight
lines, and parallel lines going in any direction appear to meet at infinity in one single vanishing-point" (Baxandall 106). Then, returning to
Dürer's etching, notice the angled positioning of the model's beckon-
ing hand, which leads our gaze toward her draped vagina. The path
of the male artist's frozen gaze is slightly more complicated. His spine
leaning forward at a sixty-degree angle to his seat, the artist stares straight
ahead through the Cartesian grid at the model, a visual path replicated
and visibly marked by the horizon lying beyond the studio's windows.
This straight path is interrupted, however, by the model's hand, which
redirects the artist's gaze toward the vagina. Just as the vanishing point

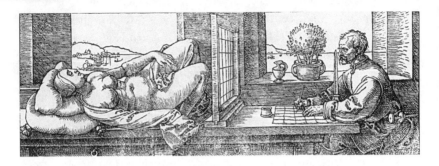

FIGURE 9. Albrecht Dürer, *Draughtsman Making a Perspective Drawing of a Woman*, 1525. Woodcut. Metropolitan Museum of Art, New York.

for us is hidden by the wall yet indicated by the position of the grid, what we might call the "vanishing vagina" is hidden from Dürer's artist yet indicated by the model's hand.

What does this sexualization of perspective imply and what are we to make of the gynophobic coincidence between the void of "infinity" and the vanishing vagina? Perhaps the German noun for "vanishing point," *Fluchtpunkt*, yields more clues than does the English. The verb *flüchten* means "to flee" or "to escape" rather than merely "to vanish," and so the German *Fluchtpunkt* suggests that its conceptual and ocular disappearance is motivated.[20] Something to evade even as it enthralls, the *Fluchtpunkt* visually elicits fear even as it arrests the attention of Dürer's artist. Not unlike the Gorgon's head of hissing snakes confronting Perseus, the "void" of female genitalia horrifies and fascinates Dürer's heroic artist as he explores a new technological frontier.

As a matter of fact, a tour of the petrifying qualities of the mythological femme fatale reveals more ways to read Dürer's appearance in Pfeiffer's essay on terror. Recall Sigmund Freud's oft-quoted 1922 description of Medusa's horrifying yet fascinating and compensatory qualities:

> To decapitate = to castrate. The terror of Medusa is thus a terror of castration that is linked to the sight of something. Numerous analyses have made us familiar with the occasion for this: it occurs when a boy, who has hitherto been unwilling to believe the threat of

castration, catches sight of the female genitals, probably those of an adult, surrounded by hair, and essentially those of his mother.

The hair upon Medusa's head is frequently represented in works of art in the form of snakes, and these once again are derived from the castration complex. It is a remarkable fact that, however frightening they may be in themselves, they nevertheless serve actually as a mitigation of the horror, for they replace the penis, the absence of which is the cause of the horror. . . .

The sight of Medusa's head makes the spectator stiff with terror, turns him to stone. Observe that we have here once again the same origin from the castration complex and the same transformation of affect! For becoming stiff means an erection. Thus in the original situation it offers consolation to the spectator: he is still in possession of a penis, and the stiffening reassures him of the fact. ("Medusa's Head" 212)

While Jean Laplanche has stressed the paradoxical reassurance ("they nevertheless serve actually as a mitigation of the horror," "he is still in possession of a penis, and the stiffening reassures him of the fact") that accompanies Freudian castration anxiety, feminist critics like Mieke Bal substantially have revised Medusa's killing looks by critiquing and destabilizing Freud's naturalized positioning of the boy as beholder and the mother as object.[21] In an essay on gender and sound, Anne Carson notes that the word "gorgon" is derived from the Sanskrit word *garg,* defined rather dramatically as a "guttural animal howl that issues as a great wind from the back of the throat through a hugely distended mouth" (quoted in Carson 120). Thus associated with loud speechlessness, the effects of Medusa begin to resemble the Kantian experience of the sublime, i.e., the confrontation with that which is uncontainable and unspeakable.[22] Primarily using examples from the 1848 Revolution and Paris Commune, Neil Hertz offers yet another way of reading the act of "facing" Medusa, whose sexual threat structures deep anxieties, which are propertied as well as gendered, about political confrontation and the possibility of mass revolution. According to Hertz, in nineteenth-century versions of Medusa's head "men of property could read . . . the provocative lineaments of power and abjection, both 'all that weakness contains of strength' and, proleptically, all that their own strength might conceal of weakness" (47).[23]

Similarly commenting on the awful predicament posed by the feminine sublime, Hal Foster argues, in his study of the compulsive nature of the "convulsive beauty" associated with Bretonian surrealism, that "like the sublime, then, convulsive beauty involves the patriarchal subject in the inextricability of death and desire. Bréton seeks to distinguish the two, to oppose to this death a beauty that is in fact bound up with it, and it is this contradiction which, never resolved, drives him to crisis after crisis" (28–29).[24]

Finally and most recently, critical race theorists have called our attention to Medusa's racial threat, which crucially escapes Bal's, Hertz's, and Foster's notice. While the Gorgon's snakes have been interpreted as penises and then pubic hair, Hiram Pérez argues that the poisonous coils also signify Blackness, the contaminating threat of Africa and Asia.[25] Dreadlocks are locks of dread. In short, Pfeiffer's essay stages a rich parody of Dürer's misogyny, which comes to contain a powerful admixture of racial anxieties and propertied appetites. For a variety of interlocking reasons, the *Fluchtpunkt* must disappear.

But this last interpretation of Medusa's "dreadlocks," which yields the prospect of Africa and Asia, can be pressed even further. Glancing again at the view from Dürer's studio windows, we note the importance of female sexuality in the ideological production of a natural order, i.e., the sectioning and mapping of land facilitated by the Cartesian grid. According to the *Oxford Encyclopedic Dictionary,* the words "grid" and "gridiron" etymologically link land (the act of partition) to the body (the act of torture, especially by fire), while the phrase "on the gridiron" denotes "a state of torment, persecution."[26] Refracted through the "idea of perspective," the gendered gaze of Dürer's artist thus acquires the voracity and racial logic of colonial possession (Baxandall 106).[27] That a substantial part of Pfeiffer's essay is devoted to Joseph Conrad's novella *Heart of Darkness* cannot then take us by surprise. Pfeiffer temporally and ideologically links this classic account of European surveying gone awry to the late-nineteenth-century emergence of the American transoceanic empire: "[Conrad's plot] takes place just as the foundations are being laid for the economic order we live in today. Contemporaneous with the Philippine-American War and with the annexation of Cuba, Guam, Hawai'i, the Philippines, Puerto Rico, and Samoa as new U.S.-controlled territories, Marlow's journey up the Congo—and by extension, up all the Congos of the world—is the precise journey into nature that makes global capitalism possible" ( *"Quod Nomen"* 281).

Yet one more turn of the screw remains in this extended reading of Dürer's quotation. Pfeiffer's parody turns into camp.[28] Ludicrous though the claim initially may seem, Dürer foreshadows the advent of Marilyn Monroe. If we follow the sequence of Pfeiffer's artistic production, the sexualized *Fluchtpunkt* of his 1998 essay predicts Monroe's disappearance two years later in *24 Landscapes.* Pfeiffer thereby cites and updates, for the American century, Dürer's gynophobic attitude toward technology. However, I would argue that, whereas the sixteenth-century hidden pudenda plays a crucial function in the *epistemology* of colonial scientific discovery, the twenty-first-century concealment of Monroe's body is a primarily *aesthetic* ploy. There are two strands to this aestheticized mobilization of her extravagant femininity and blondness, the first involving the volatility of the psychic identifications and desires that she evokes and the second exposing the mystification of the materiality of American conquest.

First, thanks to the influence of drag queen cultures, any contemporary summoning of Monroe (or, for that matter, other bombshells, like the previously cited Elizabeth Taylor and Montgomery Clift) necessarily enlists the queerness of her iconography.[29] The excessiveness of Monroe's allure lends itself all too easily to various forms of exaggeration, appropriation, and commodification, and herein lies the volatility of camp's (and Pfeiffer's) parasitical yet seditious relationship to the screen goddess. To state the obvious: Monroe elicits desire. She reminds "us"—I must underscore the range and heterogeneity of the viewing positionalities involved here—not only of our deepest longings but of the colonial structure of those desires, the blondness of our ambition. As Pfeiffer has put it, what does it mean that we, like Cinderella, still "want to be invited to the ball"?[30] For Prince Charming's ball(s) promises everything: the conferral of heterosexual romance, class mobility, and, not least of all, the execution of revenge. This last is perhaps the most powerful, if overlooked, of the rewards that are dangled before both Cinderella and Monroe's beholder, the affective and psychic dimensions of perfect revenge against the intimate, domestic oppression and sexual rivalry represented by the wicked stepmother. Pfeiffer's banishment of Monroe from *24 Landscapes* thus is a fraught act of tribute and vengeance—and does not that ambivalence define camp?

Moreover, might Pfeiffer's work propose a devotional praxis particular to queer Filipino America, perhaps a version of the *biyuti* that Martin Manalansan has studied? By "devotional praxis," I allude here to Christi-Ann Castro's scholarship on Filipino hybridity and indigeneity in the fields of dance and musicology. What makes, she asks, a particular act or object devotional?[31] This is an especially challenging question for Filipino America, given its history of multiple colonialisms and imperial forgetting, but I am intrigued by Castro's distinction between the metaphorical symbolism of an object, like the cross in traditional Catholicism, and its incarnational presence in animist faiths. In other words, in settings involving the former, the object is not unique; its authority and its call for obeisance to Christian theology inhere in its referentiality. But in animist ceremonies, e.g., Castro's example of the *subli* dance, the *Poon* (cross) is an object imbued with powers. Crucially, particular crosses possess supernatural power, hence the devotion to a specific *Poon*. I also am thinking of the possible relevance of Martin Manalansan's definition of *biyuti* ("beauty" in the gay Filipino idiom of *swardspeak*):

> My use of *biyuti* rather than the English word *beauty* faithfully captures the ways in which Filipino gay men manipulate its pronunciation and meanings. While biyuti's provenance is clearly from the English word, its precise meaning can shift depending on its context and the person for whom it is used. In this context, it means both physical feminine beauty and countenance. In many conversations, informants would refer to their person or present state of mind using the term *biyuti*. For example, if the informant wanted to show how something or someone has ruined his day or dampened his disposition, he could say, *nasira ang biyuti ko* or *naukray ang biyuti ko*. Both literally mean "my biyuti was ruined," although the latter statement utilizes the word *ukray*, which can, depending on the context, mean to ruin, to destroy, to kill, or to vilify something or someone. (*Global Divas* ix–x)

Here the relative instability and plasticity of *biyuti* correspond with the playfulness of Pfeiffer's work, while the intense vacillation between the generic and the particular that constitutes the object of hybrid devotional praxis also describes the kind of relationship that Pfeiffer constructs between the observer and the image. Pfeiffer says in an interview:

> What pushes me to use certain found images is that they have left a deep impression on me, either a long time ago, or very recently. The way that images become burned into the memory shows how porous an individual identity really is. It makes me wonder how the boundary line around an individual is drawn. In a way, all my work is a study of that process. My approach is to take an image that has penetrated my consciousness, and then to manipulate it just enough to emphasize the qualities that have impressed themselves on me, regardless of whether I wanted them to or not. (*Paul Pfeiffer* 36–37)[32]

Pfeiffer thus translates the politics of hybrid devotional praxis and *biyuti* and applies them to a critique of the worshipping of image in American popular culture.

However we may identify or disidentify with Monroe, Pfeiffer's reverential yet vengeful removal of Monroe does effect the foregrounding of the American landscape, and so my critical framing of *24 Landscapes* must account for this shift from the psychic to the material. If Dürer's woodblock captures the importance of female sexuality in the ideological production of colonial topography, Monroe fulfills a similar function in the contemporary California landscape, itself a site of multiple colonial contests. The suppression of overt female sexuality somehow enables the imperial survey and surveying of land, and perhaps closer attention to the politics of Pfeiffer's medium sheds more light on the vexed relation between the white female body and the American landscape. Describing the techniques and effects of digital editing, Pfeiffer compares computer software programs like Adobe Photoshop with the more traditional medium of oil paint:

> I think it's important to recognize that something remains after the human figure is gone. . . . Take *The Long Count* videos, for example, in which the boxers have been removed from the ring. What remains is a kind of ghost image, a trace left over from the digital editing process. Despite appearances, the editing process in those videos is not one of erasure; it's a matter of taking fragments of the background and using these to camouflage over the figure. It's really a lot like painting. The trace that remains afterwards is no longer recognizable as the figure; it's more like a ripple or disturbance on the

surface of the image. The effect is a bit like skin: tactile and seductive. That's the real transgressive potential of new imaging tools—the power to deceive the senses and elicit desire. In this sense, digital video and Photoshop are not unlike older visual media like oil paint and marble. (*Documents* 40)

Most pertinent in this rather rich interview excerpt is Pfeiffer's insistence on the "tactile" nature of digital editing, which, like oil painting, involves the application of epidermal layers to the "found" image of Monroe. If digital editing can be said to convey a message through its very materiality and not just the artist's employment of the medium, a crucial distinction emerges between the appearance of existential disappearance (we cannot see Monroe and so we naively think that she is no longer there) and perfect camouflage (we cannot see Monroe but we know that she still is there, buried underneath the reconstituted landscape).[33] How is this distinction relevant to the American clearing of indigenous and Mexican California? In the first instance, in which her ocular disappearance is confused for existential disappearance, Monroe symbolizes the racialized depopulation of the land. Thus imbued with pathos, her hyperfemininity signifies as colonized subjectivity, and *24 Landscapes* functions as a haunting memorial dedicated to the traumatic violence of that history. However, in the second instance of Monroe's existential perseverance, her hyperwhiteness signifies as imperial subjectivity and its camouflage ambivalently accentuates both the stubborn life of whiteness and its demise. In this final reading of *24 Landscapes,* California, the very land, paradoxically preserves and wreaks revenge against its colonizer. Again, it may be her camp quality that makes possible the tenacious lingering of her excessive, blond femininity. In any case, depending on the individual viewer, who decides whether or how Pfeiffer's art is successful, the fragments of digitized landscape covering over her body either corrode or conserve her corpse.

As I elaborate further in the chapter's closing section on the twenty-first-century return of a nineteenth-century expansionist aesthetic, Pfeiffer's depopulating attitude toward both the New England vista of *Morning after the Deluge* and the Californian vista of *24 Landscapes* produces the ironic restaging of the earlier aesthetic, which relies on the genocidal consolidation of a continent. A land becomes beautiful when, and because, the genocidal act of nation-building not only produces depopulated and razed "virginal" land but also disavows the violence and materiality of that process. According to the grammar of such an aesthetic, the violence of the verb "to empty" is entirely displaced by the horrifying abstraction of the noun "emptiness."[34] In other words, American notions of beauty, which rely on the boundlessness of nature, demand the emptying of a land of its peoples so as to produce the contiguous sweep and vast emptiness of a continent while the sexualized rhetoric of the now "virginal" land crucially sustains the ideological purity of manifest destiny. For this last reason, Monroe's profligate and polluting sexuality must disappear.

### Sacrilegious Sex, Ecstatic Pain, and the Slave Sublime

Two very different types of sacrilegious blonds have been discussed thus far: Lucy Reyes of chapter 1 and Marilyn Monroe. What to make, then, of the lavish blond waves in Pfeiffer's *Leviathan* that form the unlikely silhouette of a cathedral floor plan (see Plates 6 and 7)? Whereas in *24 Landscapes* Monroe's iconic curls are conspicuous for their absence, the blondness of *Leviathan* is almost palpably present. The wigs produce a strange aura of feminine corporality—they are made of dead hair, after all—that interacts in several ways with the title's reference to Hobbes.[35] Indeed, the text-image interplay that *Leviathan* generates is characteristic of many of Pfeiffer's works, which pair classic, canonical, or biblical references with contemporary images.[36] For example, *Morning after the Deluge* replies, on the one hand, to the atmospheric impressionism of the English landscape painter J. M. W. Turner, particularly the depiction of the dazzling sun in his 1843 painting *Light and Color (Goethe's Theory—The Morning after the Deluge—Moses Writing the Book of Genesis)*, and, on the other hand, to the apocryphal floods that Noah's ark survives.[37] In *Leviathan,* the striking color, uncoiling length, and undulating patterns of the arranged wigs convey sheer sensuality while the title invokes Hobbes's treatment of the body as a metaphor for the invidious division and hierarchical ordering of a body politic perpetually subordinate to a sovereign power. The body too easily symbolizes enclosure and wholeness, hence its architectural, governmental, and religious deployment in *Leviathan*. Here the body functions as the "model . . . for any bounded system," as Mary Douglas has argued, which must defend against contamination and must maintain the political fiction (or the fictional politics) of purity (116).

Drawing surprising connections between medieval and contemporary debates about the body, Caroline Walker Bynum notes that the "cultural assumption that material continuity is crucial to person made fragmentation horrifying as well as generative and didactic" (280). In *The Body and Surgery in the Middle Ages,* Marie-Christine Pouchelle writes: "In the fortress of the body, any orifice was a crack through which the external world threatened the wholeness of the individual, and through which the life force, even the soul itself, might escape" (93).[38] In proposing either an alternative to corporeal, anthropocentric totality or a different relation to that totality, *Leviathan* might be viewed as Pfeiffer's rejoinder to Bynum's important question about embodiment and identity: "In a world where we are faced with decisions about heart (and possibly even brain) transplants, about the uses of artificial intelligence, about the care of Alzheimer's patients and severely birth-damaged infants, we are forced to confront as never before the question: 'Am I my body?'" (297). For Pfeiffer, the body also and always predicts its own transgression and dissolution. In *Leviathan* and even more so in *Vitruvian Figure,* which I discuss later, the body signifies bounded integrity just as easily as it facilitates the infiltration of those boundaries, the blond locks promiscuously filling and spilling out from the sacred outline that they ironically demarcate.[39]

With closer attention to the interplay between the hair's tautness and looseness, however, another shape emerges. Down the center of the basilica, the arrangement of the wigs begins to resemble the natural parting of hair, which neatly bisects the entire print and hints at the skull that may lie beneath. Indeed, the punctured pink plastic shapes forming the edges of the cathedral resemble scalps and, as the image gains traction in the mind of the beholder, the idea of human scalping threatens to overtake the initial impression of sumptuous beauty. Medusa's capitate sublime once again enthralls and terrorizes her beholder, and in the case of *Leviathan* it poses a triple threat. In addition to the gendered psychodrama of castration anxiety, the scalping of blonds invokes a history of white paranoia and the racial savagery stereotypically attributed to Native Americans. But the third and maybe most disturbing aspect of this version of Medusa's sublime may be Pfeiffer's insight that its power lies in its philosophy and psychology of desire. However threatening Medusa's mesmerizing, freezing quality may be, the death that awaits the beholder betrayed by his or her own scopophilia is an ontological certainty. In other words, the beholder *knows* of the impending violence and yet cannot help but want to look. In its very lushness, *Leviathan* can be said to insist upon its own allure. It stubbornly insists upon the idea and desirability of beauty, especially its most normative and colonial manifestations. For in a colonial economy, the desire for blondness signals the assimilationist structuring of desire itself. Hence, if the blond wigs threaten physical violence, i.e., castration and decapitation, they also indicate the psychic life of colonial violence.

Precisely because it is such a close approximation of colonized desire, *Leviathan* plays a rather dangerous game. Pfeiffer's depictions of beauty easily lend themselves to universalist formalist interpretations, especially as they usually are coupled with classical and canonical references. The cultural specificity of the beauty, i.e., Western or white, gets waylaid by orientalist discourse such that not only do whiteness and European concepts of beauty attain the status of abstract universalism, but beauty itself becomes highly abstract. That this movement toward abstraction is itself a highly politicized process unfortunately gets lost along the way. And Pfeiffer's reviewers have shown how prematurely the interpretive act can come to a halt, generally insisting as they do on treating his work as purely formal art. Without attention to the queer politics of what must be "coded and shrouded through abstraction," the power and perils involved in Pfeiffer's double-edged gesture toward formalist beauty in *Leviathan,* its overly assimilative yet potentially liberating qualities, cannot be grasped fully (Besemer 18).[40] Hence, by way of a queer history of encoding and shrouding, the risky achievement of *Leviathan* is to "out" both the colonial structuring of desire and the politics of abstract universalism.

The basilica floor plan also appears in his 1997–98 series of digital cibachrome prints that share the title *Vitruvian Figure* (see Plates 4 and 5).[41] But in this case the architectural form is made with digitized body parts—contorted faces, open mouths, and penises—selected and assembled from hard-core gay male pornography. Again, the title refers to a classical moment in art history: Leonardo da Vinci's *Canon of Proportions ("Vitruvian Man")* (see Figure 10). Pfeiffer describes the genealogy of his title in the following way: "['Vitruvian'] is a term associated with Leonardo da Vinci's image of the human form inscribed within a circle inside a square. What's striking to me about that figure is that it presents the image of Man as synonymous with geometric

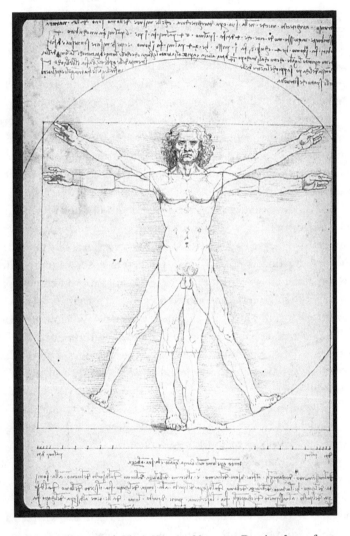

FIGURE 10. Leonardo da Vinci, *Vitruvian Man*, 1509. Drawing. Image from the Planet Art royalty-free CD-ROM *Leonardo da Vinci: Selected Works.*

order. It suggests that the Western aesthetic tradition, at its core, is anthropocentric." Intriguingly, Pfeiffer's critique of Western anthropocentrism is expressed in *Vitruvian Figure* through the proliferation of even more images of bodies engaging in carnal acts that further accentuate their corporeality. In fact, the shape of the entire floor plan is inescapably phallic. At first the gesture may seem a silly prank, sensationalist blasphemy that relies on shock value and nothing more. But I want to turn away from the too easy interpretation of sacrilege and I instead want to consider its exact opposite as an alternative: true (queer) devotion.

Far from the heretical depiction of illicit gay sex, Pfeiffer's *Vitruvian* can be seen as an instance of the kind of pious traditions established by late medieval and Renaissance artists who diversely and explicitly responded to the "spirit of incarnational theology by engaging Christ's lower body and denuding the Child from the feet up" (Steinberg 151). In the influential study *The Sexuality of Christ in Renaissance Art and in Modern Oblivion,* Leo Steinberg argues that "one must recognize an *ostentatio genitalium* comparable to the canonic *ostentatio vulnerum,* the showing forth of the wounds" (3).[42] Hence, to compel belief in Christ's incarnation as mere human, the depiction of his vulnerability to sex was as important as his vulnerability to death; so goes the standard scholarly interpretation of the period's astonishing proliferation of nude portraits of Jesus either as an infant or dying on the cross.[43] Of course, the "venial 'shamelessness'" of portrait after portrait of the naked infant, whose genitalia (in case the viewer missed them) often are indicated by the Virgin Mary's pointing finger, was possible because the Christ's sacredness was unquestioned. Steinberg declares that, "applied to Christ's body, the word 'pudenda' (Italian: *le vergogne;* French: *parties honteuses;* German: *Schamteile*—'shameful parts') is a misnomer" (18). Similarly, *Schamteile* may be a misnomer for Pfeiffer's depiction of sex and sexuality in *Vitruvian.* Viewed instead as an artifact of hybrid devotional praxis, *Vitruvian* turns out to be a most pious act of sexually shameless reverence. Just as the nineteenth-century *pasyon* lingers on in the work of Angel Shaw and Manuel Ocampo, the Renaissance tradition of sacred sexuality unpredictably manifests itself in the sexual passion of Pfeiffer's stills.

But the contorted mouths of *Vitruvian* ever so faintly suggest physical coercion even as they signal sexual pleasure, so this interpretation of nonheretical, shameless sex does not quite account for the eeriness of these eyeless, half-erased faces. And the slight uneasiness produced by these static faces develops into full-fledged horror for the viewer of Pfeiffer's moving images, like the video loop *Fragment of a Crucifixion (after Francis Bacon)*, wherein the whole body undergoes endless animated convulsion (see Figure 6). In this four-second loop, Larry Johnson's wide-open, screaming mouth and clenched fists signal sheer exultation, which is punctuated by the flickering stars of fans' cameras flashing in the background. Of course, this combination of taut musculature and extreme emotional release, expressed both facially and throughout the athlete's body, resembles the effects of torture. The title's references to the passion of Christ and to Bacon's portraits of hysterically screaming people explicitly call for such an interpretation. Yet what explains the appeal of such an image?

Loosely speculating on the biology and psychology of perceptual pleasure, Pfeiffer explains why he himself is attracted to video loops:

> The repeated image is inherently mesmerizing, like watching a fire in a fireplace, or like a moth to the flame. I'm interested in what might account for this tendency in the wiring of the mind's eye. It's like a visual addiction, something pleasurable that's hard to resist. The eye gravitates toward incessant repetition, as if it wants to lose itself in it. For me the temporality of the loop implies a kind of escape, as well as a kind of imprisonment. It's seductive, so you follow. And then you find you're locked in. (Interview with John Baldessari, *Paul Pfeiffer* 34)

What accounts for this pleasurable diminishing of the self? Why is the repetition not tedious? One way of answering these rather broad questions about identity and the consumption of images perhaps can be found in the small white flickering lights that form the backdrop of *Fragment*. Like tiny stars, the fans' flashing cameras lend a shimmering glow to the video loop, a luminescence that confirms Johnson's celebrity and that softens the otherwise slightly jerky automatism of his replayed movements. But it is the specific *rhythm* of the rapidly flaring and fading lights that enthralls the viewer. The erratic tempo of their quick life and death proves irresistible to the eye while the looped inevitability of that irregularity is a source of reassurance. *Fragment* perfectly melds erratic difference and smooth sameness, and maybe only in a medium like the video loop can these two conflicting sources of pleasure complement each other in such powerful ways for the viewer cum consumer.

Whereas stills like *Vitruvian, 24 Landscapes,* and *Leviathan* trade on the appeal of texture, color, and geometrical symmetry, *Fragment* depends upon the lure of a paradoxically frozen yet moving image. This allure has nothing to do with the magic of the movies. Four seconds is ridiculously short, and the loop forbids the unfolding of any kind of narrative. In lieu of plot development, such a tiny, dense packet of time produces the effect of the "fixed explosive," the surrealists' term for this unique combination of mobility and immobility. The athlete's convulsions are "at once disruptive and suspended," and the viewer is held in thrall by the tight temporal containment of extreme visceral affect (Foster 27). The digital entrapment of the perpetually ecstatic athlete delivers something akin to what Andre Bréton called "convulsive beauty," wherein "the animate is so close to the inanimate" (quoted in Foster 23).[44] These temporal distortions—the video's brevity as well as its perpetuity—make the athlete's voluntary movements seem painfully involuntary. Such an effect indicates that we have entered the realm of racial humiliation and trauma. *Fragment* repeats, it seems, what should not be repeated. It makes recurrent what should be the "singular presentation of a singular event" (Bal, *Narratology* 112). It loops what should remain a moment.

Given the surfacing of trauma in *Fragment,* the otherwise haphazard allusion to surrealism becomes more relevant. In his relentlessly psychoanalytic study of the surrealist uncanny, Hal Foster argues that the "convulsive beauty" and the "marvelous" sought by these artists "signaled a rupture in the natural order" and a "challenge to rational causality" (19). Foster adds that such an emphasis on disruption and shock "suggests that the marvelous also involves traumatic experience, that it may even be an attempt to work through 'hysterical' experience" (21). In *Fragment,* Johnson's "in/animation" signals the surfacing of a specific historical trauma: slavery.

The details of his uniform erased, Johnson is rendered both hypervisible and anonymous, two descriptives that in many ways still define Blackness in America. Pfeiffer himself says that he wants to call

attention to the debasement that accompanies the creation, commodification, and circulation of celebrity: "There is a kind of humiliation
in that process of simply becoming objects of admiration, or people
simply becoming consumers" *(Art 21)*. In *Fragment* the central figure
is "dissolving into the accumulation of capital until it becomes an
image," as Pfeiffer puts it *(Art 21)*. Not only is the central figure of
*Fragment* temporally trapped, its endless vacillation between mobility
and immobility recalls the forcible generation of embodied capital
and extrication of labor that define the slave economy.[45] In other
words, the silently screaming figure of *Fragment* stages a late-twentieth-
century version of what Paul Gilroy has called the "slave sublime,"
wherein "words, even words stretched by melisma and supplemented
or mutated by the screams which still index the conspicuous power of
the slave sublime, will never be enough to communicate its unsayable
claims to truth" (37).[46] Perpetually replaying four seconds of ecstatic
pain, *Fragment* distorts time to make a historical argument about the
imbrication of race and capital, bringing within disturbing proximity
of each other the diverse eras and economies of slavery, Jim Crow, and
neocolonialism.

The vague, tentative remarks of a few reviewers notwithstanding,
no critics have referred explicitly to the history of white supremacy
and racial torture like lynching that these images evoke (see Figure 7).[47]
Typically verbose and occasionally eloquent when it comes to topics
like sport as cult, the gradual dissolution of the body in contemporary
art, the impact of new technologies, and the temporal distortions particular to video loop art, Pfeiffer's critics fall silent when it comes to
the *politics* of these same topics. Clearly, there is something about their
approach to the aesthetic that produces this kind of abstract critique
of conceptual art like that of Pfeiffer's. That silence is an *unknowing*
silence, though. The origins and nature of this silence are the topic of
the next section.

## The Return of the (Repressed) Aesthetic

What story of origins can be (re)told about the American aesthetic of
emptied space, and how has this aesthetic pervaded the Filipino American
post/colonial moment? Let us begin with twenty-first-century art, glance

back at the nineteenth-century aesthetic of expansionism, and then return to the Filipino American moment.

In her sardonic, clipped, yet sweet burr, performance artist Laurie Anderson explains in the video documentary *Art 21:Art in the Twenty-First Century* the primal significance of place for contemporary artists. Making art, Anderson says, "begins with a place," and so both artistic production and critical interpretation entail understanding "how [artists] track places and make them into works of art." Place, she continues, "is about how you move through space" and about "scale," "point of view and perspective," and "exploration." So far, so good. Anderson's fondness for speaking playfully yet earnestly in aphorisms strikes the right tone of invitation as she asks the viewing public to consider broadly how one's spatial coordinates determine the way one imagines and interacts with the worlds one inhabits. Elaborating upon the allure of place and space, however, Anderson's attitude suddenly and awkwardly turns orientalist. Ambling by a squadron of Asians, mostly women, practicing Chinese martial arts and dance in a city park, Anderson uses the geopolitical place of Chinatown to describe the boundlessness of space in which "anything can happen" because they are "huge, empty, full of possibility."[48] Finally and not uninterestingly, Anderson turns hopelessly romantic. One can fall in love with a place and, "like falling in love with a person," she claims, the reasons are "passionate, irrational, hard to explain." Like a beloved person, a place "sometimes becomes part of us forever."

While this fusion of mad love, creative inspiration, and colonial setting is not unpredictable, Anderson's genuine innocence and naiveté still surprise me. In a documentary introducing a general American audience to artists, many of whom are known for the outrage that their work stirred among the political right, why did the producers choose a racial ghetto to describe the sense of creative abandon evoked by space? Why Chinatown, an exceptionally reliable guarantor of spatialized exoticism in North America? It is jarring to me that the desire to explore peopled places like Chinatown, with its history of labor exploitation, sexual marginalization, and racial exclusion, can be described in such breathtakingly apolitical ways. At the outset of the twenty-first century, the digitized dawn of Pfeiffer's *Morning,* the liberatory allure of space in the American imagination still relies on a colonial grid. The mapping, in this instance of feminized Asian bodies, sets free the imagination of the American artist, who remains innocent yet again of the politics of empire. These bodies seem particularly vulnerable to erasure, buckling as they do under the pressure of the racialized space of Chinatown. Space exerts pressure on certain bodies, which then turn into a kind of "setting"—sites for, rather than the agents of, events. In this sense, space is "raced," and the recession of racialized bodies into the background indicates the workings of colonial ideology.

This spatialized erasure of (minority) agency is abetted by the rhetorical concealment of American imperial agency, which can be dated back to the nineteenth-century era of "expansionism." There were many other euphemisms for U.S. colonization, such as "annexation," "cession," and "acquisition." In "The Beauty of Imperialism: Emerson, Melville, Flaubert, and Al-Shidyaq," a dissertation on expansionist discourse and aesthetics, Jenine Dallal focuses on the term "cession" because it effects the concealment of agency: "The term suggests a mode of consensual, non-conflictual expansion and, like the term 'acquisition,' it conceals agency. In its ideal form, cession is tautological, a transaction between two parties on the same side: settlers who occupy and willingly 'cede' territories and the United States that then 'admits' them as states, as in the case of the Northwest Ordinance or the annexation of Texas" (23).[49] Intriguingly, Dallal argues that the shift from embodied to disembodied national power occurs much earlier than the so-called experimentation with imperialism at the turn of the century. This shift occurs *during* the age of continental expansion when the topic of "expansion" shifts discursively from one of "territorial conquest to issues of constitutionality" (17). Aside from her contribution to the ongoing debate about the precise origins and dates of American imperialism, Dallal's choice of the early to mid-nineteenth century as opposed to the early twentieth century finally provides an irrefutable answer to the existentialist nature of the debates about U.S. imperialism: Is America an empire? For Dallal, the nineteenth-century controversies surrounding expansionism clearly espouse imperialist missions and desires. But her most striking insight is that the main achievement of expansionist discourse is the "internalization of conflict" or the "domestication of conflict" (16), wherein "the land itself can remain beyond dispute, entirely present because subsumed" (17). Hence, what distinguishes American imperialism from European imperialism is the conversion of self–Other rivalry into a self–self encounter. The tautology, abstraction, and self-evidence of American expansionist discourse transform rivalry between warring parties into a "drama of the self." The land is "entirely present" yet emptied, both of its native population and of its very materiality (Dallal 17). This conception of expansionism exposes the powerful sense of national entitlement to the continent, a sense of entitlement that dovetails with the ideology of manifest destiny. Ironically, the land is purged of its materiality. As part of this process of aesthetic disembodiment, the land is transformed from the site of violent contestation into an *occasion* for a self-reflexive, highly depoliticized debate about individual and national character.

In Dallal's study, Emerson is the main example of this highly individualized and abstract encounter with the self in nature. Dallal argues that her thesis on American imperialism and visual possession (i.e., Emerson's famous transparent eyeball scene in *Nature*) differs substantially from that of Mary Louise Pratt's description of the dynamics of visual possession in European imperialism. In Pratt's description of the European "anti-conquest," the imperial eye becomes all-knowing and master of the material lands before it. In contrast, Emerson's eye seems to empty the American landscape of its materiality as part of a process in radical abstraction. Rather than the outward or centrifugal forces typically associated with expansionism, American nineteenth-century imperialism operates through the inward or centripetal forces of abstraction and internalization. The landscape becomes the occasion for inward self-reflection and internalization. Thus, while Emerson critics like Richard Poirier have misinterpreted this scene as a "noble" alternate to the physical conquest of the land, Dallal argues that the Emersonian aesthetic is analogous to American imperialism (quoted in Dallal, "American Imperialism" 67). In fact, Dallal contends that the immateriality and abstraction of the Emersonian expansionist aesthetic produce an even more compelling and pervasive conception of power and imperialism than that of the European "anti-conquest."

American imperialism is animated by a powerful sense of entitlement that is profoundly bound up with the aesthetic. In other words, it is in the realm of the aesthetic that the disarticulation of imperialism succeeds most powerfully and insidiously. The relegation of imperialism to the sphere of aesthetics, the "beauty of imperialism," effects the elision of colonial violence and dispossession in ways that produce a much more insidious imperialist model than that of the Old World.

If the history of the American empire is defined by forgetting, its aesthetic is structured by double disavowal. According to the New World aesthetic, it seems possible to erase the erasure of the past. Thus, clinging to beauty, Pfeiffer's work calls for a doubled return of the repressed. By resuscitating the expansionist aesthetic and its theory of abstraction, Pfeiffer exposes the repression of genocide that is at the core of the earlier aesthetic while simultaneously reminding us of the political repressiveness of contemporary art theories of abstraction.

Space dynamically acts upon us, although we would prefer to think that we move unscathed through space. Even as the video loop transfixes us with its red and orange beauty, Pfeiffer's *Morning after the Deluge* reminds us of our uninterrogated desire for spatial fixity and neutrality, our need for physical sites to ground us epistemologically. Akin to Vicente Diaz's "moving islands" of Oceania, Pfeiffer's queer horizon goes wandering, and we feel the ground beneath us shift as our sense of perspective dissolves and the *Fluchtpunkt* literally and conceptually evaporates. Over the course of his gradually disintegrating figure studies series, Pfeiffer has us return to an emptied landscape the morning after the "complete annihilation of the world," a scene painstakingly and tenderly depopulated through the digitized erasure of racially and sexually iconic bodies (Pfeiffer, *Art 21*).[50] At the dawn of the twenty-first century, the flatness of Pfeiffer's Cape Cod landscape recalls repetition with a radical difference, the vast void associated with the geographical vocabulary of manifest destiny: the frontier, the mainland, the continent, the prairie, et cetera. The video's spatialized emptiness and timelessness owe a profound debt to the intricate workings of an American imperial aesthetic. As it turns out, the topic of his most abstract work is the imperial politics of abstraction. Despite the chorus of loud voices among his reviewers insisting that he has escaped the snares of ethnic and racial identity, it may be their own silence about the ideology of American aesthetics that is more telling. These figure studies profoundly if obliquely address the politics of sexual and racial identity, and they are deeply decolonizing. Pfeiffer cites the emptiness of American nature in ways that render the abstract, solipsistic attitude of the nineteenth-century expansionist aesthetic no longer viable. As Jenine Dallal reminds us, the expansionist aesthetic became possible only and ironically through its detachment from imperial politics and practice: "Aesthetic form . . . [is] inscribed by diverse imperial idioms, and [is] set free not *from* but *by way of* these ideological moorings" ("The Beauty of Imperialism" 14). Indeed, as I hope this chapter has shown, such abstraction itself enacts a kind of political violence. Before a work like *Morning,* we are left all alone with a wandering horizon and an unmoving sun to contemplate the horror of inextricably inter-mingled violence and beauty, such that we never again dare divorce—disarticulate—the politics of the American empire from its aesthetic.

# II
## PILIPINOS ARE PUNNY, FREUD IS FILIPINO

3

# Why Filipinos Make Pun(s) of One Another

The *Sikolohiya*/Psychology of
Rex Navarrete's Stand-up Comedy

If you pack with us, we will pack with you.
—REX NAVARRETE, *Hella Pinoy*

It is no wonder that a punning monarch produced a
race of punning and pun-admiring liege subjects.
—NICHOLAS AMHERST, *Terrae filius; or,
The Secret History of the University of Oxford, 1721–22*;
quoted in "pun," *Oxford English Dictionary*

CORNY JOKES, endless punning, and playful teasing make up the stuff of Filipino American everyday life. Polemical, aggressive, and frivolous forms of wordplay are evidence of a culture that is "alive and vibrant because of a disposition toward lighthearted bantering and joking relationships" (Enriquez, "Decolonizing the Filipino Psyche" 13). This chapter tracks the routes of Filipino American lingual decolonization by paying attention to the ephemeral phenomena of everyday *biro* (jokes) before moving to an analysis of the recorded performances of professional stand-up comic Rex Navarrete. Navarrete's stand-up comedy uses bilingual, bicultural punning structures (a variant of what Sigmund Freud calls the "double-dealing" nature of jokes) to create a hybrid community space appropriate for and peculiar to the Filipino American historical experience of being

7

"foreign in a domestic sense." To take stock of Navarrete's popularity and the cultural valence of jokes and puns, I use a combination of concepts from Freudian psychoanalysis and *sikolohiyang Pilipino,* the nationalist psychology movement that emerged under martial law in Manila in the 1970s. Popular among middle-class and working-class Filipino Americans as well as college students, Navarrete marks the emergence of a distinctive type of double consciousness that neither psychoanalysis nor *sikolohiyang Pilipino* can fully account for—what might be called *sikolohiyang P/Filipino Amerika.*[1]

What is so important about humor and wordplay in the workings of community? What are the effects of these speech acts? Is the induced laughter to be interpreted as an assimilative dissolution into passivity, a sign of communal bonding, or a joyous disruption of the mechanization of the human being? More than a century ago, Freud observed, "Thus every joke calls for a public of its own and laughing at the same jokes is evidence of far-reaching psychical conformity." Writing in the early 1980s as part of the indigenous psychology movement *sikolohiyang Pilipino,* Virgilio Enriquez argued that Filipinos "us[e] teasing as a form of socialization or even as a strategy for establishing rapport" (*From Colonial* 65).[2] More recently, Leny Mendoza Strobel has argued that part of the decolonizing process involves recognizing and respecting the orality of Filipino culture: "Sources of knowledge and wisdom such as cultural practices, folk sayings, proverbs, stories, myths and folklore, songs, dances, and humor have not been considered legitimate sources of knowledge in the colonial culture" (71).[3] In her study of Internet communities, the sociologist Emily Ignacio argues that jokes are an important "speech genre" that diasporic Filipinos use to establish membership in a group, to deal with in-group tension, to foster unity, and to resist colonial and racial assimilation. Jokes are "everyday forms of resistance," claims the performance scholar and practitioner Theodore Gonzalves ("When the Lights Go Down" 109).

Jokes also allow us to see the limits of Asian American studies for the study of Filipino American community formation and cultural production. As we are continuing to learn, assimilation means different things for different folks in Asian America. While versions of the American dream and model minority discourse are deployed regularly to contain and manage Asian presence in the United States—part of the contradictory processes of "national abjection," as Karen Shimakawa puts it—the script of immigrant assimilation sits uneasily with Filipino American legatees of the "special relationship" between the Philippines and the United States.[4] In short, Filipino presence in the United States is predicated on a history of violent inclusion rather than exclusion.[5] Thus, the exceptionalism of the United States—its New World status as singular and apart from the history of Western European empires—collides with the racialized exceptionalism of Filipinos in Asian American history. The act of reading Filipino and Filipino American histories involves what Benedict Anderson has called a "vertiginous" encounter with dizzyingly heterogeneous experiences of displacement, dispossession, collaboration, and resistance.[6] To what extent, then, might the maintenance of U.S. exceptionalism and empire depend upon the marginalization—or what Oscar Campomanes dubs the "categorical displacement"—of Filipino Americans?[7] This history—a term that here indexes both the past and the immanent—of colonialism typically is subsumed, on the one hand, by a vocabulary of bilateral foreign policy[8] and, on the other hand, by a rhetoric of consent underpinning beliefs in American opportunity and mobility.[9] Campomanes points out that the "forgotten" in "forgotten Filipino Americans" too often is interpreted as a descriptor rather than as a transitive verb (160).[10] Indeed, American imperial amnesia depends upon the peculiarities of Filipino American racial formation. But what evidence is there to muster? In other words, if Edward Said declared in 1993 that we were at the stage of "trying to inventory the interpellation of culture by empire," have the stakes and tasks before cultural critics changed today (61)? What does the case of Filipino America contribute to the process and products of this archive?

## The Differences between F and P

One way to begin answering these rather sprawling questions about culture, empire, history, and identity may lie in the distance and differences between the letters *f* and *p*. Passionate debates about identity, nationalism, and regionalism immediately proliferate when Filipinos around the world argue about the differences between the terms "Filipino" and "Pilipino," which can refer to a people, language, ethnicity, race, or nationality. At first glance, the debate seems nothing but a petty quarrel about the protocol and monikers of cultural authenticity, a version of political correctness. If I call myself "Pilipina," does that make me more authentic, more politically progressive? If I call myself "Filipina," does that make me a victim of false consciousness? Who is truly *pinoy* or *pinay*—the slang, sometimes pejorative terms for people of Filipino/ Filipina ancestry?[11] These in-group arguments about ethnic authenticity and national pride often begin (and sometimes never end!) with a discussion of whether one uses *f* or *p* ("Filipino" or "Pilipino"), indicating either one's opposition or acquiescence to the pressures of assimilation to Anglo-American values. But this binary all too quickly proves inadequate, and what at first seems a reductive choice between resistance and assimilation turns into an occasion for differences to proliferate. By arguing about the differences between identifying as "Filipino" or "Pilipino," people are trying to voice, explain, and resolve a range of problems. For example, the insistence on "Pilipino" may symbolize the potentially subversive and empowering effects of warping the sounds of a colonial language like English. On the other hand, it may signify the dominance of a regional accent and language, Tagalog, and the metropolitan elite of Manila. S. Lily Mendoza notes that Tagalog, the dominant regional language upon which much of Filipino (the national language) is based, lacks the sound "ef." This is not the case for all languages in the Philippines, however, and Mendoza argues that the shift in the Philippines from "Pilipino" back to "Filipino" signifies the "broadening of the base of the national language" (*Between the Homeland and the Diaspora* xxiv). As such, the rhetorical anti-assimilationist strategy of saying "Pilipino" rather than "Filipino" does not guarantee one's authenticity as a Filipino. Rather, the enthusiastic claiming of the *p* elides the linguistic heterogeneity of the Philippines and reinforces the hegemony of Tagalog. Furthermore, the insistence on "Pilipino" may register disdain for diasporic Filipinos several generations removed from the Philippines who do not speak any Filipino language, who may be mixed race, and whose ancestors' departure from the Philippines was part of earlier, predominantly working-class waves of migration and rural peasant displacement. That is to say, the insistence on the letter *p* as anticolonial strategy risks reinforcing other kinds of hegemonies.

Emily Ignacio's work on Internet communities and their *p* versus *f* debates usefully identifies a contemporary site for the emergence of a cybersubculture structurally defined by text and thematically obsessed with the boundaries of group membership. Internet discussions have proven especially important for the work of political mobilization and grief, for example, during the controversial trial and execution of Flor Contemplacion, a domestic worker convicted in Singapore of murdering her employer's son and Delia Maga, another maid from the Philippines.[12] Ignacio has documented the in-group arguments and criticism triggered by the Contemplacion incident, especially the turn to discussions of Filipino identity, loyalty, and essence, and even though nationality and geographic location would seem to be especially un-reliable criteria for membership in Internet communities, hard-line Philippine nationalists do attempt to exclude nonresident, diasporic Filipinos. Indeed, according to Ignacio, Filipino Americans can be marginalized by other Filipinos "because *Filipino* is usually defined against the Filipino-U.S. dichotomy. Because of this Filipino Americans occupy a marginal space more than other Filipinos in the diaspora" ("Laughter" 164). Filipino Americans hence strategically turn to jokes as a source of group unity: "Because much of the discussions revolved around the dubiousness of Filipino Americans' loyalty to the Philippines, Filipino Americans on the newsgroup needed to ground their Filipino identity in *something*. Thus, they created this list of jokes" ("Laughter" 165). The jokes managed to "ease that pain and simultaneously create a sense of community, and thus, a Filipino group identity. . . . When debates about Filipino identity became so profuse that people started questioning the very possibility of attaining a group ethnic identity as well as the unifi-cation of Filipinos, jokes were offered to show us that we Filipinos *can* and *do* share a common bond" ("Laughter" 162–63). Yet there is an important distinction between what Lois Leveen calls the "joke text" and the "joke act." Whereas the joke text consists of the "actual words of a particular joke," the joke act describes the "entire process of joke tell-ing" (31). Thus, while diasporic Filipino joke texts work to verify group membership, Ignacio importantly notes that these joke acts perform the important work of decentering and recentering:

> These jokes represent much more than just membership boundaries. They show us alternative ways of thinking about culture—as an ac-tive articulation and enfolding of issues that pertain to ourselves and others in the diaspora. Through these jokes we learned how members

of the diaspora turned the impact of colonialism and globalization on its head (albeit temporarily) through the introduction and frequent use of new words like *chedeng.* Though not structurally changing the position of the Philippines and Filipinos in relation to the world, this linguistic turn places Filipinos at the center of cultural creation instead of merely passively taking in outside cultural influences." ("Laughter" 174)

In other words, these Internet joke acts are agential in ways that refuse the marginalization of Filipinos and that create sites of cultural invention.

By underscoring the textuality of jokes and puns, I want to highlight not simply the orality but the living *literariness* of a culture that has been belittled as imitative of Anglo-American and European canonical literatures. All this bickering about two letters in the alphabet belies a complex history and problematic in the homeland and in the diaspora.[13] In Filipino America, at the heart of this dispute, are the boundaries of a racialized community with past and all too present colonial relationships to the United States that have been forgotten quite ruthlessly, both by the vanquished and the victorious.[14] If puns and jokes rely on linguistic ambivalence—their double-edged nature—for success, what can be learned from a joint analysis of "punniness," i.e., puns, wordplay, double meanings, and "funniness," here defined as socially sanctioned aggression in the form of jokes and laughter? As the stand-up comedian Rex Navarrete puts it, how does laughter produce manslaughter?

## *"My people historically butcher English": The Sound of Mans/laughter*

In a skit about the humiliating childhood experience of attending English as a second language class, Navarrete shows how immigrant children are enjoined to learn not merely the grammar of the English language but the grammar of American assimilation in a racially hierarchical society. He then transforms the scene of colonial tutelage into anticolonial resistance by observing that the word "manslaughter" contains the word "laughter." In the following excerpt from "Mrs. Scott's E.S.L. Class," Navarrete's lampooning of English-language spelling *rules*

cunningly develops into an indictment of the contradictions and violence of colonial *rule:*

> What does E.S.L. stand for? English is a stupid language. It's stupid. It
> makes no sense to me.... Really, it makes no sense. Why do we put
> such a high premium on English? It's not our language. We do the best
> we can with the invader's tongue. We do the best we can. They say,
> follow the rules. But they keep breaking it themselves. Right? Like,
> the word "laughter." Let's spell "laughter," shall we? L-a-u-g-h-t-e-r.
> Laughter. That "g-h": Is that really a "fff" sound? Ha? Is it really a "fff"
> sound? Shouldn't it be a "huh" sound? Or maybe a [silence] sound?
> What's up with that "laughter" word, huh? Nigel, tell me, what's up?
>      [In hoity-toity British accent]: Laughter, yes, it is laughter, ff-
> ff-ff-ter, laughter, l-a-u-g-h-t-e-r, laughter. We are right. You are
> wrong, silly brown monkey. Carry on.
>      [In regular speaking voice]: All right, Nigel. How about "man-
> slaughter"? It's got the word "laughter" in it. So you think I can ever
> get charged with the crime of man's laughter?
>      [In British accent]: Shit, you're right. I believe there's nothing
> we can do except take your land.
>      [In regular speaking voice]: That's always their answer. I think
> they're still pissed off that we kicked out Spain all by ourselves. And
> kept our language. *(Hella Pinoy)*

Constructing a conceptual pun out of the absurdity of spelling
rules rather than aural coincidence, Navarrete produces a chain of words
and ideas linking "laughter," "manslaughter," and "the crime of man's
laughter." This sequence exposes the hostility of laughter, which in turn
exposes the irrational violence of the colonizer and the murderous impulse subtending the response of the colonized. With the mere slip
of the tongue, mirth becomes murder. The "crime of man's laughter"
committed by the comedian, whose job after all is to "kill" the audience
with jokes, phonetically slides into "manslaughter," the act of vengeance
for the "slaughter" and genocide of colonialism. But what laws govern the "crime of man's laughter" committed by the comedian? What
law has Navarrete broken? Navarrete at first reasons that if "laughter"
is pronounced with the "fff" sound, then so too "manslaughter." But
deductive logic founders. The mistake lies in the belief that English
rules make sense. As it turns out he has broken no law but rather calls

attention to the lawlessness of the law itself. Thus, Navarrete connects the illogical irregularity of English-language spelling ("it makes no sense") with the hypocrisy of colonial law ("They say, follow the rules. But they keep breaking it themselves"). Indeed, the insistence that conventional English spelling rules make sense triggers the unleashing of racist discourse ("silly brown monkey") and territorial dispossession. The attempt by the colonized to clarify the rules ("What's up with that 'laughter' word, huh?"), followed by an example of colonial contradiction ("How about 'manslaughter'? It's got the word 'laughter' in it"), leads to the recognition ("Shit, you're right") of *flaws rather than laws* at the core of colonial governance. Navarrete's insight is that colonial regimes codify forms of domination no matter how masked they are by the rhetoric of the rule of law. The colonized exploit gaps and flaws in colonial rule opened by this foundational lawlessness. Encoded in the jokes and laughter of the colonized and in other socially acceptable forms of aggression is the threat of anticolonial insurrection leading to the death of the colonizer. It seems that we are to take Navarrete quite seriously and literally when he declares, "My people historically butcher English" ("Brian O'Brian," *Badass Madapaka*).

Rapidly oscillating between critiques of colonialism and scenes of everyday life especially in the home and classroom, Navarrete's comedy indicates the extent to which wordplay, jokes, and puns are part of the fabric of Filipino American life and culture. Navarrete's work calls for a definition of "culture" that in many ways is quite close to the tenets of the *sikolohiyang Pilipino*—indigenous psychology—movement in the Philippines. As I understand the work of *sikolohiyang Pilipino* theorists, everyday language includes classical sayings as well as everyday "folk adages" that have accumulated, sedimented, and survived over time. In other words, verbal culture constitutes the text material (as opposed to dreams and childhood memories, the stuff of the unconscious) for psychological analysis. As I explain later in more detail, *sikolohiyang Pilipino* configures language as the foundation for both culture and personhood. If these sayings and adages form the foundation of a collective *sikolohiya,* then we also need to pay attention to any instances of a common language in a heterogeneous entity like Filipino America.

In the following sections, I first present a few examples of everyday jokes that rely on what I call an "accent pun," and I initially use

Freudian psychoanalysis as an explanatory framework for the workings of humor. I then discuss the popularity of Rex Navarrete because his success means that he has found a way to express a language for and of Filipino America. What is the proof, the evidence, for this success? His ability to make people laugh. Joke theorists point out that the final and, in fact, *single* test for the comedian is whether people laugh. Navarrete's ability to make Filipino America laugh must mean that a certain vocabulary and archive of experiences have accrued over time and have reached a critical mass. His comedy has found its way to the heart of Filipino America because he knows how to deliver a joke, and so I am interested in the form/performance and content of his routine. In the final sections of the chapter, my reliance on Freud diminishes as I turn to the insights of *sikolohiyang Pilipino* and historians like Reynaldo Ileto to describe the theoretical and political significance of Filipino American expressive cultural forms. Using the connections that *sikolohiyang Pilipino* makes between language, education, and colonization and between orality and decolonization, I make the case for the advent of what I call *sikolohiyang P/Filipino Amerika* and a diasporic and minoritized concept of collective personhood as it emerges through language and aggressive types of social bonding.[15]

### Today's Road to the Promised Land Is Brought to You by the Letter **P**

So what happened to the jokes? Are Pilipinos punny or not? What follows is a dreadfully informal typology of contemporary Filipino/American gags. Let us consider jokes in the colonial language (or ESL, "English Is a Stupid Language," according to Navarrete) as an oral source of knowledge, the power of which is obtained from the punning potential of Filipino-accented English.

The first category of jokes relies on the distinctiveness of Filipino accents in English—the absence of the sounds "ef," "vee," and "th" in Tagalog, for example[16]—for their success and ambivalence, what Freud calls the "double-dealing" nature of jokes.[17] One series of jokes imitates the demands of a language exercise, asking the audience, whom Freud calls the "third person," to form sentences—meaning—out of a set of vocabulary words. For example, the third person is asked to use the words "deduct," "defense," and "defeat" in a sentence ("When **the duck** jumps over **the fence,** it uses **the feet** first"); the word "papers" in a sentence ("When you go to a gas station, you have to **pay first**"); or—my personal favorite—the word "persuading" in a sentence ("I gave my wife a necklace to celebrate our **first wedding** anniversary"). The grammatically correct answers or solutions to these corny riddles are nonsensical puns, yet—again, in my highly scientific study—they can be repeated over and over before the same audience, the laughter sometimes increasing with each repetition. Perhaps the jokes' reliance on the Filipino accent in English reinscribes the racialized inferiority of both Filipinos and Filipino languages. But I can hear my Filipino/ Pohnpeian colleague Vicente Diaz from Guam, one of the most heavily militarized parts of the United States, using one of his conceptual puns and calling these jokes a form of "base stealing," the native Chamorro reappropriation of imposed American rites (like football and baseball; hence, stealing bases), of stolen Chamorro lands turned American military bases (hence, base stealing), and of colonial languages like English and Spanish.[18]

Consider a more elaborate, if no less corny, example of an accent pun. In his recorded live concert *Hella Pinoy,* Rex Navarrete performs his greatest hits from a career in "bicultural comedy" that now spans twenty years in the United States and, more recently, in the Philippines (Lloren). Born in Manila "at a very young age," Navarrete and his family moved to California when he was two years old. He has released three comedy CDs: *Badly Browned* (1998), *Husky Boy* (1999), and *Bastos* (2001), followed by a Web cartoon "Maritess vs. The Superfriends" and his DVDs *Hella Pinoy* (2003) and *Badass Madapaka* (2006). In the dominant tradition of American stand-up, he is a master mimic who uses a particular mixture of self-deprecation, childhood or homeland nostalgia, machismo, misogyny and homophobia. Sometimes he is compliant with assimilationist values, especially in terms of gender roles and sexuality; sometimes he can be pedantic; but he also is dangerously and hilariously oppositional. Navarrete talks explicitly about sex, race, colonialism, history, and identity in ways that appeal to and bind a fractious community constituted by, paradoxically, both innumerable fault lines and a deep sense of collectivity. Filipino America is a community whose ties that bind simultaneously tear it apart—that is to say, a local community undergoing a powerful process of decolonization—and in both form and content Navarrete's brand of stand-up comedy highlights and potentially resolves the often vicious debates about identity and authenticity within Filipino and Filipino American communities often triggered by arguments about the difference between *p* and *f,* the choice to use the linguistic/racial/national descriptive "Pilipino" versus "Filipino."

Navarrete's popular skit "SBC Packers Worldwide" stages the intergenerational encounter between two stock characters in contemporary Asian America: the brash, loquacious immigrant entrepreneur and the bemused American-born or "1.5"-generation interlocutor. The latter is a reporter for a local television program that lasts only one episode, whereas the former comes to life as the inadvertently foulmouthed owner of a packing and shipping company catering primarily to Filipino Americans. If all jokes can be reduced to the simple schema of setup, delay, and punch line, Navarrete spends the "setup" portion of this skit giving an account of growing up watching local television programming and witnessing the sudden rise and demise of "Filipino American Business Journal." Aiming simply and innocuously to highlight a successful community business, the ill-fated reporter Emil Lacuesta interviews SBC Packers Worldwide owner Jojo Enriquez. Naturally (and this is so *pinoy!*), the interview is televised live to cut down on production costs. Below are extended excerpts from two versions of Navarrete's skit:

> LACUESTA: And this is Jojo Enriquez of SBC Packers Worldwide. What do you do here exactly, Mr. Enriquez, here at SBC Packers Worldwide?
>
> ENRIQUEZ: Am I on TV? I'm on the TV. Where's the camera? Oh, here at SBC Packers Worldwide, we'll pack anything. You, you bring it here, we'll pack it in front of you. We're the best packers in the world! Our motto here is, if you pack with us, we'll pack with you. That's right, that's RIGHT. But if you don't want to pack with us, you can go pack yourself. That is right. Um, we pack a lot of thing. Books, plants, furniture, animals. We're the best animal packers in the world! I pack more animals than Noah. That's right. But the most dangerous animal to pack is, uh, you, like, uh, fighting rooster. What we call in the Philippines the cock. He's a very dangerous animal

because there's a sharp blade on the ankle. But, uh, you just can't pick up that cock. You just can't grab that cock right away. You have to confuse it. Confuse that cock. You have to confuse! So we have to put it in a bag or, uh, burlap sack. So we are the best cock sackers in the world! (Excerpt from version of "SBC Packers" on the DVD *Hella Pinoy*)

LACUESTA: So here at SBC Packagers, here, what do you offer? What kind of services do you have here for the Filipino American community?

ENRIQUEZ: Oh, that is simple. We'll pack anything. That's right. You bring it here. We'll pack it in front of you. Anything. Anything. Next question.

LACUESTA: Oh. [nervous laugh] All right there, Jojo. Let's see, could you tell us, the viewers, what is the history of SBC Packers [emphasizing *p*] here? Your lineage.

ENRIQUEZ: I am the third of a long line of packers. My grandmother, she's the original grandmother packer. And then my mom, who's her daughter, she's the mother packer. And I'm just the packer. Next question.

LACUESTA: OK. [nervous laugh] All right. Let's try this. OK, what kind of services do you do here, and what kind of guarantees do you have for the Filipino American consumers here at SBC Packers?

ENRIQUEZ: That is simple, Emil. Like I said, we'll pack anything. You bring it here, we'll pack it in front of you. Sometimes you just wait and it comes back packed already without your knowing. We'll pack anything, like books, plants, animals. The most difficult animal to pack is a hamster. They got that sharp teeth. Like, the sharp is very sharp. Like an incisor! You have to be very careful when you're packing your hamster. We have a technique here at SBC where you put the hamster in front of you. You take a carrot. Put in front of the hamster. And when he's not looking, pack him quickly! Pack him quickly. Next question, Emile.

LACUESTA: [Nervous laugh] That's, that's really clever. OK there. So how do you guarantee your work here at SBC Packers?

ENRIQUEZ: OK, we keep track of everything that we pack. Nothing gets packed without me knowing. So we have this technique here, procedure. When the thing that needs to be packed needs to be shipped, we attach a piece of paper to that, you know. A sheet [pronounced "shit"], if you will. It keeps track of where it is getting

packed and where it is getting sent to. So sometimes at the end of
the day, there's all of these sheets on the ground! And no one knows
what needs to be attached to that. So I'm very mad. Very mad. I have
to scream to my children, to my workers, "Hoy! Pack that sheet! Pack
that sheet, and pack that sheet!" Next question. No more? OK. Good
night. (Excerpt from "SBC Packagers" from the CD *Husky Boy*)

The opening punch line "We'll pack anything" triggers a wave of
laughter from Navarrete's Northern California audience, and the rest
of the skit essentially consists of capping the original punch line. As in
the simpler case of the riddles, the difference between *p* and *f*—here,
between packing and fucking—is fundamental, and the skit exploits
the bicultural audience's lived experience of double worlds. Calling
"for a public of its own," the joke ultimately is about the primacy of
the group (Freud 185).[19] Laughter and amusement are, after all, ultimately defined by the group. The individual's response is irrelevant;
the group's response is "single-minded and unimpeachable" (Limon
11). In this way I propose that, in content and form, jokes allow us to
glimpse the paradox at the heart of Filipino America, defined by the
sometimes mutually reinforcing and sometimes oppositional processes
of community building and nation unbuilding: that is to say, a local
process of decolonization.

Following classical joke theory, Navarrete successfully overcomes
and exploits social inhibitions about a variety of sexual taboos, a fundamental technique of stand-up that in Asian America has been per-
fected by Korean American comedian Margaret Cho. If jokes rely on
"a ratio of manifesting and concealing," Navarrete uses his character's
accent in English and his audience's double consciousness to allude
to cross-species sex, exhibitionism, masturbation, and oral sex, all in
about two minutes (Limon 16). And if much of the "work" of jokes is
achieved by the economy of words, is not every comedian in search
of a bargain? Parsing Freud's *Jokes and Their Relation to the Unconscious,*
John Limon observes that "the penetral of tendentious jokes is less
likely to be sex or savagery and more likely to be sales, if what is on
the mind of the jokester unconscious is the hope of a bargain." (And
Limon cannot help himself from adding that the "metajoke of Freud's
book is the disguising of a lengthy Jewish joke as psychoanalysis" [21].)
Thus, a principle of economy rules the pleasure derived from jokes.

Where there is an internal obstacle, i.e., internal resistance or inhibition, an "already existing inhibition is lifted." Where there is an external obstacle, the erection of a new one is avoided (Freud 145). In both cases of erecting and maintaining inhibitions, a certain expenditure of psychic energy is necessary. Since energy is saved when inhibitions are avoided, the amount of pleasure corresponds to the amount of psychic energy saved. Thus, the "secret" of the pleasurable effect of jokes is found in this economy of energy spent on inhibition or suppression (Freud 145–46).

But Navarrete relies on a very particular kind of wordplay—punning—to elicit laughter, and the study of homonyms quite naturally leads us to the investigation of secret words that is at the heart of Nicolas Abraham and Maria Torok's *The Wolf Man's Magic Word*. Here, homonyms are the methodological basis for the decoding of the analysand's dream and the convergence upon a "taboo word" (26). The pronouncement of such a word by the analysand is nigh impossible and its discovery by the analyst is mitigated by the arbitrariness of the decoding: the word can only be guessed at since its taboo, shrouded nature (its unpronounceability) is effected by the "cryptonymic displacement" of the taboo word (26). That is to say, the sound, meaning, and existence of the taboo word are obliquely communicated through secret, complex puns and homonyms. Abraham and Torok translingually pun on the repeated appearance of the word *Nachtzeit* in the multilingual Wolf Man's German account of his dreams to Freud. *Nachtzeit* translates to *notchu* in Russian, ostensibly the Wolfman's mother tongue. It also translates to "night" in English, the first language of one of his earliest nannies. *Notchu* is then decoded back into English, and "not you" becomes the final "real" word meaning or "archeonym."

Filipino America's version of "cryptonymic displacement" turns on the aural, phonetic mobility of the signifier "tongue" in three languages: Filipino, Spanish, and English. The title of Eric Gamalinda's essay "English Is Your Mother Tongue/Ang Ingles Ay ang Tongue ng Ina Mo" serves as a terse—"packed"—example of this kind of playfulness. In Filipino, the word *tang* (which sounds like "tongue") is an abbreviated form of the commonplace insult *putang ina mo,* which is the functional equivalent of the English phrase "fuck you." But *putang ina mo* literally means "your mother is a *puta*" and of course *puta* is Spanish for "whore," that is, someone who fucks for a living. So the second half of Gamalinda's lingually miscegenous title contains five possible messages: (a) English is your first language; (b) English is your mother's language; (c) You are fucked by English; (d) You fuck with English; (e) English is fucked by your mother. While the displacement of vernacular Filipino languages by the languages English and Spanish is a form of colonial violation, if one pays attention to Gamalinda's syntax that violation in turn is structurally, formally violated by the colonized. The syntax of the second half of Gamalinda's title is grammatically correct, but it sounds stilted in Filipino because Gamalinda chooses to use English rather than Filipino syntax ("Ang Ingles Ay ang Tongue ng Ina Mo") instead of Filipino syntax (i.e., "Ang Tongue ng Ina Mo ay Ingles," or, better, "Ang Tongue ng Ina Mo ang Ingles"), which would sound more flowing and natural. In other words, Gamalinda's translation denaturalizes native syntax but in doing so calls attention to native subterfuge and tactics that undermine the English language. The independent, experimental Filipino theater troupe Tongue in a Mood, which Navarrete cofounded in 1992 with Kennedy Kabasares, Ron Muriera, and Allan Manalo, incorporates into their very name this legacy and business of "fucking" with language. Revived in 1996 by Manalo and now housed at the Bindlestiff Studio south of Market Street in downtown San Francisco, Tongue in a Mood have managed the impressive feat of staying afloat financially in a rapidly gentrifying, prohibitively expensive city for several years now; and they explain their name by asking their baffled audience to say Tongue in a Mood quickly and repeatedly until it sounds like *"'tang ina mo."*

Freud offers a theory of the translingual production of meaning. While cultural critics tend to get caught up in reading Freud for visual trauma, e.g., the glimpse of the vagina or, in Freud's misogynistic reading, the castrated penis, Freud's first example of fetishism in the 1927 essay "Fetishism" catches one's ear rather than one's eye:

> The case of a young man who had exalted a certain kind of "shine on the nose" into a fetishistic condition seemed most extraordinary. The very surprising explanation of this was that the patient had been brought up in an English nursery and had later gone to Germany, where he almost completely forgot his mother-tongue. The fetish, which derived from his earliest childhood, had to be deciphered into

English, not German; the *Glanz auf der Nase [shine on the nose]* was really "a *glance* at the nose"; the nose was thus the fetish, which, by the way, he endowed when wished with the necessary special brilliance, which other people could not perceive.

There at first seems to be no substantive connection, other than aural coincidence, between the paired words "glance" and *Glanz*. Freud initially presents the visual shine *"Glanz"* as the fetish, which is detachable and attachable from the body. The patient can endow others—anyone—with a "necessary special brilliance, which other people could not perceive." The patient eventually turns out to be "most extraordinary" when Freud discovers the "surprising explanation," which involves traveling back in time (the patient's childhood) to another country (England) as well as into another language (English). But what first catches Freud's attention is the fact that the patient can attribute a fetish to anyone and that the fetish is not a bodily attribute. The fetish is not a part of a limb, i.e., an ankle or a nose, but rather a characteristic or descriptive shine. Freud here distinguishes between metonymy (something attached to or contiguous with the body) and metaphor (something to do with the state of the bodily part rather than the bodily part itself). Such a distinction is consistent with the gynophobia of Freud's castration scene: The boy sees the vagina and is traumatized by the sight of the lack of penis (castration) and thereafter resorts to divided belief—sight and disavowal, a kind of denial whose very existence belies the existence of that which one would deny. The fetishist will not give up his attachment to that vision and so develops an alternative mechanism, another object, say, an ankle, which stands in for the vagina. In the case of the fetishist's glimpse of the ankle, the vagina travels down the body. In the case of the nose, the vagina travels upward and is something always visible.

In the case of the "glance/ *Glanz,*" Freud insists that the nose is the fetish. But this conclusion seems premature. Why not conclude that the fetish instead is the "glance"—the scopic act—at the nose? Perhaps because he must revert to a misogynist account of fetishism, Freud gestures toward but will not fully account for the significance of cross-lingual and cross-cultural travel. Freud insists upon territorialization rather than deterritorialization: the fetish must return to the female body—the vagina—instead of traveling across languages and national boundaries.

In contrast, I would argue that, rather than the bodily organ, the cross-linguistic pun "glance/*Glanz*" itself constitutes the fetish. For despite himself, Freud makes the case for the emergence of meaning-making not only through the psychoanalytic investigation of the unconscious, but also through a more fluid and conscious awareness of the traveling of meaning across cultures. In other words, Freud is Filipino.

If Freud inadvertently and briefly theorizes the translingual, transnational production of meaning, Navarrete's comedy shows us how such a "fetish" can work to highlight differences and to diminish the possibility of community. Navarrete offers *puto,* which in Spanish means "male prostitute" but in Filipino refers to an everyday *merienda* or afternoon tea snack, as another example of translingual wordplay:

> NAVARRETE: *Puto,* right? It's steamed rice-cakes. It's good for you, right? It's good for you. I mean, *puto.* What does *puto* mean in Spanish by the way? Male whore. I kid you not. Male whore. C'mon, leave it to a revolutionary-minded people like the Filipino to take something derogatory and insulting in a conqueror's language and turn it into a delectable yet nutritious treat, right? Right? So there. I had a hard time offering it to my friends next door who were Mexican. Walk up to the door.
> [In little boy's voice]: Hey Carlos, you want some *puto?*
> [In angry older voice]: Want some what, dogeater?
> [In boy's voice, on the verge of tears]: There's no comma before *puto,* Carlos. I said, you want some *puto?* I didn't say, you want some, *puto?* Just eat it, you beaner. (DVD *Hella Pinoy*)

Here, the possibility of signifying across languages and of cross-racial empathy turns into a moment of interracial, hypermasculine confrontation. While Mexicans and Filipinos share the legacy of the "conqueror's language," this moment of comparative colonialisms indicates the radical unevenness and heterogeneity of colonized experiences.

On the other hand, Navarrete also offers examples of community bonding. He opens his DVD concert *Hella Pinoy* with a recitation of the kind of behavior that is *pinoy* (Filipino) and the behavior that is *hella pinoy* (extremely Filipino). He establishes links with his audience through identification, reminding Filipino Americans of their childhood, family life, or workplace. In establishing the authentic *pinoy,* he relies on caricature that mostly has to do with class distinctions. But

Navarrete's performance is all about delivery, the way he embodies words and the way he makes the joke text something gestural and material. In particular, he does accents: Filipino accents across a range of ages (older women, older men, children); Anglo-American accents (Mormon missionaries, Sally Struthers); and perfect Cantonese. He relies on punch lines. His stories often end anticlimactically, while it is the character that emerges most powerfully through the details of mimicry.

In his opening skit in *Hella Pinoy,* Navarrete describes the distinctions between someone who is *pinoy* and someone who is *hella pinoy.* In other words, Navarrete mimics the *p* versus *f* debates about authenticity. And of course, when one is a member of his audience, laughter is the real test as to whether one really is *pinoy.* If you do not get the joke, if you cannot laugh, you are not *pinoy.* So I am interested in Navarrete's way of performing and embodying words, how his delivery and embodiment of words—joke texts, in this case—constitute community. Instead of the endless authenticity arguments over whether one uses "Filipino" or "Pilipino," Navarrete addresses these rifts and arguments by bringing together the domestic American racial construction of Filipinos as hypersexual and dangerous, i.e., always "fucking" and the transnational forces of "packing."

And still Navarrete's skit remains radically underanalyzed. "SBC Packers Worldwide" is saturated with important historical references and cultural symptoms, reduced here to a laundry list: the Filipino American obsession with celebrity ("Where's the TV?"); the sheer lack of capital backing Filipino American small-business ventures; the longstanding stereotype of Filipinos—especially Filipino men—as aggressive, hypersexual predators; and diasporic *balikbayan* (literally, "return home") practices like shipping goods to the homeland, which are signs of globalization, the brain drain, and the overwhelming dependence of the Philippine economy on the income of overseas contract workers.[20] A bargain, indeed.

## *"English is a stupid language": The Miseducation of Rex Navarrete*

Let us move on to another Navarrete skit, which features Mrs. Scott, the ESL teacher who terrorizes Navarrete as an immigrant schoolboy and who teaches both her pupils and Navarrete's audience about multiple, overlapping forms of assimilation and colonial tutelage.[21]

In the skit "Silly F.O.B.s" that immediately precedes "Mrs. Scott's E.S.L. Class," Navarrete points out generational differences and tensions in the audience. Asking the U.S.-born in the audience to identify themselves, then the immigrants, Navarrete calls up feelings of uneasiness in the audience when he makes fun of immigrants for identifying themselves. (He jokingly calls for the immigrants to be rounded up and handed over to the INS for money). And this also might be an instance of stand-up comedians' hostile attitude toward their audiences. But Navarrete then turns the tables on the audience by self-identifying as an FOB (the acronym for the pejorative "fresh off the boat)," adding that FOB stands for "FOBulous" (rhymes with "fabulous"). From this general reference to immigrant abjection and paranoia, he turns in "Mrs. Scott's E.S.L. Class" to a specific setting and moment in immigrant life: ESL graduation night. Below is an extended excerpt in which Navarrete plays the role of Mrs. Scott:

> [Sounds of tapping microphone] Hellooo! Good evening! Hello. Okay, I like to have a greeting for all of the, the, students. The parents. And the community at large. Thank you for coming to the 1977 ESL graduation evening. And I am your host and teacher, Mrs. Scott. Tonight we're going to embark on a tour, a journey if you will, of the English language. Our graduates have been practising [pronounced FRAHK-tising] for several months already. Again I am their teacher. And if you can tell by my accent I am already perfecting [pronounced "FEHR-PEKH-tining"] the English language. But enough about me. I just want to say that, you know, I am very proud [pronounced "FROWD"] of my students because they work very hard, you know. They put in a long hours, you know. Sometimes never go home, you know. So if you ask my students, they'll testify that, that, I am a very good teacher, okay. Very good, number one, okay. I am very proud of my record [pronounced "REE-cord"]. You know, just the other day, I was overlistening, I was overhearing my student, you know, talking to his parents [pronounced "FAH-rents"]. Parents [pronounced "PAH-rents"]. About how he loved my class very much, okay. He was saying, this is exact words, exact words, okay. I'm not making anything up. He said, mommy, daddy, you have to come to Mrs. Scott's class, you know. She's my favorite

teacher. You have to see her teach [pronounced "TITS"]. That really brought a tear to my eyes, okay! I just held on. Like that. I don't let gravity take it, you know. So without further ado [pronounced "JOO-JOO"], I want to bring on tonight's festivities, okay. Our first [pronounced "PURSE"] graduate, I'm very proud for him, he's kind of shy, kind of scared, okay, kind of frightened. Because he's from, he's from the Philippines, okay. For those of you who don't know where the Philippines is, you take a, look at the world map, okay. Pretend there's a map, okay. The Philippines is the southernmost island of Spain. Okay! That's enough. I'm so proud, I'm so proud. Okay, but he's from the part of the Philippines known as the jungle. So I don't know if he's gonna wear shoes or no shoes, I don't know. He's new. I don't know, you know. Sometimes they're on, some-times they're off. Sometimes only one, wow! He's like, he's a magical little boy. So without further ado. God! enough about me. I want to bring up our first graduate, Mister Rex Navarrete [pronounced "Nava-REE-TEE"], who is going to recite his very first English sentence. He working too long, okay. So please, please. Who's crying? Who's crying? Rex, are you cry—? Rex, stop that! Stop crying! Sorry. Stop crying, stop crying! I'm so embarrass. Stop crying! You want belt or the slipper? Belt or the slipper? Sorry! Okay, he's brave now. Come here! Mister Rex Navarrete. [in little boy's voice] The cow jump over the moon! *(Hella Pinoy)*

Playing the role of Rex, a cowed schoolboy, Navarrete expects an au-tomatic good grade—a "discount" from Mrs. Scott—because she also happens to be Filipino. Rex says: "I thought I was gonna get by. [in child's voice] Oooo, *pinay*! She cannot deny!" Rex thinks that he has found her out and exposed her, because as the skit continues, we see that she does deny being Filipino and distances herself from savagery, what she calls the "jungle."

The child's expectation of *utang na loob* and *kapwa*—social obliga-tion and mutual recognition—is related to the effects of globalization and the far-flung, radically vulnerable economy of the Philippines that totally confounds the metaphor set up by "diaspora," i.e., that there is a center or an "inside" from which the diaspora comes. (In fact, the Philippine economy depends on the outside, both formerly direct co-lonial powers now multinational corporate ventures as well as neo-colonial governmental powers and sources of "aid" as well as the income of overseas contract workers and diasporics with more stable sources of income and property and social capital.) Globalization has translated unevenly yet broadly for Filipinos into the idea of a collective cosmopolitanism, or, to use the language of *sikolohiyang Pilipino,* a sense of *kapwa.* Whereas *utang na loob,* which literally means "inner debt," refers to a range of interiorized feelings of social obligation, *kapwa* can be understood as a kind of friendliness and hospitality that, in the colonial context, are interpreted and exploited as naiveté rather than as an invitation and introduction to a particular economy of values based upon reciprocity (ethical, political, cultural, philosophical, and material). But at the everyday level, Filipinos draw upon both *loob* and *kapwa* to get by, economically and psychologically.

But in fact Navarrete turns out to be terrorized by Mrs. Scott ("Belt or slipper?"). During ESL graduation night, students are to perform their "very first English sentence," but Rex at first refuses to come on stage, crying backstage. Of course, within the structure of Navarrete's comedy concert, this is the second time that he is being introduced to the audience, so there is a parallel construction between the fright of the immigrant child and the fright of the professional performer, a direct reference to the stage fright that haunts all performers but perhaps especially stand-up comedians, who reportedly have an especially hostile relationship with their audience. Navarrete not only is replaying and exposing the stand-up comedian's fear of the stage, he is reconfiguring immigration and education as a theater. Both the theater and the classroom are places of interpellation, punishment, reward, tutelage, and self-(de)formation.

Navarrete dwells on the teacher's surname "Scott," his utterance of which the audience knowingly giggles at:

> She was Filipina. But, uh, her name was Mrs. Scott. [sounds of audience mumbling] Yeah. Same here. That's a really traditional, indigenous Filipino name if you ask me, though. [audience laughter] No, true! You know, I'm not gonna break her on that, you know. Because I think up in the north in the highland regions, there's probably some Filipinos named Scott, you know. They probably wear, like, a bahag and a kilt, you know. Combination. [in Scottish accent] "What are you doing here?! *'Tang ina!* Hey! This is my mountain, asshole!"

He reclaims the name as indigenous in several ways, depending on the version of the skit. In one version, he conjures the vision of a tribe of Scotsmen in the northern Philippines. But in the DVD version he makes a different kind of claim to indigeneity. He references American military presence and Amerasian children as products of liaisons between (typically) American military servicemen and Filipinas in the economy that sprang up around the bases: "Her name was Mrs. Scott. Which is a tribal, indigenous name from the Philippines, especially around the Subic naval base area. Because they immigrated to the lowlands from way up. Above the Igorot Ifugao region, there's a lost tribe of Scotsmen. Have you been there?"

Navarrete uses accented and nonstandard English in a punitive way in "Mrs. Scott's E.S.L. Class"—i.e., nonstandard accents are the object of the audience's laughter and derision—to punish Mrs. Scott for training or molding him into the racial/colonial subject via language. But he also is mocking her hypocrisy and self-delusion, a combination of the Eurocentrism that characterizes middle-class and upper-class Filipino self-hatred. She claims that her accent is perfect ("ferpect," another variation on the difference between $p$ and $f$). She highlights her Eurocentrism by explaining that the Philippines is the "southernmost island of Spain." The larger point is not that there is some kind of standard English—Navarrete spends quite a bit of time mocking standard English—but that Filipinos internalize and impart deeply hypocritical attitudes in the classroom setting. Mrs. Scott is but one in a long line of schoolteachers devoted to what Renato Constantino refers to as the "miseducation of the Filipino."

### Tutelage and the Mother Tongue

With this character and classroom setting, Navarrete brings together the primal site of Filipino colonization—the classroom—and the dualistic character of mother (signifying cultural heritage and "first" or native language) and teacher (signifying the colonizer or the colonizer's agent). But the point is that this takes place in California and so the threatening mother/schoolteacher character, Mrs. Scott, who speaks "broken" English, draws upon and modifies the historical literary/cultural relation established between language/border crossing and woman in the

Americas. Thus, there is an interesting parallel with feminist Chicana reappropriations of Malintzin and responses to Octavio Paz. Language stands between the United States and the Philippines, via gendered metaphors with which Filipino America must contend. And generally in the history of the colonial encounter between the two nations, two images or metaphors come up over and over again, both in colonial discourse and decolonizing cultural production, to describe the role/ status of language: the maternal (homeland configured as mother and the mother tongue) and education/tutelage (the classroom setting, the teacher, historical figures like the *pensionado,* and the tutelage of the infantilized Philippines as a candidate for democracy).

In a sense, Navarrete characterizes Mrs. Scott as both an assimila-tive traitor and a mother figure, echoing the figure of Malintzin, who simultaneously betrays and births the nation. Malintzin is enamored of and seduced by Spain. Like Malintzin, Mrs. Scott is enamored of Europe and has Eurocentric standards. She configures herself as civilized, using students like Rex to mark her distance and difference from the "jungle." In the two versions of the skit, she elides her ethnicity by making the Philippines dislocatable and moveable. In *Badly Browned* she literally moves the Philippines and geographically locates it in Europe on her "pretend" map ("The Philippines is the southernmost island of Spain"). But in the DVD version, while Mrs. Scott is introducing Rex, we learn that she is a Filipina from Guam and her attempt to map the world becomes even more fascinating: "He's from the part of the world known as the Philippines. Oh, you don't know where that is. I'm not from there. I'm from Guam. Hafa dei, hafa dei. Come on, let's take a look at the world map here. The Philippines is the southernmost island of Spain. It's very tiny. Very tiny. Moved near Guam now."

## Culture, Forgetting, and Resistance

Let us step back from Navarrete's work and consider solely the question of resistance and assimilation. Specifically, what kind of assimilation are these Filipino American writers, performers, and artists resisting? As I suggested above, racism and assimilation, as they generally have been nar-rated and theorized in Asian American studies, have not benefited fully from the experiences and perspectives of Filipino America. In Filipino

American studies, assimilation simultaneously indexes both colonial and racial processes of subjugation that historically bind Filipinos and Filipino Americans together, even as the highly uneven and contradictory modes of colonization and neocolonization have produced a vast range of Filipino American histories specific to locales like Honolulu, Seattle, Daly City, Chicago, Guam, and Jersey City. Yet S. Lily Mendoza notes that Filipinos and Filipino Americans are "unable to let the other one be, now and then policing each other's self-representations and contesting each other's definitions of what (ought to) constitute(s) 'Filipinoness.'" Indeed, Mendoza argues that Filipino nationals and Filipino diasporics have a "tighter transnational link" because of their "tenuous and contentious connection to a common third term: the United States—at once a site of desire(ing) as well as of lingering colonial shadows and ambivalences or what [Renato] Constantino . . . calls 'the continuing past'" (xxiii). So while the narrative of immigrant assimilation is not unconnected to the narrative of colonial assimilation, the former has overshadowed the latter in normative recitations of Asian American history, leaving underexplored this "continuing past."

Recently, critics have attempted to address this structural problem and hierarchy within Asian American studies, directly or indirectly responding to the controversy over the representation of Filipino Americans in Lois-Ann Yamanaka's fiction while also responding to Lisa Lowe's notion of heterogeneity. But I think that Asian American studies has been at a theoretical impasse for a while now, given the failure of coalitional models in a moment of exposure and crisis like the Yamanaka debacle, wherein generational, racial, sexual, and political differences devolved into (or simply revealed) profound rifts among writers, activists, and scholars. Instead, Asian American studies may need to relearn its indebtedness to feminist critiques of nationalism, for example, Rajagopalan Radhakrishnan's insight that "feminist historiography secedes from the structure [of nationalist totality] not to set up a different and oppositional form of totality, but to establish a different relation to totality" (quoted in Lowe and Lloyd 19). I am suggesting that the sheer fragmentation and diversity of the geography, culture, and history of the Philippines and the diaspora have produced a historically embedded "different relation to totality," one that the rest

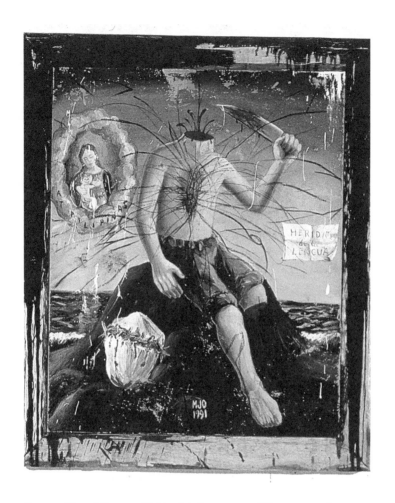

PLATE 1. Manuel Ocampo, *Heridas de la Lengua*, 1991. Oil on canvas, 180.34 x 154.94 cm. Collection of Tony Shafrazi, New York.

PLATE 2. Paul Pfeiffer, installation view of *Morning after the Deluge,* 2003. DVD projection. Projection size approximately 12 x 16 feet; loop length approximately 20 minutes. Courtesy of the artist and The Project, New York.

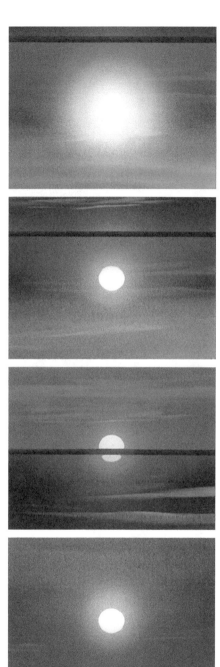

PLATE 3. Paul Pfeiffer, four stills from *Morning after the Deluge,* 2003. DVD projection. Courtesy of the artist and The Project, New York.

PLATE 4. Paul Pfeiffer, *Vitruvian Figure (after Pavia Cathedral),* 1998. Digitally generated sepia print on mylar, 72 x 36 inches (182.9 x 91.4 cm). Courtesy of the artist and The Project, New York.

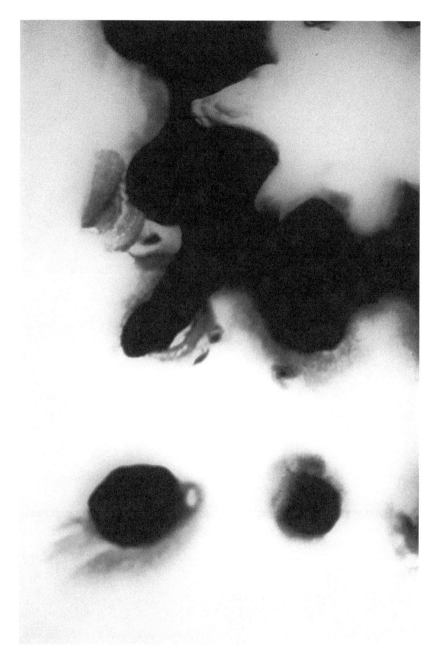

PLATE 5. Paul Pfeiffer, *Vitruvian Figure (after Pavia Cathedral)*, 1998 (detail). Courtesy of the artist and The Project, New York.

PLATE 6. Paul Pfeiffer, *Leviathan,* 1998. Digital C-print, 60 x 46 inches (152.4 x 116.8 cm). Collection of Thomas Dane, London.

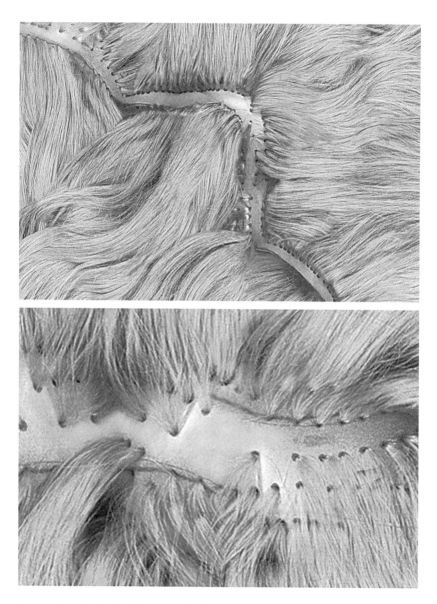

PLATE 7. Paul Pfeiffer, *Leviathan,* 1998 (details). Collection of Thomas Dane, London.

PLATE 8. Reanne Estrada, *General Tri-Corn (6)*, 2003. Ink on erasers, 4.5 x 4.5 x 0.5 inches.

PLATE 9. Reanne Estrada, *Epure Maped Oval (4)*, 2000. Pencil on erasers on wall, 4.5 x 4.5 x 0.5 inches. Collection of the Contemporary Museum, Honolulu, Hawai'i.

of Asian America can learn from instead of concocting ultimately unconvincing models of identity politics that, for example, conceive of Asian American studies as a "subjectless discourse" (Chuh 10).

What forms of resistance and assimilation are specific to Filipino American history? In the essay "The Philippine-American War: Friendship and Forgetting," Reynaldo Ileto tracks the shifting concept of "friendship" during the war when Americans used the rhetoric of banditry—or *lladrones* during the Spanish regime—to characterize the Filipino army. Ileto suggests that we take more seriously the Filipino guerrilla tactics that the Americans condescendingly dubbed "amigo warfare." The derogatory phrase refers to the shape-shifting abilities of the Filipino army, who recognized the futility of conventional warfare and also drew on similar tactics previously used against the Spanish.[22] Thus, to the Americans, the same person could be friend and/or foe. Eventually, as the war dragged on and American policy and strategy evolved, "true" friends to the Americans were only those within the "protection zones," concentration camps in which entire villages were cordoned off or relocated, a tactic similar to those used by Spanish colonial authorities. After the war, of course, "friendship" would be used to describe the relation between the United States and the Philippines, a form of colonial forgetting that obscures the power asymmetry between the two. Also, the term "friendship" refers to different ways that defeated Filipinos came to terms with the new colonizer, whether by continued "amigo warfare" or by accommodationist forgetting, literally and figuratively burying the past: "[Filipinos] could not be burdened by history as they commenced *still another* period of accommodation to colonial rule" (19).[23] Ileto usefully reclaims this history of "friendship" as a survival tactic of the colonized and of the guerrilla movement. Moreover, the war was a traumatic event that may "explain why Filipinos today seem to be so adept at handling tricky situations that demand shifting or multiple identifications and commitments" (Ileto 7). This history of survival and resistance survives in cultural forms, a legacy of the Philippine-American War. Filipinos emerged from the war as theatrical, performative subjects, using wordplay and the ambivalence of language as a matter of survival. In other words, Pilipinos are punny.

## *Orality and* sikolohiyang Pilipino

For decades now in the Philippines, scholars associated with what is called the indigenization movement have stressed the relationship between language and identity in the study of the nation's complex history of colonialisms and in the struggle for decolonization.[24] Defining the term "indigenous" as "both originating from within and directed mainly to community members" (117), S. Lily Mendoza describes the ambitious arc of the nationalist movement:

> An important tradition arising out of this decolonization impera-
> tive is the indigenization movement in the Philippine academy. Its
> purported goal is to seek to form a national(ist) discourse on civi-
> lization separate from the West. A collaborative endeavor spanning
> decades and various disciplines, it endeavored to undertake what
> Fanon (1963) refers to as "a passionate search for national culture"
> (p. 209). Comprised of several strands of interdisciplinary narratives,
> this project envisions the work of nationhood as of necessity begin-
> ning with the revision of theory as the very instrument of knowing.
> At the core of the movement's anti-colonialist thrust is an attempt
> to deconstruct centuries of colonial Eurowestern epistemological
> legacy. (11)

Because the education of Filipinos was such an important feature of American colonial policy, the university became both an important space for the emergence of the indigenization movement as well as a major object of scrutiny and debate. Mendoza reminds us that education and the academy are sites of colonization:

> Brief as the U.S. occupation may have been compared to Spain's
> protracted regime, owing mostly to its systematic ideological inscrip-
> tion in the educational system via the very instruments of knowing,
> American colonialism in the end seems to have marked the Filipino
> psyche in far more lasting ways, if not more insidiously. Thus, for de-
> cades to come, the undoing of this colonial "romance" with America
> was to become an all-consuming nationalist project. Colonial domi-
> nation having been secured most effectively through the installation
> of a colonial system of education, the academy became the logical
> site for critical contestation and intervention by Filipino nationalist
> intellectuals. (11)

Hence, the university and the schoolhouse are sites wherein colonizing and decolonizing forces are in play.

In the Philippine academy, one of the basic—and controversial—tenets of the indigenization movement is the replacement of colonial languages with Filipino languages, thereby diminishing the institutionalized power of English. For example, spearheaded in the 1970s by Virgilio Enriquez, the indigenous psychology movement *sikolohiyang Pilipino* mines Filipino languages for foundational psychological and philosophical concepts. Enriquez writes:

> A new consciousness labeled *sikolohiyang Pilipino* reflecting Filipino psychological knowledge has emerged through the use of the local language as an embodiment of the psychology of the Filipino people. A cursory examination of the Filipino language provides a basis for proposing *sikolohiyang Pilipino* as the study of *diwa* ("psyche"), which in Filipino directly refers to a wealth of ideas including the entire range of psychological concepts from awareness to motives to behavior. *Sikolohiyang Pilipino* is indeed the recognition of the importance of the Filipino mind and experience through the use of Filipino and other local languages to better analyze and understand them. (4)

Here, language is an important, even overriding variable in this approach to psychology. But even as Enriquez's revolutionary work proposes that important psychological concepts are derived from the Filipino language, how might Filipino American jokes and audiences ask us in turn to interrogate the presumption of language as epistemological ground?

But before attending to the particularities of Filipino America and the controversy ignited by the rejection of English, let us review a few more of the key insights of *sikolohiyang Pilipino.* Elizabeth Ventura, a psychology professor at the University of the Philippines, summarizes the impact of the movement:

> A reader of Philippine psychology literature will immediately note that the decade of the seventies was marked by a concern for indigenization, a recognition of language as a basic variable in personality, social psychology and testing, a broadening of the database of Filipino psychology through a concern for studying individuals in their natural social settings, rediscovering of the ties of Filipino

> psychology with other fields of study, and a greater involvement,
> on a nation-wide level, of Filipino social scientists in the develop-
> ments of the literature of Filipino psychology. . . . Along with the
> recognition of the importance of languages came a consciousness
> of the limitations and sometimes emptiness of Western theories and
> methods. (quoted in Enriquez, *Decolonizing* 4)

The argument that language precedes and constitutes selfhood may
sound familiar, even banal, to an Anglo-American academy that now
has had decades to parse Lacan. (This is, after all, Lacan's distinction between self and subjectivity. This is what I take Lacan to mean when he
writes that the cost of entry into subjectivity is the death of the self.)

But such an analogy—between Lacanian subjectivity and the collective self delineated by *sikolohiyang Pilipino*—risks missing the point
entirely. *Sikolohiyang Pilipino* proposes another kind of subjectivity,
very different from that of Lacan. This is not just about language and
the constitution of the self but also about selfhood being defined by
the rejection of a colonial language. The seismic shift from English to
Filipino language gives rise to an awareness of colonial bias, a new
consciousness that then becomes the basis for a decolonizing recapturing of the self. The emphasis on the social and cultural aspects of
language and the specific prioritization of Filipino over English reveals
the limits and limitations of Western knowledge and education. These
scholars seek to "uncover and make conscious the processes by which
the national psyche became—and to a degree has remained—captive
to a colonial imaginary" (Mendoza 60). Thus, *sikolohiyang Pilipino* proposes a transformative and oppositional methodology for analyzing
human consciousness that reveals the particularities and essentialism of
Anglo-American psychology while developing an alternative nationalist essentialism with humanist and universalist ideals.

Broadly speaking, then, the *sikolohiyang Pilipino* movement rejects
the Western emphases on the individual and on the ever elusive unconscious (accessible only through dream interpretation, hypnotism, et
cetera), and instead embraces indigenous language. Idiomatic expressions and folk sayings of the *masa* (the Filipino masses or people) become the foundation for the self and a key source of knowledge about
human consciousness. The grammar of social interactions that accrue
and evolve over time—in a word, culture—displaces the grammar of

the unconscious. The material and the text laid before the analyst radically change as the importance of repressed memories and dreams recedes. At the same time, the analyst's own priorities must change from those of one concerned with individual patients and reliant on Anglo-American training and values to one committed to a politics of decolonizing Filipino nationalism.

From the perspective of those trained in Western psychoanalysis, *sikolohiyang Pilipino* proposes a paradigm shift both in methodology and metaphor. In psychoanalysis the unconscious usually is described with figurative language that implies the unknown depths, the unexplored, the dangerous. And of course Freud at times uses the primitive (the colonized subject, the racial other) in anachronistic ways to set up an analogy between "primitive" people and the unconscious, repressed desires of civilized peoples. In contrast, *sikolohiyang Pilipino* seems to use only the conscious—what is voiced, used in conversation—and so it can be described as more "surface oriented." At the same time, *sikolohiyang Pilipino* proposes that certain "core values" are fundamental to the workings of Filipino society, and the language of depth is invoked especially in contrast with certain modes of "surface" behavior—especially more accommodative, assimilationist behavior—that colonial authorities tended to cultivate and manipulate. Generally, what makes the impact of American colonization so profound and long-lasting is that the Americans exploited and widened the gap between these "deep" values and surface behavior.[25]

Thus, *sikolohiyang Pilipino* makes two major interventions. The prioritization of the vernacular inverts the hierarchy between English and Filipino languages (and implicitly, between the elite and the masses), thereby laying bare the specificity, as opposed to universality, and biases of colonial Anglo-American values. Second, the stress on language undermines the basic premise of Western psychology, i.e., the unconscious as the source of knowledge. And so the goal of psychology, i.e., individual liberation, is rescripted as national or the people's liberation.

I am bringing together here a combination of Freud and *sikolohiyang Pilipino* to theorize both the collective and the individual. I am proposing a convergence of the unconscious in the Freudian individual/individuating subject and the collective and interpersonal in decolonizing

*sikolohiyang Pilipino.* In my reading of Freud's "Fetishism," the unconscious searches for meaning across languages and this meaning emerges
in rational and irrational ways. In Navarrete's "SBC Packers," meaning
similarly is formed through homonyms and puns and across various
accents in the same (English) language. According to the proponents
of *sikolohiyang Pilipino,* the making of meaning through language contains and conveys particular values that can change, depending upon
their interpretation and application under different colonial and post/
colonial conditions.

Clearly inspired by Virgilio Enriquez's work, education scholar
Leny Mendoza Strobel has outlined a "framework of decolonization"
necessary for the development of a "critical historical consciousness
that challenges the master narratives that have externally defined the
Filipino/Filipino American" ("Coming Full Circle" 62). Strobel's eight-
participant study advocates psychological, spiritual, and political recovery and transformation, and she prioritizes indigenous culture, values,
and research methods.[26] Strobel comments on the constructedness of
knowledge in Filipino American culture:

> The process allowed [the participants] to reflect on how sources of
> knowledge within their home cultures were either minimized or tri-
> vialized. Sources of knowledge and wisdom such as cultural practices,
> folk sayings, proverbs, stories, myths and folklore, songs, dances, and
> humor have not been considered legitimate sources of knowledge in
> the colonial culture. (71)

Perspective, in other words, is essential. There is a crucial distinction between Filipino psychology, wherein Filipino culture and history form
the basis for the study of the psychology of the Filipino, and Philippine
psychology, which denotes trends and developments in the field of psychology, mostly Anglo-American-oriented, in the Philippines. Because
the latter is privileged and much more prestigious, it took something
like the indigenization movement for scholars, individually criticizing
Anglo-American bias and dominance within their own fields, to come
together and realize that the problem existed across a wide range of
disciplines and fields.[27]

Strobel argues that part of the decolonizing process involves recognizing the orality of Filipino and Filipino American culture:

> As a residually oral culture, the Filipino American community re-
> tains its oral consciousness. Their immersion in a literate society in
> the U.S. slowly transforms this oral consciousness. The participants
> realize that their personal and family histories need to be connected
> to those memories that were never committed to texts. They now
> have the opportunity to create texts out of the recovered memories.
> ("Coming" 100)

Strobel underscores the need to recognize and value orality as a fundamental aspect of Filipino and Filipino American culture, something
that has been "passed on" to Filipino Americans.

But exactly how and how much has been "passed on" to Filipino
Americans, and is this genealogical metaphor sufficient? The indigenization movement in the Philippines is inward-looking and is about
establishing boundaries, often justifiably so, given the problem of
xenophilia rather than xenophobia in the post/neocolonial Philippines.
Enriquez discusses the universality of cultural/societal distinctions
between the outside and inside, and how every nation/culture has its
ethnocentrism. But his point is that the Philippines' problem has more
to do with "xenocentrism" rather than ethnocentrism (*From Colonial*
46). Rather than the problems of xenophobia and ethnocentrism that
tend to vex scholars in other parts of Southeast Asia, indigenization
scholars in the Philippines train and reorient themselves to be skepti-
cal of outside theories and to deem them appropriate from the outside
only when "properly nuanced": "there are 'laws' that must govern cultural borrowing" (Mendoza, *Between* 69).

So this obsession with boundaries and national/cultural identity,
not surprisingly, leads to a lot of frustration coming from both sides
of the Pacific Ocean. Responding to charges of exclusionary tactics
(one must speak Filipino to participate in *sikolohiyang Pilipino* and one
must reside in the Philippines, with the exception of overseas contract
workers), Filipinos want to know why they are being held accountable
for Filipino Americans' problems, especially when Filipino Americans
seem to have it "made" in the United States and when Filipino scholars are so strapped for resources. And Filipino Americans object in a
number of ways, including pointing out that the dispersal of Filipinos
has to do with devastating economic conditions at home and with the
rise of the Philippine nation in the first place. The Filipino American

challenge to the indigenization movement, especially via a class critique, is summarized by the California writer and editor Eileen Tabios:
"Is not the diaspora part of the Filipino history? And could not one
argue that the diaspora is (in a major way) a Philippine-based cause in
the sense that domestic policies and the situation there have not been
able to provide, say, a living otherwise for those who've had to leave
for other parts of the world? (I know that's how my granpa got to be
a *'manong'*)" (quoted in Mendoza, *Between* 192).

It is no surprise that jokes, humor, and stand-up comedy are occasions for establishing the boundaries of Filipino America, an entity that
demands the theorization of a better metaphor or concept of boundaries. In humor, there immediately is an inside and an outside, people
who get the joke and who do not, and yet those boundaries are fragile
and immediately transgressed. There is a clearly kinesthetic element to
identity in Filipino America, and it is not as if non-Filipinos or non-
Filipino-speaking people are incapable of getting the joke, because a lot
of the jokes, physical and verbal, translate. And perhaps that is another
reason for the dominance of jokes in Filipino American culture: the
constant testing of boundaries forms the hub of community, indeed,
the way that community gets formed.

Navarrete proposes a new way of theorizing and conceptualizing
national boundaries that emerges through a history of colonization. In
one of his skits, he recalls visiting the Philippines as a *balikbayan*—literally,
"return home"—for the first time after migrating to the United States:

> I realize one thing in the Philippines, you know what they got?
> Most thing *[sic]* the Philippines does have? FOBs, man. Hella FOBs.
> Damn! That place is just overrun with FOBs! God, you think there's
> a lot here. I get off the plane, FOB, FOB, FOB, FOB, FOB. When
> does it end?" *(Husky Boy)*

If the Philippines can be "overrun" with immigrants, Navarrete implies that Filipinos born in the Philippines have the same status as those
who have migrated. Just as the blond wigs in Paul Pfeiffer's *Leviathan* simultaneously demarcate and disrupt the boundaries of colonial Christian
architecture (see chapter 2), Navarrete's observation exerts tremendous
pressure on the very concept of boundaries. Similarly, in his travel memoir *Eye of the Fish* the writer Luis Francia expresses disillusion when

he arrives in the United States, finding himself already overprepared for America and then finding that recognition not at all returned or reciprocated by Americans. The disconcerting, deeply uneven blurring between the Philippines and the United States that Francia describes works the other way too, when Filipino Americans "return" to the Philippines. The FOBs are in the homeland and the natives are FOBs. In a way, Navarrete is claiming that Filipinos in America still are "foreign in a domestic sense." One need not migrate to be an "FOB" ["fresh off the boat"]. In other words, Filipino American identity needs to be understood as a kind of introjection that blurs the differences and reconstructs the boundaries between the Philippines and the United States. The very idea of what is "foreign" and what is "domestic" and how those two concepts are related to each other is thrown into crisis. For if Navarrete is proposing that the homeland rather than the United States is "overrun" by immigrants, his joke turns out to be about the history of a contradiction, what it means when a population can be "foreign for one purpose" and "domestic for another." Thus, I am proposing that we think of "foreign in a domestic sense" as a framework for thinking about the contradictory positionality of the colonized Other, one that is quite different from the metropole-colony binary dominating postcolonial studies and, to a large extent, diaspora studies. It is no mere coincidence that the company featured in Navarrete's "SBC Packers" skit is a packing and shipping company, making money off of the travel of goods; and that the popularity of the skit turns on the difference between *p* and *f* and the pun connecting packing and fucking. As I have argued in this chapter, puns travel across borders in ways that deterritorialize meaning. Puns are a vehicle for the translingual and transnational production of meaning. Constructed as "foreign in a domestic sense," Filipino America is a simultaneously inassimilable *and* assimilable vestige of American colonialism, producing a very different notion of geographical and imaginary boundaries between the colonizer and the colonized. Pilipinos are, indeed, punny.

# *"He will not always say what you would have him say"*

Loss and Aural (Be)Longing in
Nicky Paraiso's *House/Boy*

> He will not always say
> What you would have him say
> But, now and then, he'll say
> Something wonderful . . .
> . . . . . . . . . . . . . . . . . . . . . . .
> You'll always go along
> Defend him when he's wrong
> And tell him when he's strong
> He is wonderful
> He'll always need your love
> And so he'll get your love
> A man who needs your love
> Can be wonderful.
> —OSCAR HAMMERSTEIN II,
> "Something Wonderful"

I F WHAT VICENTE RAFAEL has called "white love" structures the colonial and neocolonial relationship between the Philippines and the United States, this chapter traces the alternative, if circuitous, possibilities of queer loss and love proposed by Nicky Paraiso's play *House/Boy*. A gay second-generation Filipino American writer and performer, Paraiso has developed a signature combination of cabaret and performance art over the three decades or so in which he has been involved in New York City's downtown theater scene.[1] *House/Boy* is the last in Paraiso's trilogy of full-length solo autobiographical plays about home and identity: *Asian Boys* (1994), *Houses and Jewels* (1994), and *House/Boy* (2004). While the first two plays in the trilogy highlight Paraiso's relationship with his doting, overbearing mother, the death of his near-silent father is the focus of the final play. Drawing on camp sensibility, the sentimentality of Hollywood and Visayan love ballads, and the colonizing whiteness of Hollywood musicals, Paraiso attempts to acknowledge the distance between him and his father. Concluding *House/Boy* with a moving, mournful rendition of the Richard Rogers and Oscar Hammerstein ballad "Something Wonderful" from *The King and I,* Paraiso dramatizes the failure of language to bridge that gulf while the father is alive as well as the son's refusal of material generational transmission after the death of the father. Paraiso turns to Hollywood portrayals of sexual repression and voyeurism, racism and homophobia, and idealized father-son scenes to restage the im/possibility of communication and love with the father.

Drawing on what David Román and Holly Hughes have termed the power of "o solo homo"—queer solo—performance, Paraiso uses intensely autobiographical material to reenact and rewrite the paternalism of American colonialism.[2] By dramatizing his relationship with his father and all the other "houseboys" in his life, and by alluding to the history of Filipino male domestic labor in the United States, Paraiso renders visible the impact of American paternalism on everyday kinship bonds and family structures.[3] On stage Paraiso never strays too far from his grand piano, whose closed lid is draped by a fringed shawl and littered with sheet music and family portraits (see Figure 11).[4] Closing *House/Boy* with "Something Wonderful," he "finally gets to sing for his father," as the program notes put it. Why does Paraiso conclude *House/Boy* in this way? What does it mean that emotions must be expressed—queered—only through others' emotions? Why do Filipino Americans seem to get the last word only through others' words? As I hope to demonstrate in the extended reading of *House/ Boy* that follows, "queer" in Filipino America denotes a structure of feeling that always is routed through another, usually dominant form or medium. Characteristic of the "well-organized evasiveness" that defines camp aesthetic, Paraiso's strategy of indirection is a product of

FIGURE 11. Nicky Paraiso, *House/Boy.* Photographs by Mark Roussel.

a powerful combination of forces in Filipino American history out of which have emerged the colonial structuring of the family as well as the familial structuring of colonial relationships (Babuscio 124).[5] Yet dominant cultural forms and power structures have proven again and again malleable in the hands of sexual and racial minority artists. *House/Boy* is an example of decolonizing Filipino American expressive

culture that proves as much and more. Paraiso's choice of Broadway/
Hollywood lyrics that idealize the subject's love for the king—"a man
who needs your love"—highlights the colonial psychology of "white
love." But in the song's performance (its aurality) and in what comes
before it (the variety of texts embedded in the play), Paraiso also proposes an alternative to white love. As we shall see, Paraiso's juxtaposition of two scenes of domesticity—the highly local details of a Filipino
American family alongside the grand familial narratives and metaphors
of colonialism—produce aporetic spaces that enable alternative structures of feeling, belonging, and kinship, pointing the way toward new
structures of governance and sovereignty.

## The King and I

*House/Boy* is bound spatially and psychically by the house in Queens,
New York, that his parents throw all their life savings into, something
they loudly declare his inheritance (see Figure 12). Early on in the
play, a kneeling Paraiso chalks a rude outline of a house on the floor
of the set. The outline was spotlighted in red in the 2004 production at
La MaMa Experimental Theatre Club in New York City's East Village.
But he does not want the house. Like any good gay Filipino from the
boroughs, Paraiso wants to escape his immigrant parents' home in the
outer boroughs and become a star in Manhattan. Paraiso is a failed
legatee who refuses to live up to the expectations of heterosexual re-
production that attend the parents' burdensome gift. When Paraiso's
schoolteacher mother leaves her husband and son in New York and
returns to the Philippines, the father becomes the caretaker of the
house. A registered nurse, the father is the first in a series of houseboys
who appear in the play. After both parents die, Paraiso sells the house,
and so the attempt at establishing propertied patrilineality ends rather
than begins with the death of the parents.

However, tightly interwoven throughout the autobiographical play
are popular culture references. In ways familiar to readers of Filipino and
Filipino American texts, Paraiso indicates the profundity of Hollywood's
colonizing impact on Filipinos in the homeland and the diaspora. As a
young actor, Paraiso desperately searches for role models in dominant
culture and happens upon examples of Filipino male casting in the mov-

FIGURE 12. Nicky Paraiso, *House/Boy.* Photograph by Jonathan Slaff.

ies *The King and I* (1956) and John Huston's *Reflections in a Golden Eye* (1967). Alongside his father, who is a professional caregiver, Paraiso compares and contrasts two very different celluloid houseboys. In the former movie, he discovers that the character of Prince Chulalongkhorn, a boy of the Siamese royal house, is played by a Filipino child actor. In the latter, he stumbles upon the actor Zorro David, who plays a Filipino houseboy named Anacleto, employed by the ailing white wife of a military officer. As intensely specific or local as the play at first seems, and as the details of his parents' lives unfold—such as the mother's accounts of colonial American education, her hatred of the Japanese, and the father's choice of nursing as a profession—this oscillation between autobiographical elements and popular culture indicates Paraiso's interest in indexing the global circulation of colonial discourse even within a highly personal, autobiographical solo performance.

According to the plot summary included in the promotional material for *House/Boy,* Paraiso "meets up with the characters from 'The King and I' and finally gets to sing for his father." Both *House/Boy* and its embedded text *The King and I* are about the loss of the father and the identity crisis precipitated by that loss. Paraiso converts "Something Wonderful" into a dirge for his dead father, a Filipino immigrant from the "old-timer" generation. Narratively speaking, the son finds a way to communicate with his father—"to sing for his father"—even if it is too late.[6] Interpretively speaking, however, the lyrics "He will not always say what you would have him say" can signify several things. First, at the level of plot, the son wants to hear certain words from his father, but he will never hear those words; and the father's withholding of love thus creates longing and desire. Second, at the metadiscursive level, the lyrics indicate the presence of dissembling and the deliberate, strategic use of indirection, the technique of speaking "in other words" or "others' words," which are post/colonial and queer strategies of appropriating alien, dominant languages. That is to say, Filipinos will not always say what one would have Filipinos say. In a 1951 *New York Times* article about the process of researching, writing, and composing *The King and I,* Rodgers and Hammerstein said that they found the "intangibility of [Anna's and the king's] strange union" challenging precisely because of this propensity for indirection: "In dealing with [Anna and the king] musically we could not write songs which said 'I love you' or even 'I love him' or 'I love her.' We were dealing with two characters who could indulge themselves only in oblique expressions of their feelings for each other" (3).[7] Third, since *House/Boy* explicitly presents itself as a work of mourning, the play can be said to move from "working through" to "speaking through."[8] Paraiso expresses his grief for his father through the lyrics of a dominant American cultural form like the Broadway tune, indicating that familial and filial relations as well as affective relationships are structured by the colonial and neocolonial relationship between the United States and the Philippines.

Both Lady Thiang's and Paraiso's renditions of the song thematize the subject's longing for explicit gestures and signifiers of love from the father or monarch, which are not and never will be forthcoming. In the 1951 musical and the 1956 film, the king's chief consort Lady Thiang sings "Something Wonderful" to Anna in the hopes of effecting a reconciliation between the dying Siamese king and the English widow–governess.⁹ In her appeal to Anna, Lady Thiang speaks on behalf of the state, a monarchy that must survive the transference of state power from the king to the crown prince. According to Thiang's explanation and defense of state power, the state utterly depends upon its subjects and, thus, conscripts the subject's love: "He'll always need your love / And so he'll get your love." But the problem with this economy—besides the fact that there is something very circular about its logic, i.e., the enunciation of the king's need justifies and guarantees the gratification of those needs, or, rather, the state's request for filial piety seems to constitute a reward for the subject who then must fulfill the state's mandate—is that it is a thoroughly unequal partnership. It is a transaction profoundly uncommitted to principles of reciprocity and mutuality. Rather, Thiang's song accurately delineates the psychic economy of colonialism, which relies on a combination of dependence upon and subjugation of the subject. Thus, *The King and I* works as an imperial fantasy in several ways: Thiang's conflation of filial love with romantic love elides the inequity at the heart of the relationship between the monarch and the subject. Moreover, the musical's depiction of the encounter between the male primitive (patriarchal, proslavery, misogynistic Siamese monarchy) and the female modern (abolitionist, feminist, enlightened English empire) displaces English racism onto the Siamese monarchy.¹⁰

Set in a "less-than-royal Queens household," *House/Boy* works against the imperial fantasy of male lineage and paternal benevolence in several ways (Francia, "Homebody/Queens"). The play is about a son finding a way to confess properly to his now dead parents that he has sold the house and declined the role and status of primogenitor. All his life Paraiso's parents loudly describe how hard they have worked so they can purchase and bequeath property to him. Toward the beginning of the play, he describes the pressure his parents exert upon him:

> So it's really about this house. The house that I grow up in. This house in Flushing, Queens, that my parents pour all their savings into—this little, two-story red brick house—so that I, the only son and heir, might have it. Their legacy to me. It will be their gift to me. Of course, I spend my whole life trying to escape Flushing, Queens. I say to my parents, I say, "Mom and Dad, it's really nice that you want to give me this house, but I don't know what I'm gonna do with it. I'm not going to live there." And Mom says, "Don't worry. It's your house. It's there for you if you want to stay there. Whatever you want to do with it, it's yours." Funny thing is, that after my parents pour their whole life's savings into this house in Queens—my mother decides to leave the house, and go back to the Philippines. My mother leaves this house that she and my father put all of their life's savings into and she goes back to the Philippines. And she leaves my father in the house. Alone. Because, you see, my father is the caretaker of the house. And my mother says, "Now, Daddy, you stay in the house." Dad says, "Yes. I will. I will stay here until the time that Nicky might want to use the house." (15–16)

By selling the house, Paraiso cuts off the male line in an act of repudiation that both constitutes resistance to compulsory heterosexuality and reveals the distinction and interdependence between patrilineality and patriarchy. Indeed, Paraiso poses a double threat to patriarchy because patriarchal power is reinforced by the accumulation of property and other forms of capital and by the safeguarding of patrilineality through heterosexuality.[11]

Moreover, Paraiso's act of repudiation is a response to the reversal of gender roles in his family, a reversal that is precipitated by the mother's decision to abandon the family but also underscored by the father's profession. The father is a registered nurse, a service profession associated with maternal nurturance and care.[12] A "caretaker" at home, he is a caregiver in the workplace. This combination of professional and familial feminization is fortified by the family's silence about his younger days as a bachelor. Thus, while the original Hollywood version of "Something Wonderful" reveals the allure and capaciousness of patriarchal and state power, Paraiso's version instead describes the silencing and marginalization of the father: "He will not always say what you would have him say. . . . He has a thousand dreams that won't come true." So little biographical information about his father is available to Paraiso as he is growing up. Only during his airplane flight to the Philippines to deliver his father's cremated ashes does Paraiso break this silence: "I take [the bag containing the urn] with me on the plane, and keep it with me at my seat. I put the bag with my dad's ashes between my legs, and I *talk* to my father like I have never talked to my father in my whole life. Not even when he was alive. 'Dad, Dad, we're going home. It's gonna be OK. It's gonna be alright'" (original emphasis, 23). To compensate for this silence, a portion of the play is devoted to imagining his father's life as a bachelor—stylish, brash, and carefree. He is part of the "old-timer," or *manong,* generation of Filipino men who are overwhelmingly single and young and who migrate to the United States in the 1920s before the official end of legal Filipino migration to the continent.

Upon his father's death, Paraiso becomes the *padre de familia* and his first task as such involves transporting his father's cremated ashes to his mother, who has returned to her hometown (which is also the father's hometown) in the northern Philippines. But the father's scene of disempowerment—his demotion from man of the house to houseboy—is repeated with the son. In the Philippines, Paraiso finds that his mother has developed a powerful attachment to a male domestic worker, Efren Martinez: "He is my mother's houseboy, gaunt, lanky and soft with a generous dollop of *je ne sais quoi.* Definitely *bakla*" (8). After Martinez is fired, however, she begins to confuse Paraiso for the houseboy: "After Efren Martinez leaves my mother's house, I take on the role of *padre de familia* and some kind of strange transference goes on between me and my mother. She continues talking to me as if I am Efren. By becoming the man of the house, I have actually become my mother's houseboy" (10). In other words, the models of masculinity available to Paraiso involve domestication, emasculation, and infantilization, so it is no wonder that Paraiso sells the house. My point, however, is not to demonize the mother (although Paraiso himself expresses ambivalence, hostility, and at one point visceral rage toward the mother). While the mother plays a major role in the demotion of the father within the family, the reversal of gender roles in the domestic sphere has less to do with the pathology of a particular family and more to do with the impact of twinned racism and imperialism on Filipino American family formations, models of masculinity, and structures of feelings. In other words, absent the forces of colonialism and racism that shape the lives of Filipino American men, the feminized domestication of Paraiso's father would not occur.

Paraiso's autobiographical portrait of masculinity, the home, and the family is inextricably connected to the history of American colonialism in the Philippines. American colonial rule relies on a powerful combination of patriarchal punishment and nurturance, and so the expression of paternal love is specially freighted in contemporary Filipino American texts like *House/Boy*. Yet when Paraiso says, "So it's really about this house. The house that I grow up in," his reviewers and even Paraiso himself describe *House/Boy* as a portrayal of the generational conflict between Asian parents and American children resulting from the immigrant struggle for national belonging and upward mobility, a plot structure that still tends to govern the reception and interpretation of Asian American texts (15).[13] Read instead as a post/colonial text, *House/Boy* begins to exhibit the traces of a colonial history structured by what might be called a "domestic pun," which conflates the subjectivity of the domestic worker with the spatial and ideological dimensions of the domestic sphere. That is to say, Paraiso mobilizes the idea of the "domestic" as a multivalent sign of subject and site, exploitation and reciprocity, servitude and kinship, and intimacy and expulsion. The play powerfully conflates the boundaries and internal organization of the home with the geopolitical boundaries of the state and empire.[14] This domestic pun reminds us of the fundamentally paradoxical words of the 1901 U.S. Supreme Court decision deeming territories like Puerto Rico and the Philippines "foreign to the United States in a domestic sense" *(Downes v. Bidwell)*.[15] Postcolonial studies traditionally has relied on center-periphery models and on the geopolitical distinction between the imperial metropolis "over here" and the colony "over there." *House/Boy* instead reminds us that the American empire is organized by an account of simultaneous interiority and exteriority.

Indeed, the contradictions surrounding the political formation of Filipino America are closer to the infamous formulation "domestic dependent nations" devised by the U.S. Supreme Court in the 1831 decision *Cherokee Nation v. Georgia*.[16] In response to the question as to whether Cherokees "constitute a foreign state in the sense of the constitution," the Court first found that it had the power to adjudicate such a case. It then inferred that, while the United States has a "peculiar" relationship to Cherokees and to Indians in general, Cherokees constitute an entity that is neither foreign nor sovereign:

> The condition of the Indians in relation to the United States is perhaps unlike that of any other two people in existence. In general, nations not owing a common allegiance are foreign to each other. The term foreign nation is, with strict propriety, applicable by either to the other. But the relation of the Indians to the United States is marked by peculiar and cardinal distinctions which exist nowhere else....
>
> Though the Indians are acknowledged to have an unquestionable, and, heretofore, unquestioned right to the lands they occupy, until that right shall be extinguished by a voluntary cession to our government; yet it may well be doubted whether those tribes which reside within the acknowledged boundaries of the United States can, with strict accuracy, be denominated foreign nations. They may, more correctly, perhaps, be denominated domestic dependent nations. They occupy a territory to which we assert a title independent of their will, which must take effect in point of possession when their right of possession ceases. Meanwhile they are in a state of pupilage. Their relation to the United States resembles that of a ward to his guardian.
>
> They look to our government for protection; rely upon its kindness and its power; appeal to it for relief to their wants; and address the president as their great father.

Moreover, the act of ceding land counts as evidence of Indian "dependence" upon the United States: "Treaties were made with some tribes by the state of New York, under a then unsettled construction of the confederation, by which they ceded all their lands to that state, taking back a limited grant to themselves, in which they admit their dependence." Invoking the language of paternalism, the Court declared that Cherokees are in a "state of pupilage."

As I argued in my introductory chapter, Filipino America's very existence has to do with the forcible inclusion of the Philippines into the United States, an "inclusionary racial formation built on interlocking metaphors of family, evolution, and tutelary assimilation" that must be distinguished from the paradigm of exclusion from the body politic that generally defines the study of other Asian American groups (Kramer 226).[17] A racial formation that emerges out of the colonial construction "foreign in a domestic sense," Filipino America is a simultaneously inassimilable *and* assimilable entity in the "house" of the American empire. Such a predicament resembles that of the houseboy and other domestic servants whose intimate dealings with the employer-family so easily can be seen as a threat to the family. Immediately after performing a dance sequence dedicated to the Filipino valet Anacleto in *Reflections in a Golden Eye,* Paraiso describes the bond between his mother and Efren Martinez as a "special relationship" associated with privacy in several ways:

> [Martinez] shares a private world with my mother that no one else knows, that no one neither *[sic]* inside nor outside of the family, can penetrate or fathom, much less imagine. The intimate knowledge that only he and my mother share, is a source of irritation and jealousy for my aunt Corazon, who is consumed with envy for the special relationship between Efren Martinez and my bedridden mother. He feeds her. Gives her medicine. He dresses and undresses her. Empties her chamber pot. Lifts her up from the bed and takes her for walks. Makes sure the mosquito net covers her adequately when she sleeps. Sits beside her while she says the rosary. Sometimes playing chorus to her litany of prayers. (8)

Granted special access to the mother's bedroom, Martinez is privy both to her chamber and chamber pot. He shares "intimate knowledge" with the mother while performing the most intimate of physical chores. He is entrusted with "the key to her special bureau/closet—the *aparador.* Where her Social Security checks and American Dollars are kept. Her prayer books. Her box of jewelry" (Paraiso 9). It is no wonder that his presence rouses feelings of "jealousy" and "envy."

The houseboy, Paraiso suggests, is structurally queer in relation to the household in which he labors. Martinez "knows all the secrets of the house," and he is "definitely *bakla*" (8). Rich are the ironies of such a positionality. Despite or perhaps because of the close proximity between employer and employee, the houseboy's position within the family is always precarious. The fantasy of the "special relationship," a phrase that is used regularly to describe the relationship between the Philippines and the United States and that indicates the workings of allegory in Paraiso's play, occludes the caste distinctions and labor exploitation at the heart of the economic relationship between the employer–family and the household worker. Indeed, Martinez is dismissed on the whim of a family member who accuses him of theft: "Efren packs his clothes into a small luggage case and leaves the house in a fury. He is never seen again" (Paraiso 10). The houseboy is intimately bound up with the family but always on the verge of expulsion, a permanently unincorporated part of the family.[18] He is foreign in a domestic sense. Thus, *House/Boy* allegorically proposes that Filipinos are structurally queer to the United States.

## White Love: Domesticity and Colonialism

One of the ironies brought forth by Paraiso's allegorical rendition of Filipinos' historical positionality is the phenomenon of "white love." His interlacing of references to the family, servitude, and the domestic sphere signals the presence of what the historian Vicente Rafael has called "white love," a term that captures the familial and tutelage metaphors of paternalism structuring American colonial policies and ideology. Though Paraiso insists upon specificity and the intensely local, as do other artists who have developed an oeuvre of full-length solo autobiographical performance, he offers a kind of particularity that is surprisingly worldly. *House/Boy* asks its audience to recognize and appreciate the significance of the concept of the "domestic" in the colonization of the Philippines because, according to American colonial rhetoric and policies, the home and the family structure are used as a way to narrativize the colonization of the Philippines.

Commenting on the discursive effects of the official policy of "benevolent assimilation," Rafael argues that "white love" structures the colonial relationship between the Philippines and the United States such that the Philippines is configured as the infantilized recipient of nurturance and as the subject of racial uplift:

> As a father is bound to guide his son, the United States was charged with the development of native others. Neither exploitative nor enslaving, colonization entailed the cultivation of "the felicity and

perfection of the Philippine people" through the "uninterrupted devotion" to those "noble ideals which constitute the higher civilization
of mankind." Because colonization is about civilizing love and the love
of civilization, it must be absolutely distinct from the disruptive crimi-
nality of conquest. The allegory of benevolent assimilation effaces the
violence of conquest by construing colonial rule as the most precious
gift that "the most civilized people" can render to those still caught in a
state of barbarous disorder. But instead of returning their love, Filipino
"insurgents" seemed intent on making war. (Rafael, *White Love* 21)

Thus, Filipinos' primary duty is to learn how to love colonialism. Any
rejection of the "most precious gift" of colonialism, which becomes
synonymous with civilization, is met with "discipline":

> White love holds out the promise of fathering, as it were, a "civi-
> lized people" capable in time of asserting its own character. But it
> also demands the indefinite submission to a program of discipline
> and reformation requiring the constant supervision of a sovereign
> master. Conjoining love and discipline, benevolent assimilation
> was meant to ennoble the colonizer as it liberated the colonized.
> [There is a link secured] between an ideology of benevolence and
> the repressive-productive institutions of discipline. [In other words]
> white love and native subjugation become mutually reinforcing.
> (Rafael, *White Love* 23)

"Discipline" here refers to three distinct events, the combination of
which elides the violence of colonization and narrativizes that violence
as white love. First, "discipline" is a consequential act. It is a form of
punishment for unacceptable behavior such as the rejection of the gift
of colonization. Second, "discipline" is an aspirational mode of being.
Under American tutelage, Filipinos eventually are to become a self-
disciplined people. Finally, "discipline" refers to the narrative structure
that elides the violence that is fundamental to the conquest and rule of
the Philippines. That is to say, according to the narratorial and rhetorical
structure of white love, Filipinos are disciplined—rather than oppressed
or murdered—by Americans, and a regime founded in and by violence
justifies its existence through the rhetorical, discursive, and institutional
structures of discipline.

The combination of nurturance and discipline that constitutes
"white love" makes for a particularly insidious structure of colonized

feeling, the longevity and costs of which contemporary texts like *House/ Boy* document. Paraiso moves fluidly between the intensely local(e) and the global such that the minutiae and specificity of autobiography— this particular house in Queens, this particular obsession with *The King and I,* the singular death of his father—become inextricable from the historical effects of American colonialism and neocolonialism. Any expression of love between the father and the son indirectly references these historical relations of economic and political subjugation.

## The Object of a Houseboy's Desire

Paraiso's quoting of father-son relations in *The King and I* does more than critically reproduce the colonial structure of paternal benevolence, however. Because the play is organized around the withholding of (paternal) love, such silences and gaps in communication produce longing and desire. And the play's second major embedded text, John Huston's *Reflections in a Golden Eye,* offers a breathtaking spectrum of repressed and frustrated desire.

Paraiso remembers watching *Reflections* for the first time and offers the following plot synopsis:

> I'm searching for Zorro David.
> A figure imprinted on a frame of celluloid.
> Taking the #7 train to Manhattan to go see a movie. "Reflections in a Golden Eye." The act of watching. The act of being watched. The object of desire being watched, reflected in the voyeur's eye. Zorro David in a beautiful pastel shirt and loose-fitting trousers. A deep and sonorous voice. He's talking to the mistress of the house played by Julie Harris: "Madam Allison . . . Madam Allison . . ."
> I am searching for Zorro David. Delicate, cultured, fine-boned, he flutters about like a multi-colored butterfly. He is Filipino—an actor, well, not exactly an actor, but yes, he acts and plays the part of the Filipino houseboy in the film: "Reflections in a Golden Eye."
> It's based on a novel, a story by the Southern American writer, Carson McCullers, who is a rare bird herself, odd, eccentric, brilliant. The setting of both the novel and the film is a sleepy army base in the deep white South. The kind of army base where you don't ask, and don't tell nothin'. The kind of army base where bored alcoholic officers' wives plan dinner parties and social gatherings for the other

officers and *their* wives. The kind of insular community where torrid affairs between officers and their best friends' wives are tolerated in a hothouse atmosphere of deception, recriminations, regrets, and barely kept secrets. Where voyeurism rears its curious and lustful head, and obsession becomes the rule—not the exception. The kind of story where a young enlisted soldier rides horseback in the woods completely buck naked while Marlon Brando watches totally obsessed.

In other words, my kind of story.

It's directed by John Huston in 1967 and stars an incredible cast: Marlon Brando as the repressed Captain Penderton, Elizabeth Taylor as his alcoholic wife who's carrying on an affair in the rose bushes with Brian Keith, an officer colleague of Brando's. The part of Brian Keith's fragile, sickly, and paranoid wife is played by Julie Harris who has her own personal valet and servant, an aging Filipino houseboy named Anacleto, played by Zorro David, a painter and visual artist who has never acted before in his life and, as far as I know, has never acted since.

I look for Zorro David.

In the mid-80s, my cousin Ching Valdes-Aran meets Zorro in an apartment somewhere around Times Square. Ching says he is still a painter and visual artist. Why would she lie? (5–6)

It is no coincidence that *House/Boy*'s second embedded text is a movie that relentlessly stages and thematizes scopophilia. Watching *Reflections in a Golden Eye,* Paraiso distinguishes between the voyeuristic act of looking at an object of desire and the identitarian act of looking for a self-same object with which to identify ("I look for Zorro David"). As part of his general plan to escape Queens, to become a star, and to find alternative models of Filipino masculinity, Paraiso turns to the movies, and he finds in *Reflections* many levels and types of looking: (a) Paraiso is watching the movie; (b) Marlon Brando's Captain Penderton is watching the soldier; (c) the soldier is watching Elizabeth Taylor's "alcoholic wife"; (d) Julie Harris's "fragile, sickly, and paranoid wife" is watching the soldier's surveillance of Taylor; and (e) Zorro David's Anacleto is watching over Harris. At the same time, Paraiso uses *Reflections* to set into motion many kinds and levels of desire: erotic, scopophilic, transgressive, prohibited/repressed, self-colonizing (desiring whiteness), heterosexual, homosexual, and the imperial (desiring the primitive, i.e., soldier, as a kind of primitive).

After several intervening scenes, Paraiso returns to the story of Anacleto, who has disappeared suddenly and mysteriously in the movie:

> Oh, some of the dramaturges among you are probably asking at this point, whatever happens to Anacleto, the houseboy in the story of "Reflections in a Golden Eye"? Well, Marlon Brando becomes a total voyeur, completely obsessed with the young enlisted soldier played by a young Robert Forster, who steals up to Elizabeth Taylor's room while she's asleep in a drunken stupor, which is pretty much every night. The young enlisted man just crouches down in a corner watching Elizabeth Taylor. Julie Harris sees Robert Forster's comings and goings at the Brando-Taylor home, and no one believes her, of course, and she literally goes quite mad.
>
> Her husband sends her to a fancy sanatorium with Anacleto as her inseparable companion. She dies of a heart attack almost as soon as she gets there, and Anacleto—Anacleto disappears and, like Efren Martinez [Paraiso's mother's houseboy in the Philippines], is never seen again. And that's the last we ever see of Zorro David, too.
>
> So you see why I'm obsessed. (14–15)

Here Paraiso is commenting on the fleeting appearance of gay Filipino men on screen (perhaps his version of Paul Pfeiffer's "disappearing figure studies" discussed in chapter 2). Anacleto's character is utterly dependent upon that of Julie Harris's, a symptom of Hollywood's racism and homophobia. While *Reflections* on the one hand is important to Paraiso because it signals the existence of gay Filipinos, as it turns out Paraiso discovers that Zorro David was cast for the part even though he is not a professional actor—he is a professional dancer, and it is no wonder that his acting is awful—and so David produces a horrifyingly homophobic and racist caricature. Narratively speaking, Anacleto disappears with his employer: when Julie Harris's character dies, David's character dies. Anacleto is a mere appendage to the ailing, white military wife. Anacleto's role and status are similar to that of Efren Martinez, a subjectivity constituted by simultaneous, contradictory disposability and indispensability. Indeed, the narratively aporetic presence of Anacleto is related to America's military presence in the Philippines. In McCullers's novel, the Pendertons serve in the Philippines where they meet and hire Anacleto. In a number of ways Huston's movie exemplifies how Hollywood's depiction of queer, obsessive, and/or perverse desires—

the longing for something or someone wonderful—inevitably ends in their prohibition, frustration, and thwarting. As I argue in the next and concluding section, Paraiso's juxtaposition of *Reflections* with father-son (and king-subject) scenes from *The King and I* enables the harnessing and restructuring of this proliferation of desires. Specifically, the array of marginalized desires set in motion by Paraiso's synopsis of *Reflection* is resurrected and refracted through his rendition of Lady Thiang's song "Something Wonderful."

## The Death of the King: Aporetic Spaces, Localized Plurality, and Alternative Sovereign/ty

At the end of *House/Boy*, Paraiso turns to song in order to stage the impossibility of intergenerational transmission and communication. This involves a risky turn to dominant, normative, and thus recognizable forms like the Hollywood ballad to express queer, post/colonial, and racialized subjectivity. In the extended excerpt below, Paraiso confesses that he has sold his parents' house in Queens. He then uses puppets to perform the transference of state power from king to crown prince depicted in *The King and I,* an exercise in parody that is both campy and moving. His performance of *The King and I* is interrupted by the sudden appearance (more puppets) of his parents followed by a troop of relatives, followed by Paraiso's crooning of "Something Wonderful," which closes the play:

> The very last scene of "The King and I" is one of my all-time favorites in both theater and film history. Hmm.
> I want to be Prince Chulalongkhorn. That final scene where Yul Brynner as the dying king hands his power over to his first-born son, played by the young Filipino actor Patrick Adiarte: this for me is the definitive cinematic moment where an Asian father and son share a kind of heightened flash of understanding. Perhaps it is my hope of reconciliation that I never have with my own. Of course, Mrs. Anna Leonowens, the ultimate representation of the British colonial Empire, gets the final word. It goes like this:
>
> THE KING: Several weeks I do not see you, Mrs. Anna. And now I die.
> MRS. ANNA: No! Your majesty!
> THE KING: This is not scientific! I know when I die or do not die. (Addresses the prince) Chulalongkhorn. Rise!

(To Anna) Mrs. Anna. You . . . take notes. You take notes from next king.

(Addresses the prince) Well. Suppose you are king. Is there nothing you would do?

PRINCE CHULALONGKHORN: I . . . I would make proclamations.

THE KING: Yes! Yes! . . .

PRINCE CHULALONGKHORN: First, I would proclaim for coming New Year . . . Fireworks!!!

THE KING: Hmm! Hmm?

PRINCE CHULALONGKHORN: Also boat races.

THE KING: Boat races! Why boat races for New Year's celebration?

PRINCE CHULALONGKHORN: I like boat races! And Father . . . I would like to make a second proclamation.

THE KING: Yes . . . What is second proclamation? Make it! Make it!

PRINCE CHULALONGKHORN: Regarding custom of bowing to king in fashion of lowly toad. I do *not* believe this is good thing. Causing embarrassing fatigue of body, degrading experience for soul, et cetera, et cetera, et cetera! This is bad thing.

And then my mother enters:

MAMA: You should bow to your parents. Remember, THICKER than water!

NICKY: Mama! Welcome to Siam!

And then Papa enters, looking very much like Yul Brynner.

PAPA: Customs, tradition—is a puzzlement!

NICKY: Then all my relatives march in, Lolo Domingo Quevedo Paraiso, Lola Fidela Quevedo Paraiso, all of Sarrat, Ilocos Norte, in fact, and my father's friends—Tito Ben Peña, Rosalio Quevedo, Eugenio Quevedo, Miguel Paraiso, Mark Cabanos, Ernesto Agcaoili, Juan Factora—all dressed in cute, Siamese costumes . . .

NICKY: I sold the house. My legacy. The one you poured all your life savings into. I sold it . . . You are angry with me, my Father?

THE KING (AND DADDY): Oh! Why do you ask question! When you are king, YOU are KING!!!!! You do not ask question of sick man, nor . . . of woman. Mrs. Anna, this proclamation against bowing to king, I believe to be *your* fault.

MRS. ANNA: Oh, I hope so, your majesty! I DO HOPE SO!!!!!

(Nicky speaks.)

And the music swells. And I finally get to sing for my father. (32–36)

In this highly ironized reenactment of *The King of I,* Anna recedes as the agent of Western reform and modernization, the third party who precipitates the transformation of the autocratic, slaveholding monarchy into a liberal monarchy. Instead "Nicky" gets to sing "Something Wonderful" for his father, and his refashioning of the ballad as dirge sets in motion a pluralization of object-choices. If "he will not always say what you would have him say," we really are not sure to whom the pronouns "he" or "you" refer. Sequentially, "Something Wonderful" comes at the end of the play so it is configured as closure, but the emotive and narrative power of all those different stories and object-oriented emotions begin to interact with one another. Paraiso sets all these different elements in motion, and they play and interact with each other *again*. He creates a space of bound yet free *aporetic* play. He creates the kind of aporetic spaces that produce new kinds of cathexes wherein the scattering of emotion leads to its intensification. These aporetic spaces are both bound and free, the kind that emerge from an archipelagic sensibility; they offer adeterminant spaces and openness. Precisely because there is no positive signifier, audiences can access and then inscribe themselves into these aporias. So the effect on the audience is of the possibility of play. Simultaneous or syncretic multiple longings do not compete for space and instead can live alongside one another (just as meanings live alongside one another in puns).

Aurally and tonally, Paraiso makes possible all kinds of longing, a kind of hybridity of feeling. His voice is "queer," but not in the autobiographical or anthropomorphizing sense (i.e., Nicky Paraiso is gay; therefore, his voice is gay). Rather, if the art of camp "relies largely upon arrangement, timing, and tone," the tonal quality of his voice produces an emotionally loaded plurality of desires, rooted in anger, mourning, erotic longing, racial assimilation, and kinship (Babuscio 123). Even though the writer–performer himself may report a journey in his own creative process toward claiming identity, especially gay or queer identity, I would argue that this information about the playwright is not necessarily what "authenticates" the performance and play as queer, but rather what I am calling "localized plurality" or maybe its inverse, an "archipelagic cathexis." This is a plurality of affect that, precisely because it is localized all in one voice, does not dissolve (the usual story of multiplicity) but rather intensifies.

Borrowing from the Freudian psychoanalytic concept of "determinism" or "overdetermination," wherein an "object-choice might satisfy a multiplicity of instincts" or a "fusion of instincts" or "multiple-channeled motivation," I suggest that Paraiso's work and other Filipino American texts produce the effect of "localized plurality" or "archipelagic cathexis," wherein multiplicity leads not to dissolution but rather intensification; wherein the aporetic leads to play, participation, and bonding rather than bafflement; and wherein the archipelagic and scattering lead to stronger rather than weaker cathexes.[19] Cultural producers like Rex Navarrete and Nicky Paraiso achieve this "localized plurality" through aurality, the comedian's aural play with puns and the singer's tonal quality. Such tactics create the necessary space for minority post/colonial artists to express themselves when the very conditions of cultural expression are circumscribed by imperial forgetting (or what I called "double disavowal" in chapter 2). But these spaces also allow and encourage the audience to participate and to inscribe themselves. It is this kind of localized plurality that produces an alternative or queer kind of closure, a scattering that intensifies rather than diminishes the possibilities of belonging.

Something wonderful does indeed happen at the end of Paraiso's astonishing play. In this depiction of the transfer of power from the king to the crown prince, alternative structures of feeling, genealogy, and governance become possible, an infinitival moment that makes connections between the unstable shapes that desires and drives take, on the one hand, and aesthetic form, on the other hand. Paraiso's work constructs, I think, an alternative avenue for—or perhaps a resolution of—the fundamental tension between anti-imperialist collective action and the exclusionary practices of any group formation. This alternative includes localized plurality (a multiplicity that emerges from the intensely local, the highly individuated) and archipelagic cathexis (a kind of bonding or focusing of energy that comes from the scattered or from diffuse places). By constructing aporetic spaces of freedom that attract and accommodate a variety of desires and contradictions, Paraiso radically transforms the concepts of the imperial home and the colonized houseboy. Rescripting political and personal father-son relationships and instead proposing localized plurality, a scattered structure of feeling and an archipelago of desires, Paraiso points the way toward the death of the king, toward alternative governance structures, and toward true sovereignty.

CONCLUSION

# Reanne Estrada, Identity, and the Politics of Abstraction

L IKE OTHER RACIALIZED BODIES in the United States, contemporary Filipino American artists have been subjected to what might be called a regimen of identity. They are vulnerable on the one hand to the violence of hypervisible representation, such as the recycling of stereotypes. They are vulnerable on the other hand to the violence of invisibility in the United States wrought by imperial amnesia about the colonization of the Philippines and about the racialized oppression of Filipino Americans. The visual artists featured in this book respond to this predicament of hypervisibility and invisibility in two ways: They emphasize either the presence of the body or the erasure of the body. In the work of Angel Velasco Shaw and Manuel Ocampo the body becomes exaggeratedly somatic—too full of itself—whereas the body in Paul Pfeiffer's work slowly and elaborately retreats from the gaze. In the preceding chapters, I have proposed layered ways of interpreting their art in relationship to the history of American imperialism in the Philippines and in Filipino America. For example, I have argued that Pfeiffer's work indexes the depopulating policies and aesthetics of American imperialism. Standing before Pfeiffer's gorgeously unmoving sun, empty landscape, and wandering horizon, the viewer of *Morning after the Deluge* understands that the creation and perception of a beautiful landscape are preceded by the racist, genocidal clearing of the land. Thus, one of the "messages" that the viewer can take away from Pfeiffer's art is that the making of

American beauty comes at a high cost. But what is Pfeiffer doing with and to *form*? What are the politics of form in contemporary Filipino American art, especially art that has no explicit, visible markers of Filipino American identity? In other words, what are the (identity) politics of (abstract) form?

In this concluding chapter, I turn to the work of the visual artist Reanne Estrada because her minimalist shapes and use of degradable materials propose counterintuitive ways to think about identity as a politics of evading rather than securing visibility and legibility. With her ink-mottled erasers, hair-embossed soap, and translucent packing-tape sculptures, Estrada embraces both the processes and materials by which one makes something or someone (almost) unmarked. Fascinated by erosion, Estrada is interested not in concretizing identity but rather in undoing identity. She has a minimalist aesthetic that has elicited a range of responses converging around the idea of abstraction, and there is a noticeable rift among her reviewers and audiences. In Asian American and other minority venues, Estrada, like Pfeiffer, occasionally has been accused of focusing on form at the expense of social reality and sociological content. Void of unambiguous, overt signs of things Filipino, their art is perceived as having nothing to do with being Filipino. They fail to fulfill the "mandate to represent their communities" (Wilson). Their art is apolitical, anti–identitarian, and thus "white." In contrast, establishment art critics generally are attracted to Estrada's and Pfeiffer's abstraction. For these critics, "abstract" is not a pejorative but rather a compliment because the minority artist successfully transcends her identity and her art can be evaluated solely for its aesthetic merit, unsullied by the stain of politics. What might be a way out of this series of quandaries? How have Filipino American artists negotiated the predicament between the violence of hypervisiblity and the violence of invisibility? Between being praised for producing abstract art that transcends identity and achieves universalism and being condemned for art that is "too abstract" and disavows identity?

Attempting to find a way out of these predicaments, I argue that, rather than a generic descriptive or category, abstraction is a tactic employed by artists, an aesthetic practice that is but one of a number of strategies of indirection, trickery, and mimicry at the heart of Filipino/American decolonizing cultures. These strategies I have referred to in chapter 1 as the expression of an infinitival subjectivity; aesthetically, they enable the artist to negotiate cultural meaning through abstraction. Thus, Estrada's and Pfeiffer's use of abstraction is, like camp, a way of coding and camouflaging meaning. Their art reminds us of the urgency of paying close attention to what Hayden White has called the "content of the form." In the close readings of the content of Estrada's form that follow, I argue that abstraction emerges as a practice. Indeed, the artists and writers discussed in this book collectively suggest that *identity is a decolonizing practice,* one that ironically comes most alive when identity is under erasure.

## Erasers

Like the stand-up comedian Rex Navarrete, Reanne Estrada was born in the Philippines and migrated as a child with her family to the United States. They lived for a short time in New York City before settling in Southern California. After completing a bachelor's degree in visual and environmental studies at Harvard University, Estrada eventually moved to the San Francisco Bay Area, where she and fellow Filipino American artists Jenifer Wofford and Eliza Barrios formed the guerrilla feminist art collective Mail Order Brides/MOB in 1995. For more than a decade her work both as a member of MOB and as a solo artist has appeared in group exhibitions in the United States, Canada, and the Philippines. Thus far she has had seven solo exhibitions in galleries and art museums in California, Wisconsin, Indiana, and Massachusetts with such titles as "The Allure of Obsolescence" at Lizabeth Oliveria Gallery in San Francisco, "Cut" at Lizabeth Oliveria Gallery in Los Angeles, and "Contradictory Impulses" at the Indianapolis Museum of Contemporary Art. She now lives and works in Los Angeles, where she has set up an independent consultancy that designs and develops politically progressive media-based projects that promote community empowerment and foster sustainable forms of community leadership. For example, she trained high school teenagers in filmmaking as part of a project on health and nutrition awareness programming in south central Los Angeles; she also has assisted in the development of a community-based public arts project in Historic Filipinotown in Los Angeles.

In sharp contrast with the defined goals of her consultancy and the guerrilla activism of MOB's productions, Estrada's solo art is quiet and subtle. Its allure is that of fragility, defined by what she calls "built-in obsolescence" ("About the Work"). Her simple, stark geometrical shapes are made of degradable material like packing tape, hair, soap, and erasers.[1] There is a satirical quality to her erasers series. In works like *General Tri-Corn (6)* and *Epure Maped Oval (4)* the "agent of eradication" is also the object of eradication (Estrada, "About the Work"). She laboriously pencils and inks circular gray patterns onto erasers, which look like they have sprouted either delicate flowers or disgusting mold (see Plates 8 and 9). Hence, the eraser is marked by the very materials whose markings it is meant to eliminate. Were one to pick up and use one of these carefully tarnished and arranged erasers, thereby causing the artwork to revert to its everyday function, the eraser itself would erode and eventually disappear. Thus, her work vanishes in one of two ways, either by taking on a different function and use-value—she converts everyday objects into art—or by literally disappearing. Counterintuitive as the concept initially may seem, erasure and obsolescence here work as signs of identity, which usually is associated with presence.

## Soap

With this combination of minimalist loveliness and decay Estrada says that, in making works that "aspire to be unstable," she wants to invoke in her viewer a "horror of beauty [that] is defined by the threat of its loss" ("About the Work"). She most successfully achieves this "horror of beauty" in her soap series (see Figures 13–14). In *II. One Thousand, One Hundred Eight* and *IX. Five Hundred Fifteen* she lines soap bars with strands of her hair. In the former, she wraps the mirrored pair of bars with her naturally curly hair, which has been coaxed into perfectly straight lines. The deep shadow between the soap bars laterally bisects the whole work and thus indicates that it is a three-dimensional sculpture rather than a two-dimensional drawing. But the work also is bisected horizontally by an eerily reconstituted hairline that is materially repulsive and formally beautiful in ways reminiscent of Paul Pfeiffer's *Leviathan* or Mona Hatoum's soap sculptures.

For hair does not belong on soap. Hair defiles soap. One recoils from such a combination of materials. By making formally beautiful what

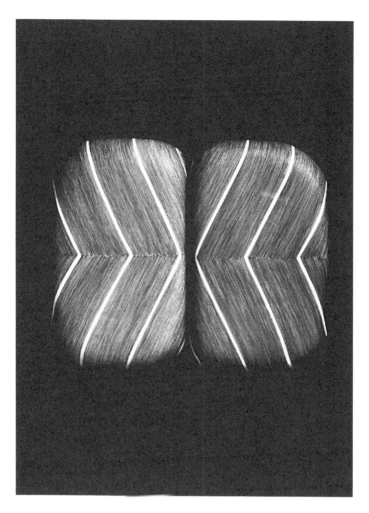

FIGURE 13. Reanne Estrada, *II. One Thousand, One Hundred Eight,* 1998. Hair on Ivory soap in shadowbox on terry cloth–covered pedestal, 37 x 10 x 11 inches.

is materially abject, Estrada finds herself in the company of other artists of color like Allan deSouza, whose materials often include his own blood, semen, nail clippings, and hair. The artist's use of such materials is a reminder of the way in which the idea of filth and excrement consolidates an arbitrary social order organized around invidious difference,

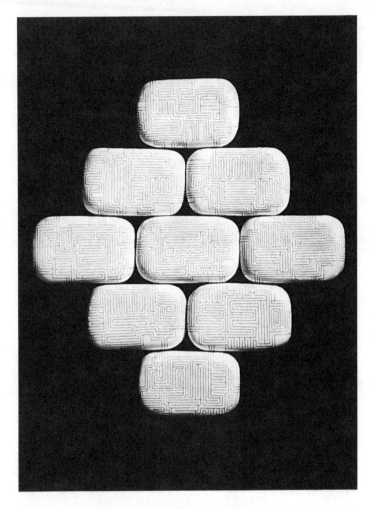

FIGURE 14. Reanne Estrada, *IX. Five Hundred Fifteen,* 1998. Hair on Ivory soap in shadowbox on terry cloth–covered pedestal, 37 x 18 x 18 inches. Private collection.

e.g., between the pure and the polluted or between the sanitary and the dirty.[2] In American newspaper and other print coverage of the Philippine-American War and its aftermath, pickaninny stereotypes were a way for Americans to understand the colonization of Asians. The noun *pickaninny* comes from the Spanish *pequeño* or the Portuguese *pequeno,* which means "little" or "tiny," and in infamous cartoons depicting U.S. president William McKinley and the new colonial subject, the dirty little Filipino must be scrubbed clean by the benevolent, slightly exasperated white father figure.[3] Hence, Estrada's choice of Ivory soap is a very nearly hackneyed metaphor for the central role of racist discourses and policies about sanitation and hygiene in the maintenance of a colonial order. But in *IX. Five Hundred Fifteen* the faint contours of the soap's brand are barely discernible. It is in just such faded traces that she references the late-nineteenth-century and early-twentieth-century American carica-tures of Filipinos that have been almost erased from dominant accounts of American history. It is with just such faint tracing, which fluctuates between the two-dimensional drawing and the three-dimensional sculp-ture, that the artist outlines what constrains her.

## Packing Tape: "You just sit there and I wrap"

Estrada claims that her sculpted objects are "of questionable pedigree and dubious archival quality." She calls them "art world interlopers with fluctuating identities and a seductively self-destructive streak" ("About the Work"). They oscillate "between two and three dimensions" and "between drawing and sculpture," and Estrada says that she thinks that her work is "best described as process-intensive high-relief drawing or low-relief sculpture" ("About the Work"). Such declarations beg the question as to the nature of the relationship between the identity of the work and the identity of the artist.

Her polypropylene packing-tape sculptures shed a little more light on this relationship, composed as they are of material that sticks to her body and picks up her hair and skin. *Tenuous (tentatively titled)* is an evolving collection of packing-tape works, which include sculptural floor- and wall-based works. At first glance *Tenuous* does resemble a line drawing (see Figure 15). Against a solid black painted backdrop, lu-cent white shards—splinters of various geometrical shapes—emanate from the exploding center of the ellipsoid, and the three-dimensional shapes turn out to be made of sticky stuff that efficiently collects and retains the bodily residue of the artist (see Figure 16). *Tenuous* thus be-gins to work as autobiography, referencing Estrada's dislocated diasporic positionality in which, simultaneously and contradictorily, there is a

FIGURE 15. Reanne Estrada, *Tenuous (tentatively titled),* 2005. Polypropylene packing tape on painted wall, dimensions variable (as shown, 7.5 x 15 feet). Installation view of *Cut,* Lizabeth Oliveria Gallery, Los Angeles, California.

center and there is no center. She has worked on *Tenuous* since 2001, and she has claimed that she continued work on it "until 2008, when [she was] a completely different person from the day [she] started." Not without a sense of mischief, she explains that both her choice of materials and the temporal span of her creative process are linked to cycles of the body:

> While making *Tenuous (tentatively titled),* my skin adheres to the tape, embedding and "encoding" my genetic material within its translucent "skin" and resulting in a kind of verifiable artist signature. Every seven years, the body changes completely on a cellular level, inside out—organs, skin and all. When my body completes such a cycle, this extended self-portrait will also be complete. ("About the Work")

Like the rest of her writing, Estrada's rationale for her choice of packing tape is clever, provocative, polished, and clearly engaged with critical theory. Rhetorically, she sounds just like other intellectual, con-

Figure 16. Reanne Estrada, *Tenuous (tentatively titled)*, 2001–6 (detail). Polypropylene packing tape on painted wall, 10 x 12 feet.

ceptual artists describing their art. When she is asked directly and informally about her choice of packing tape, however, Estrada responds with a short anecdote from her immigrant childhood. Having migrated at the age of seven with her family from the Philippines to the United States, she recounts helping her mother prepare *balikbayan* boxes—the phrase *balikbayan* literally means "return home"—full of goods to send back to relatives and friends in the homeland. Seated atop the nearly bursting boxes, the young Estrada is issued the following command by her mother: "You just sit there and I wrap. You just sit there and I wrap."[4] Wielding the packing tape, the mother reduces the daughter to mere deadweight so that she can seal the boxes more efficiently. Of course, this scene symbolically replicates the daughter's own immigrant experience: She herself was packed up and moved from one country to another.

As simple and personally revealing as it is, Estrada's anecdote is full of theoretical suggestion, complementing and in some ways exceeding the ideas about self-portraiture, identity, and transfiguration articulated in her written artist's statement. Viewed as Estrada's self-portraits as an immigrant child, *Tenuous* and the other packing-tape sculptures are subtle indictments of the mother, and these have their literary counterpart. Her mother's command "You just sit there and I wrap" recalls that of the immigrant mother in Maxine Hong Kingston's 1976 autobiography *The Woman Warrior: Memoirs of a Girlhood among Ghosts.* Kingston's notoriously verbose mother issues the command "You just translate" to the American-born narrator. Kingston's mother is deeply offended by the local drugstore, which has mistakenly delivered medication to the family's business and so has cursed them with bad luck. Instructed by her Cantonese-speaking mother to go to the drugstore and to demand free "reparation candy" from the white druggist, the daughter-narrator despairingly tries but fails to articulate the impossibility of such a request to her mother, who impatiently replies, "You just translate." In Estrada's and Kingston's scenarios, the daughter is to follow orders that are, from the mother's perspective, so simple. A dunce could "just translate" or "just sit there." As Karen Su has pointed out, however, in *The Woman Warrior* the mother's attitude toward language presumes a direct, unmediated correspondence between the "letter" and "spirit" of translation. This attitude radically devalues the work of the translator. Such work entails negotiating different contexts and "differential specificities" and hence entails "explor[ing] the epistemological parameters of knowledge in order to make sense of her own position in the world and of what that positioning forces her to negotiate" (Su, "Translating Mother Tongues, 45, 44). Both mothers render insignificant the work of translation, acculturation, and transformation that falls to the daughters and in so doing negate their daughters' subjectivities.

Kingston and Estrada have invented ways of representing and asserting subjectivity *in translation* that destabilize the very medium—language and packing tape—with which such an assertion can be made. This highly self-conscious process of destabilization successfully conveys to Kingston's reader and Estrada's viewer the invisibility, complexity, and creativity of Asian American female positionality. For example, while *The Woman Warrior* generally is configured in Asian American literary studies as the site of intense debate about the license or licentiousness (depending on the critic) with which it melds Chinese history and folklore and the phantasmatic, individuated idiosyncrasies of Kingston's own psyche, the controversial autobiography can be viewed instead as an elaborate, extended description of the hard work demanded of the translator and as a ground-clearing gesture toward the appreciation of previously devalued Asian American subjectivity. Similarly, Estrada's labor-intensive process can be viewed as a form of protest against the mother's devaluation of the child's experience. Told as a child to do nothing other than to "just sit there," Estrada's work as an artist is by contrast "absurdly labor-intensive to create." All of her works take so much time to create: "Packing tape and erasers are methodically gutted, surgically cut up, cut out and put back together again. . . . Everything is made by hand, very physical, very analog" ("About the Work"). Like Rex Navarrete's comedy skit "SBC Packing," Estrada's use of packing tape indexes the diasporic movement of goods and people that shapes so many Filipino American lives. But whereas Navarrete cuts up and remakes the English language with his puns, jokes, and other forms of wordplay ("My people historically butcher English"), Estrada slices and reassembles material like packing tape that is literally and symbolically the stuff of transnational linkages and separations. In other words, the artist creates labor where there was none and in so doing accords value where there was none. Perhaps so too does the critic.

### Packing and the Art / Act of Interpretation

In ways that nicely complement Navarrete's riotous play with language and accent in skits like "SBC Packers," Estrada's rendition of "packing" sheds light on the critical act of interpretation, which fundamentally involves packing and unpacking meaning. By investing so much physical labor into her works, Estrada calls attention to the material that she selects and the process that she and her viewer–critic undergoes. If the titles of Paul Pfeiffer's works are often highly iconographic—*Four Horsemen of the Apocalypse* or *Leviathan*—the textual description of materials perhaps is the most important part of Estrada's titles. Her choice of sticky, transparent stuff like polypropylene packing tape can be interpreted in several ways. First, the transparency of such material—

the ease with which one can see through clear tape—lends itself to thematization. Just as it is easy to see through packing tape, it is easy to see no politics in her art and to see nothing but its prettiness. One must work hard to perceive the political in her art. Yet because packing tape is sticky, it picks up bits of the artist and so there is always trace evidence of the artist that messes up everything. Obsessed with getting it right or perfect even as it necessarily is fundamentally wrong, Estrada performs a kind of camp. According to Jack Babuscio, camp aesthetic revolves around the staging of incongruity—the production of, for example, a beautiful woman who "is" a man—to celebrate amorality and to launch a "spirited protest" against the ostensibly inviolable laws of nature (123). Like the practitioners of camp, Estrada deliberately draws attention to the eternal flaw at the heart of that staging. Despite their appeal to transcendent universalist formalism, which is supposed to be emptied of sociological content and political meaning, her works inescapably bear the material signature—hair and skin—of the artist. Hence, rather than deflect attention away from identity politics, the abstract ironically calls attention to the material through which identity is thematized. In compelling if circuitous ways, her works successfully make the abstract site of meaning extraordinarily identity specific. She insists on the intrinsically, inescapably political nature of abstract form. She insists on the articulation between beauty and politics.

Oscillating between *very* abstract shape and *very* not-abstract material and between two- and three-dimensional art, works like *Tenuous (tentatively titled)* and *II. One Thousand, One Hundred Eight* reflect Estrada's dualistic life, which is divided so sharply between her formally beautiful works as a solo artist and her satirical, oppositional works as a member of the MOB collective. Enfolding that doubling into her solo works, Estrada symptomatizes the current politics of the contemporary arts in the United States, shaped as they are by the backlash against activist art starting in the 1980s that slashed state funding to the arts and humanities and that advanced a definition of the aesthetic that insisted on the separation of beauty from politics.[5] Estrada, Paul Pfeiffer, Allan deSouza, and other U.S.–based artists of color clearly want to produce works that initially are visually alluring but, upon closer inspection, are materially or experientially repulsive or abject. These are artistic interventions that together are a response to the 1980s, when the Republicans managed, in entirely unprecedented ways, to associate themselves with populism by disseminating narratives and icons of what Grant Kester calls the "shibboleth of cultural decay," the blame for which falls to the "parasitic moral depravity of young mothers on welfare, gay and lesbian artists, poor people of color, immigrant workers, and abortion doctors, overseen by a cabalistic liberal elite" (15, 14). Kester's critique of the contemporary art world and his defense of activist art practices and its oppositionality are not to be taken lightly:

> There is a not uncommon perception in the arts today that the fashion for an activist or politically engaged art has passed. On the one hand, some artists and critics are anxious to move "beyond" the perceived limitations of this work, while at the same time they are relieved to get back to the "real business" of art making.
>
> This double movement is clear in the recent call for a return to the aesthetic philosophy of the early modern period. Concepts such as beauty, taste, or the sublime that might have been previously dismissed as outdated are now being presented as the hallmarks of a new and challenging form of art that manages to be both visually seductive and politically powerful. In this view an overtly activist art practice is seen to sacrifice the unique power of the aesthetic to convey a subversive pleasure. I would argue, however, that an activist art practice, far from being antithetical to the "true" meaning of the aesthetic, can also be viewed as one of its most legitimate expressions. (7)

The very idea of allure and the concept of the art "object" or "piece"—rather than work or process—indicates that at stake is a hegemonic notion of the aesthetic wherein aesthetic culture is the means for the production of a universal subject that makes objective aesthetic judgments as to what is beautiful and what is ugly. But if it can be said that within objectivity lurks a particular if masked subjectivity, such aesthetic judgments impart and constitute colonial values. That is to say, the idea of the beautiful is coupled with that of the civilized, the idea of the ugly or bad with that of the savage. Such values and valuation would preclude the transgressive idea of the aesthetic advanced by activist art, wherein the artist has the capacity to describe, identify, and exceed the totality of systems of power and, consequently, to envision an alternate and better future.[6]

Given the stakes outlined by Kester, artists like Estrada do risk still working within the parameters of an aesthetic that would prohibit or devalue activist art as crude, ugly, and inartistic. But it is crucial to remember that Estrada *uses* abstraction. Abstraction in her work is a practice, one that lets one see the shape of things but it also lets one hide things. Through the practice of abstraction, Estrada ensures that there are no easily recognizable or legible signs of identity in her work, and by wrenching identity away from the regime of the visible she successfully politicizes perception. Perception becomes an unreliable adjudicator of racial difference and racism. It does not yield evidence so easily or directly. It does not precede knowledge but rather shapes knowledge. Rather than shoring up the colonial aesthetic, Estrada's insistence on producing abstract work that *looks* apolitical is an act of infinitival meaning-production that relies on relentlessly indirect, circuitous methods. Her practice of abstraction entails techniques of camouflage and trickery, wherein the post/colonial or minority artist uses stolen signs from the dominant culture both for and to other purposes.

In his scholarship on the Philippine-American War, Reynaldo Ileto has pointed out that Filipinos developed ways of feigning friendship, playing dead, and hiding and waiting. What the Americans derogatorily called "amigo warfare" denotes a Filipino style of resistance, which relied on decentralization from town centers as well as a bicultural mode of living in the towns—friends and collaborators to the Americans during the day and enemies during the night. Ileto speculates that this history "might even explain why Filipinos today seem to be so adept at handling tricky situations that demand shifting or multiple identifications and commitments" (7). But it was "illegal to remember the war," as Ileto baldly puts it in Angel Shaw's 2007 documentary *Stay the Course*. In the encounter with the violence of imperial forgetting, Filipinos have turned to shape-shifting of many kinds. But these sorts of resistance tactics do not lend themselves to memorialization. I would put it even more baldly: Bicultural, decentralizing modes and infinitival subjectivity do not lend themselves to history. Thus, Filipinos necessarily have moved out of history by turning to culture and form, developing a relationship to form and ideas about meaning-production that can survive the onslaught of the illegality of remembering.

Throughout this book, I have described artists' and performers' use of the overly visible and the overly invisible, and I have moved from representations of the body in visual economies to the representation of speech in linguistic economies. By emphasizing the artistic and everyday forms that Filipino Americans choose and use to keep track of that which has been lost to history, I hope to have demonstrated that, embedded within identitarian practice, is a history of resistance strategies. Defined as a *practice,* identity can and must change and so it contains history.

In decolonizing cultures, shape-shifting is a mode of survival as well as the basis for racism, e.g., Filipinos are nothing but first-rate mimics. And so attention to shape and form is paramount. It is a tautology: Filipino culture survives *through* culture, using dominant shapes, genres, and languages as sites of meaning, including abstract forms that lend themselves to universalism (which, of course, is Eurocentric and, thus, culturally specific) but in fact are the means for expressing both the specificity and wild heterogeneity of Filipino America. So while Reanne Estrada's retreat from the gaze at first looks like a retreat from politics, it is quite the opposite. Her retreat allows the preservation of politics in the form rather than content of her works. By outlining what constrains them, these artists remind us of the politics of form, even and perhaps especially in its most "abstract" manifestations. Reanne Estrada and all of the artists and performers in this book remind us that, in the case of decolonizing Filipino America, identity has everything to do with form.

And form has embedded in it a long history of resistance.

EPILOGUE

## *Lost in St. Louis: Pilipinos Are Punny, Especially on Cell Phones*

Like Judy Garland, I went to St. Louis. Unlike Garland, I met up with Filipino Americans flocking to Missouri in the summer of 2004 to attend the annual weeklong Filipino American National Historical ("Hysterical," quipped one member) Society conference. Milling around the University of Missouri student center on a humid Saturday evening, we had gathered to commemorate the centennial of the 1904 World's Fair, which imported and displayed a thousand Filipinos in the "Philippine Exhibit" (see Figures 17 and 18). Most of us learned for

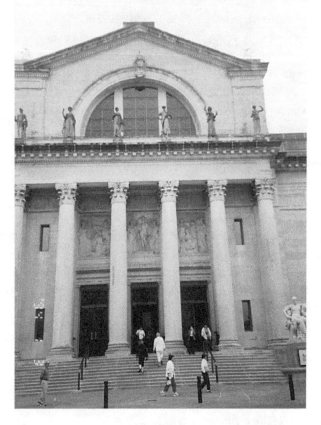

FIGURE 17. Museumgoers, including participants in the Filipino American National Historical Society (FANHS) conference, at the entrance to the Missouri Historical Society Museum, St. Louis, July 2004. Photograph by Cynthia Marasigan.

the first time that the mascot for one of the local middle schools was until very recently the "Igorot." We marveled at the photographs of Geronimo, a U.S. prisoner of war in 1904. We found out that a special law had to be passed for him to be transported to the fair so that he could sign autographs. I chatted with a seventy-seven-year-old war bride from Springfield, Illinois. I looked down at her tired, wrinkled

FIGURE 18. Banner advertising the exhibit "The 1904 World's Fair: Looking Back at Looking Forward," back entrance to the Missouri Historical Society Museum. Photograph by Cynthia Marasigan.

feet. ("I don't know why I buy new shoes; they hurt my feet so bad, honey!") She had met and married her American husband in the Philippines in 1946. She knew how to tell her story. Efficiently boasting about her children and grandchildren's education and white-collar jobs, she confessed that she had skipped out on the conference that morning. She had "gone gallivanting" to the local casino with friends.

By Sunday morning, I was in a van crammed with fourteen other brown bodies, mostly high school students from San Diego, ready to tour the original fairgrounds that had covered more than a thousand acres of central St. Louis. The official tour bus was fully booked, so the rest of us decided to form a caravan of sedans and minivans behind the bus. I was filled with doubt. I have learned to be frustrated by the Filipino predilection for ambitious yet haphazard planning and overly mediated connection, which always seem to doom us to tribalized failure. Why, for example, do I always find myself conveying messages from my mother to her sister and back again when they both have telephones, the technology for direct, unmediated correspondence? Why does it take at least four separate parties for a box of Christmas presents to wend its way from a living room in New York City to a living room in Quezon City? But the Californian teenagers in the van were nattily dressed and surprisingly well behaved. My prejudice against their adolescent species slackened. That is, until I remembered that it was ten o'clock in the morning and that they were drugged by exhaustion. They had not slept for five days, and who knows what kind of trouble their hormones had incited in five nights.

Confirming my fears, our van arrived at the rendezvous spot too late. The bus and its convoy had left without us. I should have known that the happy Hollywood version—meet me in St. Louis, indeed—would not work in real life. No one in the van was from St. Louis. We were lost. I grabbed the city map from Joanie Cordova, the directionally challenged occupant of the front seat, and looked at the location of St. Louis for the first time, trying to figure out where we were. We knew that the tour would conclude at the Missouri Historical Society Museum. I called out directions to the driver and the van helplessly rolled forward. *Where* was the official tour bus with the official tour guide?

A girl in the back of the van had the wits to call her mother, one of the lucky ones on the bus. Stilled witnesses to the ensuing exchange between daughter and mother, we immediately sensed the generational, language, and accent differences between them:

DAUGHTER: "Ma! What road are you on now?"
MOTHER: "We're on Skincare Road! Where are you?"
DAUGHTER: "Skincare? What kind of a name is that? Are you sure?"
MOTHER: "Yes!"

We could hear the mother's rising irritation. We were disrupting her morning and interrupting the tour. The girl hung up: "I think she's getting angry." The van sighed; fifteen pairs of shoulders slumped. No more information would come from the bus. Flailing around with the wholly unfurled map, I cast my eyes desperately up, down, and around the gridded topography of St. Louis. What could she have meant by "Skincare"?

But my eyes found what my ears heard. I found "Skinker Road." I cried out directions to the wondrously composed driver, and ten minutes later we caught up to the bus. The teenagers whooped and yelled, "You really know how to read a map!" Our van joined the convoy.

But then we realized, as St. Louis flitted by our windows, that we had no idea what we were looking at because the tour guide was on the bus. Once again, the teenagers came through with their cell phones. A boy called the bus and got someone there to hold their phone up to the guide. His droning voice came through loud and clear on speakerphone. The guide was white and male. The van's euphoria slowly dissolved. He did not understand what might be important to Filipino Americans. The teenagers started to look sleepy and even younger again. Heads leaned against the van's windows. We got bored. We got annoyed. We snickered. We added footnotes to the guide's commentary:

"Who's this *haole* guy?"
"Why isn't the bus stopping here? This is what Filipinos want to see!"
"I'll just edit out all the garbage and tell you what's important."

The van woke up again. I lifted my eyes from the map that I still gripped in my hands. We understood that it was okay that we were not on the bus. We had been late and lost and we had found the bus. But even after we caught up with the tour, we found ourselves perpetually behind. There was a permanent lag between our 2004 experience of the 1904 World's Fair and the guide's narrative, and so we had begun to fill the gaps in by ourselves. Our chatter constituted our experience.

Yet we had one more lesson to learn. Fifty minutes into the tour we realized that the cell speakerphone was two-way. The bus could hear everything we were saying. Too late, we heard laughter coming over the speakerphone. The van fell into a horrified silence. We realized how rude we had been. Then the silence passed, the contagion set in, and we started to laugh too.

In Filipino America, as it turns out, one can find oneself. One would not think it, but puns make it possible to communicate. One first must learn to be patient with the puns: the built-in layers of mediation, misdirection, and multivalence. One must be prepared for the possibility of finding a self utterly different from what one expected. No narcissistic echo here. No mirror. No reflection. Just a crackling cell phone exchange between people divided by difference, struggling to communicate in the bent sounds and forms of a colonial *lengua* like English.

## Introduction

1. In my extended analysis of Pfeiffer's *Leviathan* and other works in chapter 2, "A Queer Horizon: Paul Pfeiffer's Disintegrating Figure Studies," I argue that the blondness of the wigs is part of Pfeiffer's meditation on the iconic blondness of Marilyn Monroe, whom Norman Mailer dubbed the "Great American Body."

2. For analyses of the *Insular Cases,* see Allan Isaac's definitive study "Disappearing Clauses: Reconstituting America in the Unincorporated Territories" in *American Tropics: Articulating Filipino America;* Paul Kramer's "Dual Mandates: Collaboration and the Racial State" in *The Blood of Government: Race, Empire, the United States, and the Philippines;* and Amy Kaplan's *The Anarchy of Empire in the Making of U.S. Culture,* especially the introduction.

3. For example, Angel Shaw has lived and worked both in the United States and the Philippines since she began gathering materials for her 1992 video-documentary *Nailed.* Shaw also organized a major author reading and signing event in Manila's Cultural Center of the Philippines to mark the 2002 publication of the aforementioned *Vestiges of War* anthology. Paul Pfeiffer's recent works, such as the 2006 video loop installation *Live from Neverland,* is composed of materials he has been gathering in the Philippines. (*Live from Neverland* features the juxtaposition of a 1993 video of Michael Jackson denouncing his arrest and treatment by the police with a video of a choir of young, formally dressed Filipino men and women chanting, with eerie perfection, Jackson's monologue. Pfeiffer has shown his work several times in the Philippines—for example, in the 1995 exhibition "14 Artists: Sugod sa Katapusan" in Dumaguete City and in the 2001 "Refresh" exhibition at Silliman University. He also won a 1994–1995 Fulbright-Hays Fellowship in the Philippines. Born and raised in the Philippines, Manuel Ocampo has lived

in the United States and Europe, but he currently is based again in the Philippines. Based in California, Reanne Estrada is one of several Filipina American artists participating in "Galleon Trade," a series of international arts exchange and exhibition projects between the Philippines, United States, and Mexico organized and curated by Jenifer Wofford beginning in the summer of 2007 with an exhibition in Manila featuring thirteen Filipino American and Mexican American artists.

4. For an overview of the continuities and divergences between British and American constitutional law across the (American) colonial period, focusing on the colony of Rhode Island, see Mary Sarah Bilder's *The Transatlantic Constitution: Colonial Legal Culture and the Empire.*

5. For an overview of these cases, see Avelino Halagao Jr., "Citizens Denied: A Critical Examination of the Rabang Decision Rejecting United States Citizenship Claims by Persons Born in the Philippines during the Territorial Period." For a very useful complementary account of the forms of "foreigner discrimination" experienced by Filipino American immigrants, see Angelo Ancheta's "Filipino Americans, Foreigner Discrimination, and the Lines of Racial Sovereignty."

6. In his dissent in the 1994 case *Rabang v. INS,* which I discuss forthwith, Justice Harry Pregerson argues in favor of the Filipino plaintiffs suing for American citizenship based upon their or their parents' birth in the Philippines during the territorial period; and he cites Baldwin's article as an example of "scholars writing around the time of [the United States'] acquisition of the Philippines [who] recognized precisely this outcome" *(Rabang v. INS).*

7. On *Calvin's Case* see Polly J. Price's "Natural Law and Birthright Citizenship in *Calvin's Case (1608)."*

8. For a useful, compact essay on American modernism, see Daniel Singhal's "Towards a Definition of American Modernism." See also Erika Doss's *Twentieth-Century American Art.*

9. Jacqueline Francis's research in the forthcoming monograph *Race-ing Modernism: Malvin Gray Johnson, Yasuo Kuniyoshi, Max Weber, and Racial Art in America* draws renewed attention to the unsettled nature of the definition of modernism by way of the work of artists of color that is part of and apart from the mainstream of modernism.

10. For example, one of Pfeiffer's reviewers discusses even a work like Pfeiffer's *Four Horsemen of the Apocalypse,* which features Black basketball players, in relation to minimal abstraction (Prince "Feint Art"). See chapter 2 for a further discussion of Pfeiffer's *Four Horsemen.*

11. See Dallal's "The Beauty of Imperialism: Emerson, Melville, Flaubert, and Al-Shidyaq."

12. I am indebted to Kimberly Alidio for drawing my attention to James's comments in "Governor Roosevelt's Oration," *Boston Evening Transcript* (April 15, 1899): 9.

13. See also Sharon Delmendo's chapter "Marketing Colonialism: Little Brown Brothers in the Kodak Zone" in her *The Star-Entangled Banner: One Hundred Years of America in the Philippines,* 47–85.

14. The representation of Filipino sexuality in Lois-Ann Yamanaka's novels and poetry has been a source of controversy for more than fifteen years now, ever since the Association for Asian American Studies (AAAS), a national organization of academics, gave Yamanaka an award for her 1993 collection of poetry *Saturday Night at the Pahala Theatre,* and especially after the AAAS awarded and then, after protests, rescinded its 1998 fiction prize to Yamanaka for her 1997 novel *Blu's Hanging.* The entire governing board of AAAS resigned soon after, and the *New York Times, Atlantic Monthly, Newsweek, Chronicle of Higher Education,* and *Time* ran articles on the dispute. See, for example, Somini Sengupta's "An Author Who Gathers Prizes and Protests" and Jamie James's "This Hawaii Is Not for Tourists." For a range of academics' stances on the controversy in Asian American studies, see Darlene Rodrigues's "Imagining Ourselves: Reflections on the Controversy over Lois-Ann Yamanaka's *Blu's Hanging*"; Candace Fujikane's "Sweeping Racism under the Rug of 'Censorship': The Controversy over Lois-Ann Yamanaka's *Blu's Hanging*"; Erin Suzuki's "Consuming Desires: Melancholia and Consumption in *Blu's Hanging*"; Crystal Parikh's "Blue Hawaii: Asian Hawaiian Cultural Production and Racial Melancholia"; and Mark Chiang's "Autonomy and Representation: Aesthetics and the Crisis of Asian American Cultural Politics in the Controversy over *Blu's Hanging.*"

15. Examples of the "wild heterogeneity" of the Philippines include the oft-repeated facts that the archipelago is composed of more than seven thousand islands, is home to at least seventy (documented) languages, and was occupied and colonized by Spain, the United States, and Japan. When I studied Filipino under Professor Adelwisa Weller at the University of Michigan, I learned that the number of letters in the alphabet is not stable, reflecting both the impact of colonial languages like English and Spanish and the efforts to indigenize the national language. As recently as 1987, three letters were removed from the alphabet.

16. Though unvoiced explicitly here, I am indebted to African Americanist literary scholarship on the problems and possibilities of identifying the ethos and historical emergence of a racialized cultural moment, such as the Harlem Renaissance and the Black arts movement. In posing questions about diaspora, remembrance, and expressive culture and in proposing a Filipino American aesthetic, I also am retracing the lines of enquiry opened by Paul Gilroy in *The Black Atlantic: Modernity and Double Consciousness.*

17. Sibylle Fischer. Interview with Gina Ulysse in *Bomb: Art and Culture Interviews.*

## *1. An Open Wound*

1. A note on punctuation: While I mostly use the less distracting, unhyphenated "Filipino American," and occasionally "U.S. Filipino," I employ the solidus ("Filipino/American") at the beginning of this chapter to indicate both the presence of Filipinos in the United States and the imperial presence of the United

States in the Philippines. This term encompasses minority racial status, colonial status, and the post/colonial legacy of invisibility produced by the amnesia that distinguishes American history in relation to empire. Conceiving of the term Filipino/American solely as a designation of racial minority status risks repeating the erasure of a history of colonization, a massive omission that too typically characterizes many historical treatments of American imperialism at the turn of the century. Though I use the term "Filipino American" throughout most of the book, mostly because the solidus becomes too distracting, I would argue that the terms "Filipino-American" and "Filipino American" are misleading and tautological, for being "Filipino" in some sense also means being "American" or, to be more precise, a racialized subject of an American colony. (The asymmetry of the rhetorical relationship between "Filipino" and "American" becomes clear when one realizes that the inverse is ludicrous: Being "American" emphatically does not always also mean being "Filipino.") While this claim has its limitations, I think it is important because it reveals the misleading effects of characterizing the relationship between the American rhetoric of democratic citizenship and the reality of its colonized subjects as one of antithesis rather than of interdependence. More anecdotally, I regularly am confronted by various forms of the inevitable interrogation "Where are you from?" While much Asian Americanist deconstruction of this accusatory question rightly focuses on racial formation and on the perpetually alien status of Asians in America, it does not benefit fully from Filipino/American critical perspectives that might emphasize a legacy of colonization. That is to say, the response "I am an American" can be perceived as a declaration of citizenship that may or may not involve an embracing of assimilationist values. What if the respondent is thinking, "I am an American (subject)," a subordinate subject, not a citizen of the American empire?

2. For a range of theoretical, anecdotal, and historical discussions of imperial forgetting, see Oscar Campomanes, "The New Empire's Forgetful and Forgotten Citizens: Unrepresentability and Unassimilability in Filipino-American Postcoloniaities"; the work of Ambeth R. Ocampo in general but especially *Bones of Contention: The Bonifacio Lectures;* Marlon Fuentes's faux interview with the (fictional) Mia Blumentritt, "*Bontoc Eulogy,* History, and the Craft of Memory: An Extended Conversation with Marlon E. Fuentes"; and Kimberly Ann Alidio, "'When I Get Home, I Want to Forget': Memory and Amnesia in the Occupied Philippines, 1901–1904."

3. Sigmund Freud, "Mourning and Melancholia," *General Psychological Theory: Theories on Paranoia, Masochism, Repression, Melancholia, the Unconscious, the Libido, and Other Aspects of the Human Psyche.* All quotations from Freud in this chapter are from "Mourning and Melancholia" and are cited in the text using page numbers from this edition.

4. Of course, one need not necessarily turn to psychoanalysis to understand the intrinsic connection between mental and physical wounds. In everyday usage,

the term "trauma" denotes both emotional and bodily damage as a host of U.S. television hospital dramas demonstrate weekly. The etymology of "trauma" is informative: originally a Greek noun, "trauma" means "wound." "Trauma" also is linked to the Greek verbs *titroskein* (to wound) and *tetrainein* (to pierce). So why psychoanalysis? I consider both the Filipino/American texts and the Freudian text as wonderfully unstable and richly layered. In juxtaposing them, however, I regard the Filipino/American texts as politically inspiring, whereas Freud's writings are here configured as anxiously authoritarian texts. To me, the use of Freud's writings (and Western psychoanalysis in general) forces an engagement with compulsory heterosexuality, whiteness, and imperial forgetting that reveals both their workings and their failures. Nothing works harder to reinforce and to undercut its own remarkably persistent grand claims than does Freudian psycho-analysis. Freud's canon is filled with hundreds of contradictions and awkward hiccups that interrupt the smooth delivery of a singular, authoritative voice and that threaten any sustained rationale for what Kaja Silverman has called the "dominant fiction." Though the term is risky, I attempt to cast Freudian texts as "fictive" because they seem to operate in the same ways that most compelling narratives and art do. They attempt to tell us, both prescriptively and descrip-tively, who we are.

5. I should note that Ocampo and his former partner, Sherry Apostol, lived in New York City in the mid-1990s and that they are friends with Shaw. The itinerant couple then moved back and forth between the San Francisco Bay Area; Seville, Spain; and Manila, Philippines. In the 1990s, Ocampo was represented by Annina Nosei Gallery in Manhattan and, in informal conversation, Apostol has described some of the challenges and difficulties they encountered while nego-tiating the elite, overwhelmingly white world of dealers, collectors, and critics in New York City. At one of his exhibition openings, Ocampo donned the uniform of a security guard and convincingly patrolled the margins of the mingling crowd for quite a while. Some of these problems are captured by the 1999 documentary *God Is My Co-pilot* by Phillip Rodriguez, an hour-length exploration of Ocampo's work and life.

6. See Anne Cheng's *The Melancholy of Race,* Judith Butler's *The Psychic Life of Power: Theories in Subjection,* Douglas Crimp's essay "Mourning and Militancy," Jeff Nunokawa's essay "'All the Sad Young Men': AIDS and the Work of Mourning," José Muñoz's chapter "Photographies of Mourning: Melancholia and Ambivalence in Van DerZee, Mapplethorpe, and *Looking for Langston*" in his book *Disidentifica-tions: Queers of Color and the Performance of Politics,* and, more generally, David Eng and David Kazanjian's edited volume *Loss: The Politics of Mourning.*

7. See Vicente Rafael's chapter "'Your Grief Is Our Gossip': Overseas Fili-pinos and Other Spectral Presences" in his book *White Love and Other Events in Filipino History,* and Paul Gilroy's *Postcolonial Melancholia.*

8. See chapter 1 "The Dominant Fiction" in Kaja Silverman's *Male Subjectivity at the Margins.*

9. For a discussion of Freud's "primitive," see the introduction to David Eng's *Racial Castration: Managing Masculinity in Asian America.*

10. Here, I borrow from Elaine Scarry's work on torture and the inexpressibility of pain in *The Body in Pain: The Unmaking and Making of the World.*

11. This statement is monumentally reductive, but my intention here is to characterize the radical denigration of Philippine vernacular languages as an experience of violence and loss that is constitutive of post/colonial subjectivity. As Vicente Rafael has argued in *Contracting Colonialism: Translation and Christian Conversion in Tagalog Society under Early Spanish Rule,* however, the heterogeneity of Philippine vernacular languages made it impossible for the Spanish to adopt and codify a single language in its colonizing and Christianizing mission. Too, the geographical diversity of the archipelago and the relatively small Spanish population prevented the marginalization of Philippine languages. Rather, competence in Spanish (and later, with the advent of U.S. colonization, English) marked the formation of language-based class hierarchies, which continue to stratify metropolitan and rural life in the Philippines.

12. I am not arguing that Ocampo's painting repeats the violence of colonization. Rather, the painting is a reenactment of colonial violence, one that contains powerful anticolonial sentiment.

13. In an edited collection of essays titled *Disenfranchised Grief: Recognizing Hidden Sorrow,* the gerontologist Kenneth J. Doka focuses on radically unacknowledged kinds of bereavement and grievers, people who "experienc[e] a sense of loss but d[o] not have a socially recognized right, role, or capacity to grieve" (3). Doka's interest in both the "intersocial" and the "intrapsychic" aspects of disenfranchised grief is illuminating: "Disenfranchisement can occur when a society inhibits grief by establishing 'grieving norms' that deny such emotions to persons deemed to have insignificant losses, insignificant relationships, or an insignificant capacity to grieve. But . . . there is an intrapsychic dimension as well. The bereaved may experience a deep sense of shame about the relationship or they may experience emotions, perhaps reflecting societal norms, that inhibit the grieving process" (xv). As in traditional psychoanalysis, in grieving there are certain "norms" that determine not merely the line between normal and pathological but between normal and "insignificant." This social insignificance easily translates into a perceived innate inferiority or "incapacity," further pathologizing and harming sexual and racial minority communities precisely during crisis periods that require tremendous support and resources. While the authors in the above-mentioned collection primarily focus on the individual, the family, or other small social units, I argue that colonial melancholia is a communal, political form of disenfranchised grief.

14. See Anne Cheng's *The Melancholy of Race.*

15. See Timothy Mitchell's *Passional Culture: Emotion, Religion, and Society in Southern Spain* for a study of penitentiary rites, pain, and emotion in the southern Spanish context. See Peter Fraser's *Images of the Passion: The Sacramental Mode in Film* for an eclectic series of analyses of major and minor films that evince what Fraser calls the "sacramental" or "incarnational" mode.

16. See Hayden White's *The Content of the Form: Narrative Discourse and Historical Representation.* For works on the politics of style, see Kobena Mercer's *Welcome to the Jungle: New Positions in Black Cultural Studies* (especially chapter 4, "Black Hair/Style Politics"), Pearl Cleage's "Hairpiece," Angela Y. Davis's "Afro-Images: Politics, Fashion, and Nostalgia," and Deborah Grayson's "Is It Fake? Black Women's Hair as Spectacle and Spec(tac)ular."

17. In the introduction to their edited anthology *The Politics of Culture in the Shadow of Capital,* Lisa Lowe and David Lloyd gesture toward the theorization of new forms of political subjectivity other than those proposed by conventional conceptions of modernity, i.e., the "citizen of the nation or the proletarian class subject" (18). By connecting "passional potentiality" and "infinitival subjectivity" with a coherent cultural moment like the Filipino American cultural moment, I am interested in elaborating upon what Lowe and Lloyd have called "the possibility of forms of agency that inhere in the longer duration of social forms that have emerged in resistance and in relation to modern institutions" (15).

18. I am aware of my suspiciously structuralist tendency here to reduce agency and subjectivity to a grammatical sentence. But I am interested in not too quickly abandoning the idea of deep structures in cultural analysis—hence, my forays in this book into Freudian psychoanalysis, *sikolohiyang Pilipino,* narratology, and critical race theory. If art and expressive culture afford us a sideway or peripheral glimpse of these "deep structures," I think it the task of the critic to learn anew and repeatedly how to look.

19. With this idea of "infinitival subjectivity," I want to lend a specificity to the debates about the valence of W. E. B. Du Bois's influential concept of "double consciousness" in Filipino American history. I also am gesturing toward important distinctions between East Asian American, South Asian American, and Southeast Asian American experiences of double consciousness. For example, Traise Yamamoto's argument about "masking" in Japanese American women's literature powerfully draws upon and departs from DuBois. Yamamoto describes the "exceptionally closed" face of her grandmother in a 1938 family photograph. She muses the im/possibilities of reading a face that "understands its own readability." This face recognizes that it has no control over how it will be read, and it habitually constructs a protective mask. It is a historical product of the sheer need to survive the twinned forces of racism and sexism. Ironically, however, this impassivity is all too easily appropriated by Orientalism and converted into stereotype. Thus, Yamamoto revists a crucial question with which scholars of African American and Asian American literature still grapple: How

are we responsibly to read such wary texts? The book's title—*Masking Selves, Making Subjects: Japanese American Women, Identity, and the Body*—puns on "masking" as an act or process emanating from dominant fiction as well as from the self; the title "suggests a process enacted by an agency separate from the socially defined self as well as a self whose agency is enacted in the process of masking." Thus, Yamamoto selects a trope—the mask—that relies on a basic division between surface and depth, a binary that becomes problematic since it invokes essentialist notions of "humanist interiority." Yamamoto wants to retain both a sense of constructedness *and* a kind of interiority—a "place for the self." Such an approach to double consciousness is quite distinct from the kind of performative and kinetic theory that a number of Filipino American critics, such as Elisabeth Pisares, Theo Gonzalves, Karen Tongson, Christine Balance, and Lucy Burns, are proposing for the study of Filipino American cultural forms.

20. Ocampo was born in 1965 in the Philippines and moved to the United States in 1985. After living in several cities in the United States and then in Europe, Ocampo moved back to the Philippines in the early 2000s. In the late 1980s and especially in the 1990s, Ocampo developed what one *Art in America* reviewer calls a "vocabulary of images specific to his accounting of the colonialist legacy of the Philippines, producing complex, tortured paintings expressive of his native archipelago's troubled history" (Leffingwell 138). He achieved a certain degree of fame in the 1990s, when he became known or labeled as a "multicultural artist dealing with academic postcolonial discourse through his unapologetic confrontation with his bi-cultural identity" (Bright 95). However, commentary has tailed off since, and this signals the extent to which his work is engaged with and understood within the multicultural moment of the late 1980s and early 1990s. Much critical attention at the time was paid to the religious content of his work. An *Artforum International* reviewer described his 1994 series of paintings "Stations of the Cross" as a "blasphemous send-up of Catholic excess, particularly the pious self-mortification practiced yearly by penitent Filipinos who reenact each of the Fourteen Stations of the Cross—including the crucifixion, nails and all" (Borum 102). In a 1994 *Flash Art* interview, Ocampo said of his paintings that they "are not meant to be didactic. I think in that sense they become performance art, like a Passion Play" (Scarborough 84). In the 1990s, Ocampo's work also stirred up much controversy because of his use of swastika imagery; at the 1992 Documenta, Ocampo's work was "condemned to a basement storeroom because of curatorial fears that his swastika imagery might offend the German public" (Duncan 139).

21. Ocampo famously began painting while working as a youth in the Philippines for a church. In an interview, he says, "A priest was looking for artists to copy paintings, icons, and stuff in the church. It was supposedly conservation" (Ocampo, "Manuel Ocampo: Sheer Art Attack" 66). He then began producing and selling convincing, deliberately distressed or aged imitations of Spanish colonial

folk painting to Western tourists. In response to a 1994 *Flash Art* interviewer's question about whether he felt like he was "selling out," Ocampo said: "Hey, that's exchange, like what I used to do in the Philippines. I seriously wanted to become a painter. I used to copy all these antiquated colonial paintings to sell to European dealers who knew they were fake, and they would sell them to the public as authentic antiques from the Philippines. I'd even put them in the oven, with egg tempera, to make them look old" (Scarborough 85).

22. However, there are two "whole" figures in *Heridas:* the floating, framed Madonna and child. The Madonna looks down at her child in a classic portrait of feminine nurturing. But her gaze could also extend further, focusing attention downward to the wrapped, severed head carefully placed upright on the ground. (I thank Benigno Trigo for his comment that this thematic of maternal nurturing appears in most of the images I have selected for this chapter.) The image of Madonna and child seems to function as a counterpart or counterpoint to the fragmented, violent images of the *pasyon.*

23. My attempt at narrating these visual signs is very much influenced by Mieke Bal's interweaving of visual and narratological studies in *Double Exposures.* See, for example, Bal's analysis of vision and focalization in chapter 8, "His Master's Eye," 255–88.

24. I began noticing the visual "logic" of blood after reading Mieke Bal's analysis of Michelangelo da Caravaggio's painting *Judith Beheading Holofernes;* see chapter 9 "Head Hunting" in *Double Exposures,* especially 292–93.

25. I elaborate upon this debate in the next chapter on Paul Pfeiffer's re-invocation of sacred sexuality.

26. For example, Christ's penis may have been viewed primarily as the object of circumcision and not necessarily as a sexual organ. Thus, controversy in the Middle Ages over "bodily stirrings" was not over their location, i.e., specific bodily organs, but over whether their source was "inspired or demonic" (Bynum). Contending that people of the Middle Ages approached gender more fluidly, which had a "symbolic richness" rather than depended on "modern dichotomies," Bynum finally argues that we "turn from seeing body as sexual to seeing body as generative" (117).

27. Bynum's argument in fact goes further: "There may be warrant in the Christian tradition for equating the penis with maleness and maleness with humanity, but I would argue that medieval theology at least as explicitly equates the breast with femaleness and femaleness both with the humanity of Christ and with the humanity of us all" (117).

28. I am indebted to Liza Johnson's video *Fernweh: The Opposite of Homesick* for the initial idea of exploring the "opposite of homesick."

29. Born in 1966 in the United States, Angel Shaw has a bachelor of fine arts degree from the California Institute of the Arts. Since the late 1980s she has been

regularly traveling between the United States and the Philippines, living and working for extended periods in both countries. She has made several experimental videodocumentaries, including *Nailed* (1992); *Asian Boys* (1994), which is a collaboration with performance artist Nicky Paraiso; and *Umbilical Cord* (1998); she has also screened her more recent productions *The Momentary Enemy, Blowback,* and *Balikbayan/Return to Home.* She has taught at Hunter College, Columbia University, the New School for Social Research, New York University, and Pratt Institute. In 2000–2001, she worked as acting executive director of the nonprofit media arts organization Asian CineVision, which is based in New York City and since 1977 has annually held an Asian American International Film Festival. She is a coeditor of the 2002 anthology *Vestiges of War: The Philippine-American War and the Aftermath of an Imperial Dream, 1899–1999.*

30. It is no accident, I think, that the "angels" of the dream coincide with the videomaker's first name "Angel."

31. Mary Louise Pratt uses the term "autoethnography" in her influential *Imperial Eyes: Travel Writing and Transculturation* as does Françoise Lionnet in *Autobiographical Voices: Race, Gender, and Self-Portraiture.* More recent examinations of autoethnography can be found in the work of Catherine Russell; see chapter 10, "Autoethnography: Journeys of the Self," in Russell's *Experimental Ethnography: The Work of Film in the Age of Video.* Also see chapter 3, "The Autoethnographic Performance: Reading Richard Fung's Queer Hybridity," in José Muñoz's *Disidentifications: Queers of Color and the Performance of Politics.*

32. When I have shown this video in the undergraduate classroom, it is at this point that my American students seem to become much more aware of their nationality and identity as Americans. That is to say, they become more aware of the United States as an imperial and neo/colonial entity. Thus, while up to this point in class discussion my students tend to distance themselves from *Nailed* by characterizing the documented images and events as "pagan," "barbaric," and "blasphemous," the sight and sound of the singing schoolchildren for some reason close this distance, and my students generally find their familiarity discomfiting and disturbing.

33. Quoted in Gail Okawa's essay "Resistance and Reclamation: Hawaii 'Pidgin English' and Autoethnography in the Short Stories of Darrell H.Y. Lum" (192). I refer to Okawa's use of Pratt here because Okawa's discussion of the recuperative use of Hawai'i pidgin English is an example of another growing body of literature and criticism on U.S. colonization.

34. Here I respectfully disagree with Rolando B. Tolentino's reading of *Nailed* in his survey of the different "waves" of Asian American and Filipino/American media production; see Tolentino's "Identity and Difference in 'Filipino/a American' Media Arts."

35. The Filipino term for diasporics, *balikbayan,* literally means "return home."

36. In the essay "Trying Whiteness: Media Representations of the 1996 Okinawa Rape Trial," I elaborate on the historical and ideological connections between the Civil War and Reconstruction eras and the late-nineteenth-century rise of the transoceanic American empire, including the function of the romance of the Lost Cause of the Confederacy.

## 2. A Queer Horizon

1. Pfeiffer's compelling, even saturated analyses of his own work explicitly influence my own readings. Of *Morning* he says: "I have also been playing with panoramic horizons in the video I've been working on called *Morning after the Deluge*. In a sense, *Morning after the Deluge* is a study of the human figure: its place in the history of Western art, and its disintegration at the dawn of the digital age. In classical one-point perspective, all sight lines come together at the horizon, at the theoretical vanishing point where all things recede to infinity. The horizon is the primary visual reference for centering oneself within a landscape. In *Morning after the Deluge* this relationship is flipped: the horizon line is uprooted and allowed to wander across the picture plane, while the sun becomes the still point, the visual anchor in an upside-down world. In this spatial scheme, there is the reality of the sun rising and setting behind the earth's horizon, and the opposing reality of the earth's horizon moving across the surface of the sun" (*Paul Pfeiffer* 38–39).

2. A journalist for the Philippine-based *Inquirer* calls Pfeiffer the "toast of international contemporary art" (Casocot).

3. There generally is a stunning silence about race in the reviews of Pfeiffer's work on Black male celebrity.

4. The use of the term "flexible" here is a quick allusion to the work of Aihwa Ong on labor and the flexibility of global capitalism. While Pfeiffer explicitly has voiced his interest in critiquing the simultaneously lucrative and racially humiliating cultural labor that the image of Black celebrity performs, especially in high-profile sports like basketball that have attained the status of commercially profitable entertainment, I suspect that his critics' stunning silence about the imbrication of race and capital indicates the flexibility of American formalism. There is either something about the image itself that outdoes critical theory or something about American aesthetics, as this chapter finally argues, that allows the emergence of Pfeiffer's work only to manage it.

5. For example, in her comprehensive review of the 1998–1999 exhibition "At Home and Abroad: Twenty Contemporary Filipino Artists," Eleanor Heartney argues that the "unique history of the Philippines has inspired these artists to forge a contemporary art tradition that is all their own" (67). However, Heartney has remarkably little to say about Pfeiffer's work in the context of that history and the forging of that tradition. See Heartney's "Archipelago and Diaspora." In her review

of the same exhibition, Collette Chattopadhyay groups Pfeiffer's work with that of several other Filipino or Filipino American artists exploring the "relationship between the politics of power and concepts of nationhood and identity." She writes of Pfeiffer's *Vitruvian Figure (After Pavia Cathedral):* "Transforming the symbolic spirituality of the church into an emblem of physical and sexual abuse, Pfeiffer's work discloses the often sublimated narrative of Filipino adaptation of Catholicism through political subjugation and tyranny" (21). See Chattopadhyay's "At Home and Abroad: Contemporary Filipino Views." Note that I use scare quotes around "diasporic" to indicate that nationalist Filipino reviewers, for sometimes good and sometimes bad reasons, tend to associate the diaspora with the periphery. Such strategies reinforce the boundaries of the Philippines and risk a kind of policing surveillance of the homeland, which, of course, is to be distinguished from the necessary, if complex, importance of the concept of homeland in decolonizing projects, especially given the radical vulnerability of the Philippine economy to multiple forms of external and internal colonialisms.

6. For example, Pfeiffer exhibited work in the 1991 group show "Dismantling Invisibility: Asian Americans Respond to the AIDS Crisis"; the 1992 exhibition "Made in America: Remembering Vincent Chin" at Art in General in New York City; and the 1993 group show "Kayumanggi Presence" at the Academy of Art in Honolulu.

7. Pfeiffer himself notes, however, that critics' emphasis on his "multicultural" background erases the colonial histories that shaped him. In an interview in the German journal *Kunst und Kirche,* Pfeiffer says: "Für mich ist meine Biographie aber weniger eine Spur multikultereller Ideale, sondern vor allem ein Rest von Kolonialgeschichte." [But for me, my biography is less a sign of multicultural ideals and rather, above all, a remainder of colonial history] (73).

8. Notable exceptions to this pattern include the critic–scholars Jennifer Gonzalez and Joan Kee. In an interview with Pfeiffer in *Bomb,* Gonzalez suggests that his work is "about remembrance and forgetting, raising the question of the after-image of history and how that inevitably shapes the vision and consciousness of the present—in particular the discourse of the visual that itself structures conceptions of race" (22). Kee calls attention to Pfeiffer's "past participation in Godzilla, the New York–based Asian American arts group known for its advocacy for and by Asian American artists" (66). But even Kee insists that "much of Pfeiffer's current work has little if any visible ethnic content" (66). Even when she addresses the "tendency to erase Pfeiffer's ethnic origin in discussions of his work," she continues to understand his use of erasure "as a means of commenting on the fundamentals of human nature" (67).

9. Pfeiffer's sudden fame is, indeed, monied. The amount he received in the Whitney Museum's inaugural Bucksbaum Award of 2000 (US$100,000) is cited regularly. According to Sotheby's Web site, *Morning after the Deluge* fetched GBP48,000

in a February 2004 auction in London. At the same time, however, the negative criticism of Pfeiffer's high-budget, high-profile entry at the Cairo Biennial must be understood as a much larger indictment of the United States' occupation of Iraq and support of Israel. See Turner, "Dust in the Desert."

10. For example, the following reviews reduce the question of race to the question of celebrity: Arthur Danto's "Art of the Free and Brave" and Katy Siegel's "Paul Pfeiffer." Writing on Pfeiffer in the *Nation*, Danto compares Pfeiffer's *Fragment* to the imperial spectacle of entertainment in the Roman Coliseum instead of situating the work in the context of U.S. chattel slavery as well as the violence and terror of the Jim Crow era. Pedro Velez's "Looking Good" reduces Pfeiffer's *The Long Count (I Shook Up the World)*, which uses footage from Cassius Clay's famous 1964 bout with Sonny Liston, to a "haunting examination of idolatry in sports." In a review of a 2001 exhibition at the UCLA Hammer Museum, Jody Zellen first notes that Pfeiffer's works "use film and television as a point of departure, often focusing on a moment or gesture," and then adds, "Less interested in the who than in the what Pfeiffer's complex works are about the manipulation of spectacle and the presentation of the banal." Though topically emphasizing the "creation of the spectacle," Zellen conspicuously omits any reference to race in the discussion of works that directly invoke the spectacle of Black celebrity. For example, the discussion of videos, including *The Long Count (Rumble in the Jungle)*, which features Pfeiffer's digital near-erasure of all trace of Muhammad Ali from video footage of his famous fight with Joe Frazier, Zellen comments on Pfeiffer's "recombining the elements to make evocative 'reconstructions' of sports events without players, audience or even ball at times." See Zellen's "Paul Pfeiffer: UCLA Hammer Museum." In another version of this tendency to erase race, Karen Rosenberg asserts that Pfeiffer "transforms NBA players into Northern Renaissance men." See Rosenberg's "Paul Pfeiffer." In his interview with Jennifer Gonzalez, however, Pfeiffer insists on the relation between race and spectacle. Invoking the writings of Frantz Fanon on the hypervisibility of the Black man, Pfeiffer remarks that "a special relationship exists between black bodies and spectacle. It's almost as though the spectacle could not exist without them."

11. For example, the following reviews focus on Pfeiffer's use of new, especially video-loop techniques: Anne Barlow's "Circle as Cycle," David Goldberg's "Refresh: The Art of the Screen Saver," Michael Rush's "New Media Rampant," and Barbara Pollack's "Back to the Future with 'BitStreams.'"

12. I of course am referring here to Norman Mailer's caustic description of Monroe's and Arthur Miller's marriage as that between the "Great American Body" and the "Great American Brain."

13. My invocation of Derrida is deliberate: Pfeiffer's narration of Western art history is "supplementary" in that it parasitically follows but also modifies the main trajectory of that governing history.

14. It is not entirely accurate to refer to the digital modification of Barris's photos as "erasure," for Pfeiffer reconstitutes the beach background by covering over—rather than rubbing out—Monroe's image. And so Pfeiffer can claim that "digital video and Photoshop are not unlike older media like oil paint and marble" (interview with Basilico 40). I take up the politics of medium further on in the chapter.

15. I rely throughout this chapter on Crary's flexibly historicizing and spatially responsive definition of vision: "Whether perception or vision actually change is irrelevant, for they have no autonomous history. What changes are the plural forces and rules composing the field in which perception occurs. And what determines vision at any given historical moment is not some deep structure, economic base, or world view, but rather the functioning of a collective assemblage of disparate parts on a single social surface. It may even be necessary to consider the observer as a distribution of events located in many different places. There never was or will be a self-present beholder to whom a world is transparently evident. Instead there are more or less powerful arrangements of forces out of which the capacities of an observer are possible" (*Techniques* 6).

16. Crary is, of course, writing on modernism and the nineteenth century, and I am aware of the achronicity of this chapter. But my larger point is that the scattered archipelagic and achronic sensibilities of the Filipino American renaissance are productively baffling. Both time and space go mad, as Pfeiffer's work so clearly demonstrates. For an account of modernism and postmodernism that corresponds and resonates with the Filipino American cultural renaissance, see Santiago Colás's "The Third World in Jameson's *Postmodernism, or the Cultural Logic of Late Capitalism.*"

17. The Latin phrase *"Quod nomen mihi est?"* (What is my name?) of Pfeiffer's essay title hails from the 1973 horror movie *The Exorcist*. To Pfeiffer, the crucial scene is of the priest posing the identity question to the demon-possessed child (*"Quod Nomen"* 285–86).

18. In *The Life and Art of Albrecht Dürer,* Erwin Panofsky argues that the Italian-influenced northern painter, engraver, and woodcut designer "managed to describe complicated geometrical constructions more briefly, more clearly and more exhaustively than any professional mathematician of his time" (245). For a more compressed and chronological and pictorial overview of Dürer's innovations and creative development, see the collected essays in the Dürer section of the catalog *Gothic and Renaissance Art in Nuremberg 1300–1550* (264–337).

19. John Berger reminds us of Dürer's monstrous partitioning and reassembly of the human model: "Dürer believed that the ideal nude ought to be constructed by taking the face of one body, the breasts of another, the legs of a third, the shoulders of a fourth, the hands of a fifth—and so on"; for an overview of Dürer's theory of human proportions, see Panofsky 260–70. Analyzing dioramas in New York's American Museum of Natural History, Haraway's essay on the technologies

of domination also works well alongside Pfeiffer's ode to Central Park in *Figure Study (Theodore Roosevelt Memorial)* (1999) and *Perspective Study (After Jeremy Bentham)* (1998), which consist of dioramas encased in museum-quality display cases. I thank Jan Bernabe for suggesting this connection to Haraway.

20. Since I discuss a wide range of rhetorical, ideological, and artistic strategies of disappearance in this chapter, I use the German for "vanishing point" to stave off possible confusion. My turn to German also reflects the fact that a significant number of reviews, interviews, and essays on Pfeiffer have appeared in German newspapers and journals. See Curiger, "Aus der Schiene gekippt," and Pfeiffer, "A Void That Looks Back . . . ."

21. I rely here on Neil Hertz's summary of Laplanche's castration complex (31); Mieke Bal uses Medusa as a point of departure for a discussion of uninterrogated subject- and object-positionings in both museum exhibitions and "new museology" scholarship (*Double Exposures: The Subject of Cultural Analysis* 57–86).

22. For more on the relation between the sublime and the unspeakable, see Trinh Minh-ha's discussion of the "void" in an interview with Nancy Chen. I thank Vivian Chin for this citation.

23. I thank Susan Najita for pointing the way, via Hertz's essay, toward a politics of the sublime.

24. In his psychoanalytic study *Compulsive Beauty* of the surrealists, Foster proposes a definition of the sublime vis-à-vis the "uncanniness" of "convulsive beauty," the basic principle of Bretonian surrealism that "superceded automatism" (19): "In/animate and im/mobile, the veiled-erotic and the fixed-explosive are figures of the uncanny. Bréton recodes the 'morbid anxiety' provoked by this uncanniness into an aesthetic of beauty. And yet finally this aesthetic has to do less with the beautiful than with the sublime. For convulsive beauty not only stresses the formless and evokes the unrepresentable, as with the sublime, but it also mixes delight and dread, attraction and repulsion: it too involves a 'momentary check to the vital forces,' 'a negative pleasure.' In surrealism as in Kant, this negative pleasure is figured through feminine attributes: it is an intuition of the death drive received by the patriarchal subject as both the promise of its ecstasy and the threat of its extinction. However transformed the map, the terrain of this surrealist sublime is not much changed from that of traditional beauty: it remains the female body" (19).

25. In some ways, Pérez's insight is anticipated by Frantz Fanon's account of the white child's traumatic encounter with the Black man in *Black Skin, White Masks*.

26. Known for her use of "modernist gestural grids" in paintings often compared with Mondrian, the contemporary New York City–based artist Denyse Thomas says that the grid represents her engagement with the history of slavery, particularly various architectural forms of incarceration and transportation, acts of physical torture, and the signifying language and coding patterns that emerged with traditions of quilting (Besemer 16). Responding to her categorization in the

art world as the "black woman of formalism," Thomas describes her use of the grid as a personal, political, and particularist engagement with history, an approach and motivation completely at odds with her reception as an artist of color working with the universality of formalism: "I link my personal history with my historical past. Slavery marks the start of my history. . . . Each stroke, a lash; each mark [is a sign of] resilience in the fields" (quoted in Besemer 16).

27. In his chapter "The Period Eye," Baxandall describes the close relationship between the idea of perspective and the practice of architectural and topographical surveying: "Many Quattrocento people were quite used to the idea of applying plane geometry to the larger world of appearances, because they were taught it for surveying buildings and tracts of land. There is a typical exercise in Filippo Calandri's treatise of 1491. . . . There are two towers on level ground. One is 80 feet high, the other 90 feet high, and the distance from one tower to the next is 100 feet. Between the towers is a spring of water in such a position that, if two birds set off one from each tower and fly in a straight line at the same speed, they will arrive at the spring together. One is to work out how far the spring is from the base of each tower. The key to the problem is simply that the two hypotenuses or bird-flights are equal, so that the difference of the squares of the two tower heights—1700—is the difference of the squares of the two distances of tower from spring. The idea of perspective, of imposing a network of calculable angles and notional straight lines on a prospect, is not outside the grasp of a man able to handle such an exercise in surveying" (107–108).

28. For a quick overview of the politics of camp, see Nikki Sullivan's *A Critical Introduction to Queer Theory* (193–96). Though there are intense divisions and debates about camp, especially around its appropriation and dilution as well as between lesbians and gay men, for my purposes I generally define camp as a politically valent, antinormative signifying praxis with a distinctly performative sensibility whose historical emergence is indebted to drag queen subcultures, including the crucial participation and contribution of queers of color. For the specific purposes of this chapter, I am influenced by Steven Drukman's definition of camp as "a 'means' or a 'method' for the gay gaze" (quoted in Sullivan 196).

29. I reinvoke Taylor's and Clift's sexual iconography to gesture once again toward their racial and colonial symbology in the Manila of *Dogeaters* and, more generally, in the colonial Filipino imaginary.

30. In an unpublished paper at the 1999 *Vestiges of War* conference at New York University, Pfeiffer conducted a reading of the television-movie version of Cinderella produced by Whitney Houston, who played the role of fairy godmother (not, apparently, on crack). The role of Cinderella went to Brandy and the highly forgettable and marginal—though not, clearly and happily, to viewers like Pfeiffer—Prince Charming was played by the Filipino American actor Joel Torres.

31. See Castro's Ph.D. dissertation "Music, Politics, and the Nation at the Cultural Center of the Philippines."

32. Pfeiffer here echoes Goethe's early-nineteenth-century description of the dissolution between external stimuli and internal perception in *Farbenlehre:* "Let the observer look steadfastly on a small coloured object and let it be taken away after a time while his eyes remain unmoved; the spectrum of another colour will then be visible on the white plane . . . it arises from an image which now *belongs to the eye*" (quoted in Crary, *Techniques* 68–69). Pfeiffer makes the connection to Goethe in *Morning after the Deluge,* whose title is a reference to J. M. W. Turner's 1843 painting *Light and Color (Goethe's Theory—The Morning after the Deluge—Moses Writing the Book of Genesis).* In fact, I suspect that Pfeiffer's layers of quotations actually originate with Jonathan Crary's *Techniques of the Observer,* which conducts a reading of Turner's painting in a chapter on Goethe's wresting of vision from the technology of the camera obscura, thus heralding the modernist emergence of the observer. According to Crary, Goethe "insistently cites experiences in which the subjective contents of vision are dissociated from an objective world, in which the body itself produces phenomena that have no external correlate" (*Techniques* 71).

33. Micol Hebron usefully points out that, though the question and concept of medium often are bandied about in reductive or naturalized ways, a recognition of the discursive instability of "medium" is crucial: "Does *medium* mean *material*—or the effect of the material? Is the medium *really* the message?" (24). Hebron lists the changing definitions of "medium" from the sixteenth to the nineteenth centuries: In 1854, "medium" meant "middle ground"; in 1605, "intermediate agency; channel of communication"; in 1853, "a person who conveys spiritual messages"; and in 1854, "a substance through which something is conveyed" (25). In Pfeiffer's case, where the image is everything, there emerges a rather eerie connection between the impossibility of human agency and communication, the increasing materiality of the medium, and the allure of the image (both still and moving).

34. I discuss the politics of abstraction in the chapter's conclusion, but I want to insert here Linda Besemer's deceptively simple formulation of the following question: "Is it . . . 'genuinely queer' to speak about politics and abstraction?" (15).

35. I tentatively gesture here toward Walter Benjamin's idea of "aura" and the art object, especially via Hal Foster's reading of Benjamin's "A Short History of Photography" and "On Some Motifs in Baudelaire," because Pfeiffer's work often seems to take as a point of departure Benjamin's description of the nostalgia for human restoration either in nature or in a "primary relationship to the body, to the *maternal* body" that defines the auratic experience (Foster 196).

36. Commenting on the material that he amasses, Pfeiffer says: "I borrow so much of what I use. I think of myself much less as an author and more like a poacher, a mediator, or translator" *(Art 21).*

37. In fact, Pfeiffer's derivative relationship to Turner itself seems a riff on the work of Jonathan Crary, who offers the following interpretation of Turner's famed 1843 painting of the sun: "In Turner all of the mediations that previously had distanced and protected an observer from the dangerous brilliance of the sun are cast off. . . . Turner's direct confrontation with the sun . . . dissolves the very possibility of representation that the camera obscura was meant to ensure. . . . [In *Light and Color (Goethe's Theory)—The Morning after the Deluge*] the collapse of the older model of representation is complete: the view of the sun that had dominated so many of Turner's previous images now becomes a fusion of eye and sun. On one hand it stands as an impossible image of a luminescence that can only be blinding and that has never been seen, but it also resembles an afterimage of that engulfing illumination. If the circular structure of this painting and others of the same period mimic the shape of the sun, they also correspond with the pupil of the eye and the retinal field on which the temporal experience of an afterimage unfolds. Through the afterimage the sun is made to belong to the body, and the body in fact takes over as the source of its effects. It is perhaps in this sense that Turner's suns may be said to be self-portraits" (*Techniques* 139–41). This last claim about self-portraiture must inform, I think, Pfeiffer's description of *Morning* as a figure study.

38. I cannot help interjecting, perhaps too frivolously, the Leonard Cohen lyric that, by expressing abiding faith in imperfection, seems a perfect rejoinder to Pouchelle's "fortress of the body": "There is a crack, a crack in everything; that's how the light gets in" (quoted in Nehring 9).

39. Deleuze and Guattari's notion of a "body without organs (BwO)," as well as their critique of psychoanalysis in its failure to understand the emergence of such a phenomenon, may be relevant for a fuller reading of Pfeiffer's *Leviathan* and *Vitruvian Figure:* "The organs distribute themselves on the BwO, but they distribute themselves independently of the form of the organism: forms become contingent, organs are no longer anything more than intensities that are produced, flows, thresholds, and gradients. . . . It is not at all a question of a fragmented, splintered body, of organs with the body (OwB). The BwO is exactly the opposite. There are not organs in the sense of fragments in relation to a lost unity, nor is there a return to the undifferentiated in relation to a differentiable totality. There is a distribution of intensive principles of organs, with their positive indefinite articles within a collectivity or multiplicity, inside an assemblage and according to machinic connections operating on a BwO. *Logos spermaticus.* The error of psychoanalysis was to understand BwO phenomena as regressions, projections, fantasies in terms of an *image* of the body" (quoted in Reust 143).

40. In an essay on the politics of abstraction, Linda Besemer recounts the history of formalism and abstract expressionism among gay artists for whom the "choice of abstraction as a vehicle for describing the social and political construction of the homoerotic functions both as a marker of personal and gay cultural memory." Far

from universalist, Pfeiffer's work participates in a tradition of strategic abstraction that "outs" the "discursive cloak of 'universal' formalism" (18).

41. C-print, or cibachrome print, is an archival-quality print and process that ensures that the image will not fade and will last for a very long time.

42. Crucially, however, the representational exposure of Christ's sexuality underscores his imperviousness to the temptations of sex. According to the theology, Christ's power inheres in his virtuous attitude toward sex, the perfect virginity he maintained throughout his short life: "Chastity consists not in impotent absence, but in potency under check" (Steinberg 18). Expounding upon the significance of Christ's unsullied sexuality, Steinberg argues that "the divine Father's only-begotten is (as theology has it) a virgin, virginally conceived; enfleshed, sexed, circumcised, sacrificed, and so restored to the Throne of Grace; there symbolizing not only the aboriginal unity of the godhead, but in its more dramatic, more urgent message, a conciliation which stands for the atonement, the being-at-one, of man and God" (106).

43. For a feminist critique of Steinberg's influential study that takes more fully into account the role of lactating, generative or procreative, and bleeding women in these representations of Christ's sexuality, see chapter 3, "The Body of Christ in the Late Middle Ages: A Reply to Leo Steinberg," in Caroline Walker Bynum's *Fragmentation and Redemption: Essays on Gender and the Human Body in Medieval Religion*.

44. According to Breton's manifesto, there are three categories of "convulsive beauty": the "veiled-erotic, fixed-explosive, magical-circumstantial" (quoted in Foster 23). I focus on the surrealist concern with mobility and temporality suggested by the second category, which "involves an 'expiration of motion'" (Bréton, quoted in Foster 25).

45. Terry Eagleton argues that the economic vacillation between mobility and immobility is a relentlessly aesthetic project. M. Keith Booker usefully summarizes Eagleton's reading of the Kantian "beautiful" and the "sublime": "The beautiful, Eagleton suggests, supports the imaginary identification, shoring up the subject and giving it the confidence it needs to compete in a free market, whereas the sublime performs a humbling function, reminding the subject that, free or not, there are limits that are not to be crossed. This double movement is for Eagleton essential to the ideology of bourgeois society: 'For one problem of all humanist ideology is how its centering and consoling of the subject is to be made compatible with a certain essential reverence and submissiveness on the subject's part'" (85).

46. For a useful reading of Gilroy's rather gestural description of the "slave sublime," see Paul Anderson's "Ellington, Rap Music, and Cultural Difference."

47. Two reviewers—one from the *Nation* and one from the *New York Times*—refer to Johnson as a hunted animal. See Arthur Danto's "Art of the Free and the Brave" and Roberta Smith's "Art in Review: Paul Pfeiffer."

48. If this depiction of Chinatown is intended to be absurd or ironic, the

choreography and editing of this sequence simply do not succeed. Any attempts to work against the colonial scene are undone by the crowding of orientalist symbols and sound, e.g., painted fans, flowers, Asian-sounding music, and faceless and voiceless Asians.

49. The extensive attention paid to a Ph.D. dissertation may seem odd, but Dallal's thesis is the most compelling study that I have found on American imperialism and aesthetics.

50. In an interview, Pfeiffer cites two cultural references for *Morning:* the British painter Francis Bacon, perhaps especially his series of screaming figures; and Noah's ark, hence the "morning after the complete annihilation of the world" *(Art 21).*

## 3. Why Filipinos Make Pun(s) of One Another

1. In recent years, Navarrete has enjoyed stunning popularity among wealthy, elite *Manileños* ("wannabe Americans," according to one former Navarrete fan), especially after he toured in the Philippines with the film *The Flip Side* (2002). Whereas in the United States his lowbrow comedy primarily is identified and reverberates with working-class and middle-class Filipino Americans, he clearly is developing a bifurcated audience. Some fans now seem disillusioned with these enormous class divisions in his fan base because they feel that the elite *Manileños* do not "get" his humor and are drawn to his miming of heavily accented, first-generation Filipino Americans because such caricatures shore up the *Manileño* desire to become (unmarked) Americans.

2. Though I do not have the space here, I also am interested in queer (i.e., drag queen and king) cultural practices of aggressive teasing and criticism, such as "reading" and "throwing shade." I more explicitly discuss their relevance in the next chapter on Filipino American gay male dramatic performance and writing.

3. In *Decolonizing the Filipino Psyche: Philippine Psychology in the Seventies,* Virgilio Enriquez quotes Elizabeth Ventura, who writes, "A reader of Philippine psychology literature will immediately note that the decade of the seventies was marked by a concern for indigenization, a recognition of language as a basic variable in personality, social psychology and testing, a broadening of the data base of Filipino psychology through a concern for studying individuals in their natural social settings, rediscovering of the ties of Filipino psychology with other fields of study, and a greater involvement, on a nation-wide level, of Filipino social scientists in the developments of the literature of Filipino psychology. . . . Along with the recognition of the importance of languages came a consciousness of the limitations and sometimes emptiness of Western theories and methods" (4).

4. See introductory chapter to Karen Shimakawa's *National Abjection.*

5. In her chapter "Fraternal Devotions: Carlos Bulosan and the Sexual Politics of America," Rachel Lee addresses this inversion of—or counterpart to—the

predominant exclusion/immigrant paradigm in Asian American studies in *The Americas of Asian American Literature: Gendered Fictions of Nation and Transnation*.

6. Vicente Rafael refers to Anderson's characterization of Philippine history as "vertiginous" in *White Love and Other Events in Filipino History*.

7. More recently, of course, American imperial amnesia about the Philippines has changed, especially since the American declaration of war on Iraq in 2003. While the Philippine-American War and the American colonization of the Philippines (among other peoples and nations within and without North America) essentially has been eradicated from dominant narratives of American history, the George W. Bush administration released several official statements attempting to recuperate and rewrite the colonial regime in the Philippines as an example of the successful dissemination and realization of American democratic principles in the global arena. Enthusiastically abetting this revisionism, the Macapagal administration in turn appropriated the rhetoric of the "global war on terror" to bolster its own campaign against a variety of long-standing armed movements within the Philippines and to secure the continued flow of American advisers and funding. Consequently, the Philippine congressional resolutions to end U.S. neocolonial exploitation and dependency—resulting in the 1991 closure of massive U.S. military bases such as Clark and Subic—gradually have been rolled back, most noticeably with the illegal arrival of American troops and agents in the southern Philippines.

8. By "rhetoric of bilateralism," I refer to the way American neo/colonialism in the Philippines is rewritten as foreign policy, a game of diplomacy with participants of equal footing.

9. Here, I refer to Werner Sollors's distinction in his study *Beyond Ethnicity: Consent and Descent in American Culture* between vertical lines of "descent" and horizontal lines of "consent," a difference invoked when describing the United States as a land of opportunity for immigrants regardless of class status. In *Racial Formation in the United States: From the 1960s to the 1990s*, Howard Winant and Michael Omi point out how the promise of "consent" depends upon the elision of racial difference (67).

10. Fred Cordova's *Filipinos: Forgotten Asian Americans* is a groundbreaking account of Filipino American history.

11. In an informal conversation about racial mixture and racial ambiguity among Filipinos, Christy Carillo, a friend of mine who is a Filipino American from North Carolina, settled all these identity issues quite effectively and efficiently by observing, "Either you are Filipino or you're not."

12. For further discussion of the impact of Flor Contemplacion's trial and execution, see also Vicente Rafael's chapter "Your Grief Is Our Gossip: Overseas Filipinos and Other Spectral Presences" in his *White Love and Other Events in Filipino History*.

13. I am dissatisfied with both scholarly and everyday practices of identifying the Philippines as "home" or "homeland" and everywhere else as the "diaspora." The problem is embedded in the etymology of "diaspora," which comes from *spora*—"seeds"—that are scattered around the world. This model privileges men and heterosexuality and also sets up a too strict and calcified relation between the idea of home and place; in other words, between the signifier and signified. While this may be interpreted as an argument against indigenous claims and worldviews, this is not at all my intention. Rather, I want to expose and disrupt the hierarchy of authenticity between Filipinos and Filipino Americans. What if, as Vicente Diaz asks, Guam is home? (And, frankly, I think that, given Guam's status as a U.S. territory, this is a different question from someone who would ask, say, what if California is home?) That is to say, supposedly universal questions of home, identity, and place in the world interact with—and are transformed by—local conditions and histories in ways that in turn affect the "homeland." And this is doubly so for the Filipino diaspora (I need to use the term; there is no other for now) and the Philippine economy, extremely vulnerable as it is—even iconic—of the workings of globalization, militarization, mass migration within and without the Philippines, and neocolonialism. See, for example, Rhacel Parreñas's *Servants of Globalization*.

14. Indeed, the very number of letters in the Filipino alphabet—which has varied from 20 to 31 to 28—is no settled matter.

15. For the Filipino American context, one could also coin the phrase *sikolo-hiyang Filipina America,* deliberately choosing *f* (instead of *p*) and feminizing the nation ("Filipina" instead of "Filipino"). One would do so to emphasize the heterogeneity of Filipino languages and accents; for example, the letter *f* does exist in some accents and languages.

16. For a discussion of Internet *p* and *f* debates, see Emily Noelle Ignacio's "*Pilipino ka ba?* Internet Discussions in the Filipino Community."

17. In *Jokes and Their Relation to the Unconscious* Freud writes, "A joke is thus a double-dealing rascal who serves two masters at once" (190).

18. See Vicente Diaz, "Fight Boys, 'til the Last . . .': Islandstyle Football and the Remasculinization of Indigeneity in the Militarized American Pacific Islands."

19. I am grateful to Hiram Pérez for pointing out the etymological connection between the words "public" and "pubic," which share the Greek root word *pubes*. Both etymologically and politically, the public sphere is conceived of as an exclusively male domain. In this chapter, I am interested in how a Filipino American performer like Rex Navarrete capitalizes on and contests the historically homophobic, sexist, and Eurocentric cultural arena of stand-up comedy.

20. See Navarrete's Web animation "Maritess vs. The Superfriends," http://www.rexnavarrete.com/soundsandsights/maritess.surf; and Parreñas, *Servants of Globalization*.

21. The reference in the heading is to the nationalist historian Renato Constantino's influential pamphlet "The Miseducation of the Filipino."

22. In *Pasyon and Revolution,* Reynaldo Ileto describes different examples of guerrilla warfare against the Spanish, e.g., elite *mestizo* strategies in urban settings versus peasant uprisings in rural settings.

23. Ileto cites the example of Philippine-American War veterans interviewed in the 1960s–1970s who kept attributing torture and violence from the American war to the Japanese. Ileto points out the basic fact that, because Japan lost, there was a liberation phase for people to remember the horrors. But in the case of the Philippine-American War, of course, America won.

24. See below for a more detailed account of the emergence of the indigenization movement in the 1970s in the Philippine academe. Motivated by leftist, anticolonial nationalism, this multidisciplinary group of scholars generally sought to reconceive and transform the object, objective, and methodology of scholarship in and about the Philippines.

25. Generally speaking, many Filipinos describe—with admiration—those who speak Tagalog, without any Spanish or English references or idioms, as fluent in "deep" Tagalog. Note the use of the adjective "deep" as opposed to, say, "pure."

26. For example, Strobel's methodology in this eight-participant study is grounded in the "Filipino core values of *pakikiramdam* (shared perception) and *pakikipagkapwa-tao* (shared identity)" (64).

27. See Mendoza, especially chapter 5, "Re-Narrating the Filipino Nation: Theory Revision and the Project of Indigenization," for an overview of the indigenization movement that blossomed in the Philippines in the 1970s. Along with her survey of the movement's theoretical and political interventions, Mendoza notes that Marcos's declaration of martial law, including travel restrictions, inadvertently fostered leftist scholars' sense of collectivity and intellectual growth. Thus, though this enforced isolationism during the Marcos regime was intended to contain and control intellectual and artistic expression, the less porous national boundaries led to important concepts like *papaloob* ("inwards") and, generally, to the development of an interdisciplinary, self-reflective, and oppositional critique of Anglo or colonial biases in academe (Mendoza 49).

## 4. *"He will not always say what you would have him say"*

1. After completing dual bachelor's degrees in music and theater at Oberlin College (where he was in the same cohort with Bill Irwin) and a master's degree in theater at New York University, Nicky Paraiso worked with Meredith Monk for about a decade, and he has been affiliated with La MaMa Experimental Theatre Club for about three decades, where he now works as a curator. In 1988

Paraiso wrote and performed in *20th Century Blues* at La MaMa, putting on what he calls a "Las Vegas–style cabaret" and an "Olympic song marathon" backed by a full band and three singers, in which he sang "thirty songs in ninety minutes." In his *Village Voice* review of *House/Boy,* the poet–journalist Luis Francia dubbed *House/Boy* a "cabaret memoir"; and Paraiso says that longtime friend and fellow artist Jessica Hagedorn calls him the "Joel Grey of Tondo" (interview). Paraiso also was a member of *Kambal sa Lusog* (Pilipinas Lesbians, Bisexuals, and Gays for Progress), an organization founded in New York City in the late 1980s and an important site of Filipino American cultural and political activism during the height of the HIV/AIDS crisis and epidemic. To date there has been no sustained attempt to document Paraiso's extensive body of work, at least partially because of a general marginalization of performance art and other forms of "alternative theater" that create what Theodore Shank calls "a new cultural movement outside the dominant culture" (quoted in Esther Kim Lee 110). In *Performing Asian America: Race and Ethnicity on the Contemporary Stage,* Josephine Lee points out that the politics of publishing has hindered the development of Asian American dramatic literature, or perhaps more accurately has obfuscated the history of that development; she notes that "the traditional relationships between playwright and theatrical company, which encourage a 'finished' playscript—detachable from its initial performance venue and marketed to individual readers and theaters for re-production—do not allow for a more probing investigation of performances such as the many one-actor pieces by Asian Americans such as 'Charlie' Chin, Amy Hill, Nobuko Miyamoto, Lane Nishikawa, Jude Narita, Nicky Paraiso, Canyon Sam, and Denise Uyehara" (25). In scholarship on Asian American theater that mentions Paraiso, his work typically is cited briefly as an instance of such marginalization. For example, in *A History of Asian American Theatre,* Esther Kim Lee refers to Paraiso in a chapter section titled "Performance art, multimedia theatre, and alternative theatre" (110). In dissertations, published essays, and forthcoming monographs, critics like Theodore Gonzalves and Lucy Burns are addressing and filling in these tremendous gaps in the scholarship on Asian American "alternative theater." Publishers like Kaya Press (www.kaya.com) must be applauded for their commitment to one-actor publications; for example, in 2004 Kaya published Denise Uyehara's *Maps of City and Body: Shedding Light on the Performances of Denise Uyehara.* Personal interview, July 15, 2005.

2. In his ethnographic fieldwork with Filipino gay men whose "discourses and behavior have presented a persistent performative view of the world," Martin Manalansan argues that performance is "part of citizenship" (15). Insisting on the "primacy of the everyday" in his study of the "dramaturgy of Filipino gay men's lives," Manalansan wants to make less distinct the boundaries between everyday, quotidian performance and staged performance, arguing that performance is "not only a matter of just 'acting,' but rather is about the aesthetics of Filipino gay men's struggles for survival" (16).

3. The title and themes of *House/Boy* reference the history of male Filipino domestic labor in the United States. In her groundbreaking study *Creating Masculinity in Los Angeles's Little Manila: Working-Class Filipinos and Popular Culture, 1920s–1950s*, Linda España-Maram notes that during this period of intense overt racism (and racialized sexism) against Filipino men who had few employment options before them, domestic and service work as "houseboys" and "fountain pen boys" was an important alternative to the highly unstable world of migratory seasonal labor in canneries and farms. So while early Filipino immigrant labor usually (and rightly) is associated with fish processing and fruit picking, España-Maram points out that immigrant men (and women) also found jobs in the service profession, which offered a more stable life even as they often worked extremely long hours; and, like their counterparts in the fields and canneries, labor exploitation was a regular feature of their lives. Jobs as "houseboys" in private homes made it more possible for these immigrant men to continue to go to school and to keep up with their studies, their lives made up of "work, school and wages" (España-Maram 25). In the early 1930s, my maternal grandfather, Pastor Echavez, obtained a college degree in the United States by working as a "houseboy" in Kansas; his employer was a former president of Silliman University, which was founded in Dumaguete, Negros Oriental, in the Philippines by American Presbyterian missionaries.

4. This and subsequent descriptions of the production and set are based on a November 2004 staging of *House/Boy* at La MaMa Experimental Theatre Club in New York City.

5. See also Martin Manalansan's discussion of New York City drag pageants in the chapter "'To Play with the World': The Pageantry of Identities" in his *Global Divas: Filipino Gay Men in the Diaspora*.

6. According to the playwright's notes in the script, a section of *House/Boy* "could be called 'Song for My Father'" (15).

7. Such declarations by Rodgers and Hammerstein explain the attraction as camp of musicals like *The King and I*. Also of interest in their *New York Times* article is the parallelism between the "strange union" of Anna and the king and that between the librettist and composer.

8. Briefly, the psychoanalytic concept of "working through"—*Durcharbeiten*—refers to the defense mechanisms and recovery process that result from the experience of trauma. I am thinking especially of Sigmund Freud's 1914 essay "Remembering, repeating and working-through (Further recommendations on the technique of psycho-analysis II)" (*SE*, 12: 145–56).

9. Note that Anna's whiteness crosses several national boundaries. The real Anna Leonowens, whose published memoirs were the source for Margaret Landon's 1943 novel, which in turn inspired the libretto for Rodgers and Hammerstein's musical, claimed that she was born in Wales. But she in fact was English, born and raised in India. Karen Manners Smith notes that Leonowens's memoirs are a "blend

of memory, folklore, and imaginative self-invention" (1060). Christina Klein points out that, in all versions, "although an Englishwoman, Anna is an Americanized figure who uses the politics and culture of the Civil War—Lincoln's struggle to free the slaves, Harriet Beecher Stowe's *Uncle Tom's Cabin*—as her frame of reference" (194–95).

10. Along with *South Pacific* (1949) and *Flower Drum Song* (1958), Rodgers and Hammerstein's *The King and I* completes the collaborators' trilogy of "Oriental musicals" (Klein 8). Sheng-mei Ma dubs them "'Chopsticks' musicals" (17). The musical version of *The King and I* opened in 1951 in New York City, and its script draws on several sources: a pair of published memoirs by Anna Leonowens, who worked as a teacher in the Siamese court in the 1860s and published *The English Governess at the Siamese Court* in 1870 and *The Romance of the Harem* in 1873, both of which are controversial for their fictionalized elements, historical errors, or contradictions; and Margaret Landon's 1943 *Anna and the King of Siam,* a reworking of Leonowens's memoirs. The 1956 movie version was directed by Walter Lang and swept the Oscars and box office records. It relied heavily on Rodgers and Hammerstein's script and less so on a 1945 film version *Anna and the King of Siam* directed by John Cromwell and on an 1853 travel memoir by Frederick Arthur Neale, an Englishman who visited Bangkok. See Christina Klein's *Cold War Orientalism: Asia in the Middlebrow Imagination, 1945–1961* for an account of the cultural work performed by the musical *The King and I* during the cold war as a representative example of the "pervasive sentimentalism of middlebrow depictions of Asia" and the rise of a "vision of interconnectedness" rather than enmity or difference between Asia and the West (15, 12); see especially 11–15 in the introduction and chapter 5, "Musicals and Modernization: *The King and I.*" In her explanation of the popularity of the musical in the 1950s, Klein also describes the emergence of Thailand as a staunch ally and a major recipient of U.S. aid.

11. I thank Jodi Kim and Maylei Blackwell for their questions about whether Paraiso affirms or poses a threat to queer neoliberalism. While I do not pursue further this line of inquiry in this chapter, I, in brief, would argue that Paraiso inverts the investment that neoliberalism has in privacy, property, and heteropatriarchal formulations of the domestic sphere, including the investment of queer liberalism in "petitioning the neoliberal state for rights and recognition before the law" (Eng with Halberstam and Muñoz 10), and I must gesture toward the important scholarship of Lisa Duggan, especially *The Twilight of Equality? Neoliberalism, Cultural Politics, and the Attack on Democracy,* and the special issue "What's Queer about Queer Studies Now?" of *Social Text,* edited by David Eng, Judith Halberstam, and José Muñoz.

12. Note, however, that the father's profession is not the same in the two productions of *House/Boy* in 2004 at La MaMa Experimental Theatre Club in New York City, both of which were directed by Ralph Peña. In the April–May run, the

father was a "Pullman porter for the New Haven Railroad," but in the November run the father worked as a registered nurse.

13. In *Immigrant Acts* Lisa Lowe points out that the narrative of generational conflict gets so much play in dominant American culture that histories of racism and material oppression are obscured (64). For a description of the ideological work performed by popular Asian American narratives of ethnicized conflict and resolution, see David Palumbo-Liu's chapter "Model Minority Discourse and the Course of Healing" in his study *Asian/American: Historical Crossings of a Racial Frontier.*

14. In his review of *House/Boy,* Luis Francia remarks that the term "houseboy" has "larger metaphorical significance, with implications of not being quite a man in a house (read: America) that won't quite accept him."

15. Note that the dissenting justices in *Downes v. Bidwell* point out the crucial contradiction of the decision, that a territory can be "domestic for one purpose and foreign for another."

16. Paul Kramer makes the important cautionary point that the tendency in the historiography of U.S.-Philippine relations to make analogies between domestic and transoceanic racial formations—for example, between U.S. policy toward Native Americans and that toward Filipinos—not only risks producing caricature rather than analysis of relations of power, but "reinforces rather than undermines the 'insularity' of Philippine-American history" (19). More specifically, in his account of the formation of the Bureau of Non-Christian Tribes in 1900 by the Philippine Commission during the Philippine-American War, Kramer notes that, although Secretary of War Elihu Root recommended that the commission adopt domestic U.S. models of "tribal governance," the bureau's first director, David Barrows (an anthropologist and political scientist who would go on to become an acting president of the University of California, one of many positions in an extraordinarily varied colonial administrative, higher education, and military career), eventually recommended against the adoption of "Indian policy" in the Philippines after a six-month tour of Native American reservations and educational institutions (212–14). For a critique of the use of such analogies in the historiography of the U.S. empire, see Kramer's distinction between and discussion of what he calls the "historiography of 'export' or 'projection'" and the "colonial discourse" approach (19–20) as part of his larger project on race, U.S. empire, and the "politics of recognition," which denotes "relations of power ... defined not by the hegemon's outright political exclusion of the less powerful but by its ability to establish and adjust standards or criteria for inclusion" (18). On the other hand, Dean Saranillio importantly emphasizes instances of linkages between coeval anti-American resistance movements in his research on U.S. colonialism, racism, and Hawai'i statehood, citing, for example, correspondence between the Cherokee Nation and Queen Lili'uokalani and between Hawaiian nationalist Robert Wilcox and Filipino nationalist Emilio Aguinaldo.

17. In his account of the "Philippine-American War as Race War," Paul Kramer shows how the American construction of a colonial state in the Philippines involved major shifts and innovations in race theory that would enable the transition from war to colonial governance: "New political circumstances called especially for different visions of race. As one expression of its expertise, the civilian leadership had developed a new vision of Filipinos, casting them not as a 'savage' bloc to be routed and suppressed as a whole but as a divided population of 'little brown brothers' deserving of American benevolence and tutelage. This new vision required dispensing officially with the exclusionary and exterminist racism to which at least some Americans remained prone but that was incompatible with the success of collaboration [with Filipino elites]. It meant developing an inclusionary racial formation built on interlocking metaphors of family, evolution, and tutelary assimilation" (226).

18. I use the phrase "permanently unincorporated" here to make an analogy between the political and economic hierarchies within a household and those within the U.S. empire (such as the past and present existence of incorporated and nonincorporated territories, organized and unorganized territories, states, and occupied nations).

19. I am interested in Freud's description of multiple causes of an "inhibition" (or a "symptom") and the various responses to that "inhibition" or "symptom" because this is a nonlinear conceptualization of causality or "multiple-channeled motivation." Note that the definition of "determinism" or "overdetermination" is that of an "object-choice [that] might satisfy a multiplicity of instincts."

## Conclusion

1. Not surprisingly, in a personal conversation/interview Estrada expressed her admiration for the sculptor Eva Hesse, who famously chose to work with material like latex because she knew it would deteriorate.

2. I am paraphrasing ideas from Mary Douglas's influential study *Purity and Danger: An Analysis of the Concepts of Pollution and Taboo.*

3. For an excellent compilation of these images, see Abe Ignacio's *The Forbidden Book: The Philippine-American War in Political Cartoons.*

4. Personal interview with the artist August 18, 2006.

5. For a summary of the relationship between the state and the arts—especially from the perspective of activist artists—from the 1960s to the late 1990s, see Grant Kester's edited volume *Art, Activism, and Oppositionality.*

6. In his introduction to *Art, Activism, and Oppositionality,* Kester offers a powerful reclamation of the idea of the aesthetic from the vantage of activist art, which, he argues, has the four following potentialities and capabilities: (1) the artist has the capacity to describe, identify, and exceed the totality of systems of power;

(2) activist art implicates the viewer; (3) the aesthetic has transgressive power that exceeds the current system of domination and, thus, envisions an alternate and better future; (4) disseminating icons of parasitism, e.g., the Black single mother and the Latino immigrant, and the icons of elite amorality, e.g., angry feminists and the liberal elite, the Republican right successfully channeled white working class and lower-middle-class anger and despair and displaced it onto communities of color, and progressive artists have the training and are in the perfect position to produce counterimages.

# BIBLIOGRAPHY

Abraham, Nicolas, and Maria Torok. 1986. *The Wolf Man's Magic Word: A Cryptonymy.* Minneapolis: University of Minnesota Press.

Alejo, Albert. 2000. *Generating Energies in Mount Apo: Cultural Politics in a Contested Environment.* Quezon City, Philippines: ADMU Press.

Alidio, Kimberly Ann. 1999. "'When I Get Home, I Want to Forget': Memory and Amnesia in the Occupied Philippines, 1901–1904." *Social Text* 17, no. 2: 105–22.

Ancheta, Angelo. 2006. "Filipino Americans, Foreigner Discrimination, and the Lines of Racial Sovereignty." In *Positively No Filipinos Allowed: Building Communities and Discourse,* ed. Antonio Tiongson Jr. et al. 90–107. Philadelphia, Pa.: Temple University Press.

Anderson, Laurie. 2001. Interview. *Art 21: Art in the Twenty-first Century.* Season 1. Videodocumentary, director Susan Sollins.

Anderson, Paul A. 1995. "Ellington, Rap Music, and Cultural Difference." *Musical Quarterly* 79 (1): 172–206.

Appadurai, Arjun. 1986. "Introduction: Commodities and the Politics of Value." In *The Social Life of Things: Commodities in Cultural Perspective,* ed. Arjun Appadurai, 3–63. New York: Cambridge University Press, 1997.

Babuscio, Jack. 2004. "Camp and the Gay Sensibility." In *Queer Cinema: The Film Reader,* ed. Harry Benshoff and Sean Griffin, 121–36. New York: Routledge.

Bal, Mieke. 1996. *Double Exposures: The Subject of Cultural Analysis.* New York: Routledge.

———. 1997. *Narratology: Introduction to the Theory of Narrative.* 2nd ed. Buffalo, N.Y.: University of Toronto Press.

Balce-Cortes, Nerissa. 2002. "Savagery and Docility: Filipinos and the Language of the American Empire after 1898." Ph.D. dissertation, University of California, Berkeley.

Baldwin, Simeon. 1899. "The Constitutional Question Incident to the Acquisition and Government by the United States of Island Territory." *Harvard Law Review* 12 (6): 393–416.

Barlow, Anne. 2002. "Circle as Cycle." *Afterimage* 29 (5): 12.

Baxandall, Michael. 1988. *Painting and Experience in Fifteenth-Century Italy: A Primer in the Social History of Pictorial Style.* 2nd ed. New York: Oxford University Press.

Berger, John. 1977. *Ways of Seeing.* New York: Penguin.

Besemer, Linda. 2005. "Abstraction: Politics and Possibilities." *X-TRA* 7 (3): 14–23.

Bilder, Mary Sarah. 2004. *The Transatlantic Constitution: Colonial Legal Culture and the Empire.* Cambridge, Mass.: Harvard University Press.

Blumentritt, Mia. 1998. "Bontoc Eulogy, History, and the Craft of Memory: An Extended Conversation with Marlon E. Fuentes." *Amerasia Journal* 24 (3): 75–90.

Booker, M. Keith. 1996. *A Practical Introduction to Literary Theory and Criticism.* White Plains, N.Y.: Longman.

Borum, Jenifer P. 1994. "Manuel Ocampo: Annina Nosei Gallery." *Artforum International* 33, no. 2: 102.

Bright, Susan. 1999. "Manuel Ocampo." *Art Asia Pacific* 22: 95.

Burns, Lucy Mae San Pablo. 2004. "Community Acts: Locating Pilipino-American Theater and Performance." Ph.D. dissertation, University of Massachusetts, Amherst.

Butler, Judith. 1997. *The Psychic Life of Power: Theories in Subjection.* Stanford, Calif.: Stanford University Press.

Bynum, Carolyn Walker. 1991. *Fragmentation and Redemption: Essays on Gender and the Human Body in Medieval Religion.* Cambridge, Mass.: MIT Press.

Campomanes, Oscar. 1995. "The New Empire's Forgetful and Forgotten Citizens: Unrepresentability and Unassimilability in Filipino-American Postcolonialities." *Critical Mass* 2 (2): 145–200.

Carson, Anne. 1995. "The Gender of Sound." In *Glass, Irony and God.* New York: New Directions, 119–42.

Casocot, Ian Rosales. 2007. "Cultural Awakening in Dumaguete." *Inquirer.* May 20. http://showbizandstyle.inquirer.net/lifestyle/lifestyle/view_article.php?article_id=67047. Accessed January 27, 2008.

Castro, Christi-Ann. 2001. "Music, Politics, and the Nation at the Cultural Center of the Philippines." Ph.D. dissertation, University of California, Los Angeles.

———. 2004. Public lecture. University of Michigan, Ann Arbor. June 24.

Chattopadhyay, Collette. 1999. "At Home and Abroad: Contemporary Filipino Views." *Art Asia Pacific* 22: 20–22.

Cheng, Anne. 2001. *The Melancholy of Race.* New York: Oxford University Press.

*Cherokee Nation v. Georgia.* 1831. 30, U.S. 1. U.S. Supreme Court. Online Lexis-Nexis Academic, February 22, 2007.

Chiang, Mark. 2006. "Autonomy and Representation: Aesthetics and the Crisis of

Asian American Cultural Politics in the Controversy over *Blu's Hanging.*" In *Literary Gestures: The Aesthetics in Asian American Writing,* ed. Rocío Davis and Sue-Im Lee. Philadelphia, Pa.: Temple University Press.

———. 1998. "Trans/National Crossings of Asian America: Nationalism and Globalisation in Asian American Cultural Studies." Ph.D. dissertation, University of California, Berkeley.

Choy, Catherine Ceniza. 2000. "Asian American History: Reflections on Imperialism, Immigration, and 'The Body.'" *Amerasia Journal* 26 (1): 119–40.

Chuh, Kandice. 2003. *Imagine Otherwise: On Asian Americanist Critique.* Durham, N.C.: Duke University Press.

Cleage, Pearl. 1993. "Hairpiece." *African American Review* 27 (1): 37–41.

Clifford, James. 2001. "Indigenous Articulations." *The Contemporary Pacific* 13 (2): 468–90.

Colás, Santiago. 1992. "The Third World in Jameson's *Postmodernism, or the Cultural Logic of Late Capitalism.*" *Social Text* 31/32: 258–70.

Constantino, Renato. 1982. *The Miseducation of the Filipino.* Quezon City, Philippines: Foundation for Nationalist Studies.

Cordova, Fred. 1983. *Filipinos: Forgotten Asian Americans, a Pictorial Essay, 1763–circa 1963.* Dubuque, Iowa: Kendall/Hunt.

Coxhead, Gabriel. 2004. "Paul Pfeiffer: *The Morning after the Deluge.*" *Contemporary Magazine* 60. http://www.contemporary-magazines.com/reviews60_3.htm. Accessed June 9, 2009.

Crary, Jonathan. 1990. *Techniques of the Observer: On Vision and Modernity in the Nineteenth Century.* Cambridge, Mass.: MIT Press.

Crimp, Douglas. 1989. "Mourning and Militancy." *October* 51: 3–18.

Curiger, Bice. 2002. *"Aus der Schiene gekippt: Erzählen und Erinnern als Fallen der Wahrnehmung."* In *Sammlung Ackermans.* Dusseldorf: Hatje Cantz Verlag, 73–85.

Dallal, Jenine. 2001. "American Imperialism UnManifest: Emerson's 'Inquest' and Cultural Regeneration." *American Literature* 73 (1): 47–83.

———. 1996. "The Beauty of Imperialism: Emerson, Melville, Flaubert, and Al-Shidyaq." Ph.D. dissertation, Harvard University.

Danto, Arthur. 2000. "Art of the Free and the Brave." *The Nation* 270 (18) (May 8): 45–49.

Davis, Angela Y. 1996. "Afro-Images: Politics, Fashion, and Nostalgia." In *Names We Call Home: Autobiography on Racial Identity,* ed. Becky Thompson and Sangeeta Tyagi. New York: Routledge.

Delmendo, Sharon. 2004. *The Star-Entangled Banner: One Hundred Years of America in the Philippines.* New Brunswick, N.J.: Rutgers University Press.

Diaz, Vicente. 2002. "'Fight Boys, 'til the Last . . .': Islandstyle Football and the Remasculinization of Indigeneity in the Militarized American Pacific Islands." In *Pacific Diaspora: Island Peoples in the United States and across the Pacific,* ed. Paul

Spickard, Joanne Rondilla, and Deborah Hippolyte Wright. Honolulu: University of Hawaii.

———. *Moving Islands.* Unpublished manuscript.

Doka, Kenneth J. 1989. *Disenfranchised Grief: Recognizing Hidden Sorrow.* Lexington, Mass.: Lexington.

Doss, Erika. 2002. *Twentieth-Century American Art.* Oxford, UK: Oxford University Press.

Douglas, Mary. 1966. *Purity and Danger: An Analysis of Concepts of Pollution and Taboo.* New York: Praeger.

*Downes v. Bidwell.* 182 U.S. 244. No. 507. U.S. Supreme Court. 1901. Online Lexis-Nexis Academic, February 22, 2007.

Duggan, Lisa. 2003. *The Twilight of Equality? Neoliberalism, Cultural Politics, and the Attack on Democracy.* Boston, Mass.: Beacon Press.

Duncan, Michael. 1993. "Manuel Ocampo at Salander-O'Reilly/Fred Hoffman." *Art in America* 81 (11): 137–38.

Eng, David. 2001. *Racial Castration: Managing Masculinity in Asian America.* Durham, N.C.: Duke University Press.

Eng, David, Judith Halberstam, and José Muñoz, eds. 2005. "Introduction: What's Queer about Queer Studies Now?" *Social Text* 23 (3–4): 1–17.

Eng, David, and David Kazanjian, eds. 2003. *Loss: The Politics of Mourning.* Berkeley and Los Angeles: University of California Press.

Enriquez, Virgilio. 1982. *Decolonizing the Filipino Psyche: Philippine Psychology in the Seventies.* Quezon City, Philippines: Philippine Psychology Research House.

———. 1992. *From Colonial to Liberation Psychology: The Philippine Experience.* Diliman, Quezon City: University of the Philippines Press.

España-Maram, Linda. 2006. *Creating Masculinity in Los Angeles's Little Manila: Working-Class Filipinos and Popular Culture, 1920s–1950s.* New York: Columbia University Press.

Estrada, Reanne Agustin. 2006. "About the Work." Artist's statement. July.

Fanon, Frantz. 1968. *Black Skin, White Masks,* trans. Charles Lam Markmann. New York: Grove Press.

Fischer, Sibylle. 2004–2005. "Interview with Gina Ulysse." *Bomb: Art and Culture Interviews* (Winter): 72.

Foster, Hal. 1993. *Compulsive Beauty.* Cambridge, Mass.: MIT Press.

Francia, Luis. 2001. *Eye of the Fish.* New York: Kaya.

———. 2004. "Homebody/Queens: A House Is Not a Home in Nicky Paraiso's Cabaret Memoir." *Village Voice* April 27. Accessed February 2, 2007. http://www.villagevoice.com/theater/0418,francia,53181,11.html.

Francis, Jacqueline. *Race-ing Modernism: Malvin Gray Johnson, Yasuo Kuniyoshi, Max Weber, and Racial Art in America.* Unpublished manuscript.

Fraser, Peter. 1998. *Images of the Passion: The Sacramental Mode in Film.* Westport, Conn.: Praeger.

Freud, Sigmund. 1927. "Fetishism." In *Standard Edition of the Complete Psychological Works of Sigmund Freud*. Vol. 21, 147–58. London: Hogarth Press, 1953.

———. 1905. *Jokes and Their Relation to the Unconscious*, trans. James Strachey. New York: Norton, 1963.

———. 1922. "Medusa's Head." In *Sexuality and the Psychology of Love*, 212–13. New York: Collier-Macmillan, 1963.

———. 1917. "Mourning and Melancholia." *General Psychological Theory: Theories on Paranoia, Masochism, Repression, Melancholia, the Unconscious, the Libido, and Other Aspects of the Human Psyche*. New York: Collier-Macmillan, 1963.

———. 1914. "Remembering, repeating and working-through (Further recommendations on the technique of psycho-analysis II)." In *Standard Edition*. Vol. 12, 145–56. London: Hogarth Press, 1953.

Friis-Hansen, Dana. 1998. "Adrift in the Pacific." In *At Home and Abroad: 20 Contemporary Filipino Artists*, ed. Dana Friis-Hansen, Alice Guillermo, and Jeff Baysa, 17–31. San Francisco, Calif.: Asian Art Museum of San Francisco.

Fujikane, Candace. 2000. "Sweeping Racism under the Rug of 'Censorship': The Controversy over Lois-Ann Yamanaka's *Blu's Hanging*." *Amerasia* 26 (2): 158.

Gamalinda, Eric. 2002. "English Is Your Mother Tongue /Ang Ingles Ay Ang Tongue Ina Mo." In *Vestiges of War: The Philippine-American War and the Aftermath of an Imperial Dream, 1899–1999*, eds. Angel Shaw and Luis Francia. New York: New York University Press, 247–59.

Gilroy, Paul. 1993. *The Black Atlantic: Modernity and Double Consciousness*. Cambridge, Mass.: Harvard University Press.

———. 2004. *Postcolonial Melancholia*. New York: Columbia University Press.

Goldberg, David. 2001. "Refresh: the Art of the Screen Saver" at the Cantor Center for the Arts, Stanford University. *Artweek* 32 (January 1): 14–15.

Gonzalez, Jennifer. 2003. "Paul Pfeiffer." *Bomb* 83: 22–29.

Gonzalves, Theodore. 2001. "When the Lights Go Down: Performing in the Filipino Diaspora, 1934–1998." Ph.D. dissertation, University of California, Irvine.

*Gothic and Renaissance Art in Nuremberg 1300–1550*. 1986. New York: Metropolitan Museum of Art.

Grayson, Deborah. 1995. "Is It Fake? Black Women's Hair as Spectacle and Spec(tac)ular." *Camera Obscura* 36: 13–31.

Greenberg, Clement. 1940. "Towards a Newer Laocoon." In *Art in Theory, 1900–2000: An Anthology of Changing Ideas*, 2nd ed. Ed. Charles Harrison and Paul Wood, 562–68. Malden, Mass.: Blackwell, 2003.

Guillermo, Alice G. 1998. "Filipino Art at the Centennial of the Revolution and into the Twenty-first Century." In *At Home and Abroad: 20 Contemporary Filipino Artists*, ed. Dana Friis-Hansen, Alice Guillermo, and Jeff Baysa, 33–43. San Francisco, Calif.: Asian Art Museum of San Francisco.

Hagedorn, Jessica. 1991. *Dogeaters*. New York: Penguin.

Halagao, Avelino Jr. 1998. "Citizens Denied: A Critical Examination of the Rabang

Decision Rejecting United States Citizenship Claims by Persons Born in the Philippines during the Territorial Period." *UCLA Asian Pacific American Law Journal* 5: 77–98.

Hall, Calvin. 1954. *A Primer of Freudian Psychology.* New York: New American Library, 1979.

Haraway, Donna. 1993. "Teddy Bear Patriarchy: Taxidermy in the Garden of Eden, New York City, 1908–1936." In *Cultures of United States Imperialism,* ed. Amy Kaplan and Donald Pease, 237–91. Durham, N.C.: Duke University Press.

Harrison, Charles. 2003. "Modernism." In *Critical Terms for Art History,* 2nd ed., ed. Robert Nelson and Richard Shiff, 188–201. Chicago: University of Chicago Press.

Heartney, Eleanor. 1999. "Archipelago and Diaspora." *Art in America* 87 (9): 64–67.

Hebron, Micol. 2005. "Artspeak: Meditations on Medium." *X-TRA* 7 (3): 24–25.

Hertz, Neil. 1983. "Medusa's Head: Male Hysteria under Political Pressure." *Representations* 4: 27–54.

Ho, Christopher H. 2003. "'Paul Pfeiffer': MIT List Visual Arts Center." *Modern Painters* 16 (2): 125.

Ignacio, Abe, et al., eds., 2004. *The Forbidden Book: The Philippine-American War in Political Cartoons.* San Francisco, Calif.: T'Boli.

Ignacio, Emily Noelle. 2003. "Laughter in the Rain: Jokes as Membership and Resistance." In *AsianAmerica.Net: Ethnicity, Nationalism, and Cyberspace,* ed. Rachel Lee and Sau-ling Wong, 158–76. New York: Routledge.

———. 2002. "*Pilipino ka ba?* Internet Discussions in the Filipino Community." In *Contemporary Asian American Communities: Intersections and Divergences,* eds. Linda Trinh Vo and Rick Bonus. Philadelphia, Pa.: Temple University Press.

Ileto, Reynaldo. 1979. *Pasyon and Revolution: Popular Movements in the Philippines, 1840–1910.* Quezon City, Philippines: Ateneo de Manila University.

———. 2002. "The Philippine-American War: Friendship and Forgetting." In *Vestiges of War: The Philippine-American War and the Aftermath of an Imperial Dream, 1899–1999,* eds. Angel Shaw and Luis Francia, 3–21. New York: New York University Press.

Isaac, Allan. 2006. *American Tropics: Articulating Filipino America.* Minneapolis: University of Minnesota Press.

James, Jamie. 1999. "This Hawaii Is Not for Tourists." *Atlantic Monthly* 283 (2): 90+.

James, William. 1899. "Governor Roosevelt's Oration." *Boston Evening Transcript,* April 15, 9.

Johnson, Liza. 2000. *Fernweh: The Opposite of Homesick.* Video.

Jones, Gayl. 1975. *Corregidora.* New York: Random House.

Kaplan, Amy. 2002. *The Anarchy of Empire in the Making of U.S. Culture.* Cambridge, Mass.: Harvard University Press.

Kaplan, Amy, and Donald Pease, eds., 1993. *Cultures of United States Imperialism.* Durham, N.C.: Duke University Press.

Kee, Joan. 2001. "Processes of Erasure: Paul Pfeiffer's Narratives of Global Art." *Art Asia Pacific* 32: 64–69.

Keizer, Arlene. 2004. *Black Subjects: Identity Formation in the Contemporary Narrative of Slavery.* Ithaca, N.Y.: Cornell University Press.

Kester, Grant H. 1998. "Ongoing Negotiations: *Afterimage* and the Analysis of Activist Art." In *Art, Activism, and Oppositionality: Essays from* Afterimage, ed. Grant Kester, 1–19. Durham, N.C.: Duke University Press.

Kingston, Maxine Hong. 1976. *The Woman Warrior: Memoirs of a Girlhood among Ghosts.* New York: Vintage, 1989.

Klein, Christina. 2003. *Cold War Orientalism: Asia in the Middlebrow Imagination, 1945–1961.* Berkeley: University of California Press.

Koelbl, Alois, and Johannes Rauchenberger. 2004. "'A Void That Looks back at You . . .': Paul Pfeiffer im Gespraech mit Alois Koelbl und Johannes Rauchenberger." *Kunst und Kirche* 2: 70–77.

Koh, Karlyn. 2004. "At the Edge of a Shattered Mirror, Community?" In *Asian North American Identities: Beyond the Hyphen,* eds. Eleanor Ty and Donald Goellnicht, 149–69. Bloomington and Indianapolis: Indiana University Press.

Kramer, Paul. 2006. *The Blood of Government: Race, Empire, the United States, and the Philippines.* Chapel Hill: University of North Carolina Press.

Latham, R. E. 1965. *Revised Medieval Latin Word-List: From British and Irish Sources.* London and New York: Oxford University Press, 1980.

Laurence, Michael. 1991. "Manuel Ocampo at Christopher John." *Art in America* 79 (1): 143.

Lee, Esther Kim. 2006. *A History of Asian American Theatre.* New York: Cambridge University Press.

Lee, Josephine. 1997. *Performing Asian America: Race and Ethnicity on the Contemporary Stage.* Philadelphia, Pa.: Temple University Press.

Lee, Rachel. 1999. *The Americas of Asian American Literature. Gendered Fictions of Nation and Transnation.* Princeton, N.J.: Princeton University Press.

Leffingwell, Edward. 2001. "Manuel Ocampo at Jack Shainman." *Art in America* 89 (2): 138.

Legasto, Priscelina Patajo. 1992. "The Pasyon Pilapil: An-'other' Reading." In *Women Reading . . . Feminist Perspectives on Philippine Literary Texts,* ed. Thelma Kintanar, 71–89. Quezon City, Philippines: University Center for Women's Studies.

Leveen, Lois. 1996. "Only When I Laugh: Textual Dynamics of Ethnic Jokes." *MELUS* 21, no. 4: 29–55.

Limon, John. 2000. *Stand-up Comedy in Theory, or, Abjection in America.* Durham, N.C., and London: Duke University Press.

Lionnet, Françoise. 1989. *Autobiographical Voices: Race, Gender, and Self-Portraiture.* Ithaca, N.Y.: Cornell University Press.

Lloren, Jason W. "Rex Navarrete: Filipino American Comedian." SFGate.com, June 23, 2002.

Lowe, Lisa. 1996. *Immigrant Acts: On Asian American Cultural Politics.* Durham, N.C.: Duke University Press.

Lowe, Lisa, and David Lloyd, eds. 1997. *The Politics of Culture in the Shadow of Capital.* Durham, N.C.: Duke University Press.

Lukacher, Brian. 2002. "Landscape Art and Romantic Nationalism in Germany and America." In *Nineteenth-century Art: A Critical History,* eds. Steven F. Eisenman et al., 143–59. London and New York: Thames and Hudson.

Ma, Sheng-mei. 2003. "Rodgers and Hammerstein's 'Chopsticks' Musicals." *Literature/Film Quarterly* 31 (1): 17–26.

Manalansan, Martin. 2003. *Global Divas: Filipino Gay Men in the Diaspora.* Durham, N.C.: Duke University Press.

Mendoza, S. Lily. 2002. *Between the Homeland and the Diaspora: The Politics of Theorizing Filipino and Filipino American Identities: A Second Look at the Poststructuralism-Indigenization Debates.* New York: Routledge.

Mercer, Kobena. 1994. *Welcome to the Jungle: New Positions in Black Cultural Studies.* New York: Routledge.

Mitchell, Timothy. 1990. *Passional Culture: Emotion, Religion, and Society in Southern Spain.* Philadelphia: University of Pennsylvania Press.

Molina-Azurin, Arnold. 1988. Review of Reynaldo Ileto's *Pasyon and Revolution: Popular Movements in the Philippines, 1840–1910. Philippine Daily Inquirer,* July 1.

Molon, Dominic, and Jane Farver, eds., 2003. *Paul Pfeiffer.* Chicago: Museum of Contemporary Art.

Muñoz, José Esteban. 1999. *Disidentifications: Queers of Color and the Performance of Politics.* Minneapolis: University of Minnesota Press.

Navarrete, Rex. 2006. *Badass Madapaka.* DVD.

———. *Badly Browned.* CD.

———. 2003. *Hella Pinoy: A Live Comedy Concert.* DVD.

———. 1999. *Husky Boy.* CD.

———. 2002. "Maritess vs. the Superfriends." Web animation. http://www.rexnavarrete.com/soundsandsights/maritess.swf.

Nehring, Cristina. 2005. "Love Hurts." *New York Times Book Review,* February 13, 8–9.

Ngai, Mae M. 2002. "From Colonial Subject to Undesirable Alien: Filipino Migration, Exclusion, and Repatriation, 1920–1940." In *Re/collecting Early Asian America: Essays in Cultural History,* ed. Josephine Lee et al., 111–26. Philadelphia, Pa.: Temple University Press.

Nunokawa, Jeff. 1991. "'All the Sad Young Men': AIDS and the Work of Mourning." In *Inside/Out: Lesbian Theories, Gay Theories,* ed. Diana Fuss. New York: Routledge.

Ocampo, Ambeth R. 2001. *Bones of Contention: The Bonifacio Lectures.* Manila: Anvil.

Ocampo, Manuel. 2005. Interview. "Manuel Ocampo: Sheer Art Attack." *Giant Robot* 39: 62–70, 80.

Okawa, Gail. 1997. "Resistance and Reclamation: Hawaii 'Pidgin English' and Autoethnography in the Short Stories of Darrell H.Y. Lum." In *Ethnicity and American Short Story,* ed. Julie Brown. New York: Garland.

Omi, Michael, and Howard Winant. 1994. *Racial Formation in the United States: From the 1960s to the 1990s.* 2nd ed. New York: Routledge.

Ong, Aihwa. 1999. *Flexible Citizenship: The Cultural Logics of Transnationality.* Durham, N.C.: Duke University Press.

Palumbo-Liu, David. 1999. *Asian/American: Historical Crossings of a Racial Frontier.* Stanford, Calif.: Stanford University Press.

Panofsky, Erwin. 1995. *The Life and Art of Albrecht Dürer.* Princeton, N.J.: Princeton University Press.

Paraiso, Nicky. *House/Boy.* Unpublished script.

Parikh, Crystal. 2002. "Blue Hawaii: Asian Hawaiian Cultural Production and Racial Melancholia." *Journal of Asian American Studies* 5 (3): 199–217.

Parreñas, Rhacel. 2001. *Servants of Globalization: Women, Migration, and Domestic Work.* Stanford, Calif.: Stanford University Press.

Pérez, Hiram. 2002. "On the Tip of Our Tongue: Topographies of Race and Forgetting in the Americas." Ph.D. dissertation, Columbia University, N.Y.

Pfeiffer, Paul. 2001–2. "A Conversation with Paul Pfeiffer." Interview with Stefano Basilico. *Documents* 21: 30–43.

———. 2001. "*Quod Nomen Mihi Est?* Excerpts from a Conversation with Satan." In *Vestiges of War: The Philippine-American War and the Aftermath of an Imperial Dream, 1899–1999,* ed. Angel Shaw and Luis Francia, 278–89. New York: New York University Press.

———. 2003. Interview. *Art 21: Art in the Twenty-first Century.* Season 2. Video documentary, director Susan Sollins.

———. 2004. "'A Void That Looks Back at You . . .': Paul Pfeiffer im Gespräch mit Alois Kölbl und Johannes Rauchenberger." *Kunst und Kirche* 2: 70–77.

Pfeiffer, Paul, with Valeria Liebermann, Stefano Basilico, and Thomas Ruff. 2003. *Paul Pfeiffer.* Chicago, Ill.: Museum of Contemporary Art.

Pisares, Elizabeth. 1999. "Daly City Is My Nation: Race, Imperialism, and the Claiming of Pinay/Pinoy Identities in Filipino American Culture." Ph.D. dissertation, University of California, Berkeley.

Pohl, Frances K. 2002. "Black and White in America." In *Nineteenth-Century Art: A Critical History,* ed. Steven F. Eisenman et al., 179–203. London and New York: Thames and Hudson.

————. 2002. "Old World, New World: The Encounter of Cultures on the American Frontier." In *Nineteenth-Century Art: A Critical History,* ed. Steven F. Eisenman et al., 160–78. London and New York: Thames and Hudson.

Pollack, Barbara. 2001. "Back to the Future with 'BitStreams.'" *Art in America* 89 (9): 60–63.

Pouchelle, Marie-Christine. 1990. *The Body and Surgery in the Middle Ages.* Trans. Rosemary Morris. New Brunswick, N.J.: Rutgers University Press.

Pratt, Mary Louise. 1992. *Imperial Eyes: Travel Writing and Transculturation.* New York: Routledge.

Price, Polly J. 1997. "Natural Law and Birthright Citizenship in *Calvin's Case* (1608)." *Yale Journal of Law and the Humanities* 9: 73–145.

Prince, Mark. 2003. "Feint Art." *Art Monthly* 267: 1–5.

*Rabang v. INS.* 1994. No. 91-16125. U.S. Court of Appeals for the Ninth Circuit. September 20.

Rafael, Vicente. 1993. *Contracting Colonialism: Translation and Christian Conversion in Tagalog Society under Early Spanish Society.* Durham, N.C.: Duke University Press.

Rafael, Vicente, ed. 1995. *Discrepant Histories: Translocal Essays on Filipino Cultures.* Philadelphia, Pa.: Temple University Press.

————. 2000. *White Love and Other Events in Filipino History.* Durham, N.C.: Duke University Press.

Reust, Hans Rudolf. 2002. *"Körper und Geister."* In *Sammlung Ackermans,* 57–71. Dusseldorf: Hatje Cantz Verlag.

Richard, Frances. 2001. "Paul Pfeiffer: The Project." *Artforum International* 39 (7, March): 143–44.

Roach, Joseph. 1996. *Cities of the Dead: Circum-Atlantic Performance.* New York: Columbia University Press.

Rodgers, Richard, and Oscar Hammerstein II. 1951. "About 'The King and I.'" *New York Times,* March 25, sec. 2: 1, 3.

————. 1995. *The King and I. Six Plays by Rodgers and Hammerstein.* New York: Random.

Rodrigues, Darlene. 2000. "Imagining Ourselves: Reflections on the Controversy over Lois-Ann Yamanaka's *Blu's Hanging.*" *Amerasia* 26 (2): 195.

Rodriguez, Phillip, director, 1998. *God Is My Copilot.* Videodocumentary.

Román, David, and Holly Hughes. 1998. "*O Solo Homo:* An Introductory Conversation." In *O Solo Homo: The New Queer Solo Performance,* ed. David Roman and Holly Hughes. New York: Grove.

Rosenberg, Karen. 2008. "Paul Pfeiffer." *NewYorkMetro.com.* http://www.newyork metro.com/nymetro/arts/art/10259. Accessed January 27, 2008.

Rowe, John Carlos. 2000. *Literary Culture and U.S. Imperialism: From the Revolution to World War II.* New York: Oxford University Press.

Rush, Michael. 2000. "New Media Rampant." *Art in America* 88 (7, July): 41.

Russell, Catherine. 1999. *Experimental Ethnography: The Work of Film in the Age of Video.* Durham, N.C.: Duke University Press.

Said, Edward. 1993. *Culture and Imperialism.* New York: Knopf.

Saranillio, Dean Itsuji. 2007. "Visualizing Settler Nation Narrations: Hawai'i State-hood at the Intersections of U.S. Racism, Settler Colonialism and Empire." Dissertation prospectus, University of Michigan, Ann Arbor.

Scarborough, James. 1994. "Manuel Ocampo: One-Man National Movement." *Flash Art* 27 (176, May/June): 84–85.

Scarry, Elaine. 1987. *The Body in Pain: The Unmaking and Making of the World.* New York: Oxford University Press.

Schueller, Malini. 1998. *U.S. Orientalisms: Race, Nation, and Gender in Literature, 1790–1890.* Ann Arbor: University of Michigan Press.

See, Sarita. 1998. "Trying Whiteness: Media Representations of the 1996 Okinawa Rape Trial." *Hitting Critical Mass: A Journal of Asian American Cultural Criticism* 5 (2): 57–78.

Sengupta, Somini. 1999. "An Author Who Gathers Prizes and Protests." *New York Times,* February 8: E1.

Shaw, Angel Velasco. 2007. *Stay the Course.* Videodocumentary.

Shimakawa, Karen. 2002. *National Abjection: The Asian American Body Onstage.* Durham, N.C.: Duke University Press.

Shohat, Ella, and Robert Stam. 1994. *Unthinking Eurocentrisim: Multiculturalism and the Media.* New York: Routledge.

Siegel, Katy. 2000. "Paul Pfeiffer." *Artforum International* 38 (10, Summer): 174–75.

Silverman, Kaja. 1992. *Male Subjectivity at the Margins.* New York: Routledge.

Singhal, Daniel Joseph. 1987. "Towards a Definition of American Modernism." *American Quarterly* 39 (1): 7–26.

Smith, Karen Manners. 2000. Review of *Anna and the King. American Historical Review* 105 (3): 1060.

Smith, Roberta. 2000. "Art in Review: Paul Pfeiffer." December 15, sec. E: 41.

Sollors, Werner. 1986. *Beyond Ethnicity: Consent and Descent in American Culture.* New York: Oxford University Press.

Steinberg, Leo. 1996. *The Sexuality of Christ in Renaissance Art and Modern Oblivion.* Chicago: University of Chicago Press.

Strobel, Leny Mendoza. 1997. "Coming Full Circle: Narratives of Decolonization among Post-1965 Filipino Americans." In *Filipino Americans: Transformation and Identity,* ed. Maria P. P. Root. Thousand Oaks, Calif.: Sage.

Su, Karen. 1999. "Translating Mother Tongues: Amy Tan and Maxine Hong Kingston on Ethnographic Authority." In *Feminist Fields: Ethnographic Insights,* ed. Sally Cole et al., 33–50. Peterborough, Ontario: Broadview Press.

Sullivan, Nikki. 2003. *A Critical Introduction to Queer Theory.* New York: New York University Press.

Suzuki, Erin. 2006. "Consuming Desires: Melancholia and Consumption in *Blu's Hanging.*" *MELUS* 31 (1): 35–54.

Tiongson, Antonio T. Jr. 2006. "On Filipinos, Filipino Americans, and U.S. Imperialism: Interview with Oscar V. Campomanes." In *Positively No Filipinos Allowed: Building Communities and Discourse,* ed. Antonio Tiongson Jr. et al., 26–42. Philadelphia, Pa.: Temple University Press.

Tolentino, Rolando. 2002. "Identity and Difference in 'Filipino/a American' Media Arts." In *Screening Asian Americans,* ed. Peter Feng, 111–32. New Brunswick, N.J.: Rutgers University Press.

Trinh T. Minh-ha. 2000. "Speaking Nearby." Interview with Nancy Chen. In *Feminism and Film,* ed. E. Ann Kaplan. New York: Oxford University Press.

Turner, Grady T. 2004. "Dust in the Desert: 9th Cairo Biennale." *Flash Art* 37 (235): 41.

Uyehara, Denise. 2004. *Maps of City and Body: Shedding Light on the Performances of Denise Uyehara.* New York: Kaya Press.

Velez, Pedro. 2005. "Looking Good: Interplay at Museo de Arte de Puerto Rico." *Artnet* January 31. http://www.artnet.com/magazine/reviews/velez/velez6-12-03.asp#2. Accessed January 27, 2008.

Vergara, Benito. 1995. *Displaying Filipinos: Photography and Colonialism in Early Twentieth-Century Philippines.* Diliman, Quezon City: University of the Philippines Press.

White, Hayden. 1987. *The Content of the Form: Narrative Discourse and Historical Representation.* Baltimore, Md.: Johns Hopkins University Press.

Wilson, Megan. 2007. Review of "Worlds in Collision 2." http://www.stretcher.org/archives/r9_a/WIC_mw.php. Accessed March 17.

Wong, Sau-ling. 1993. *Reading Asian American Literature: From Necessity to Extravagance.* Princeton, N.J.: Princeton University Press.

Yamamoto, Traise. 1999. *Masking Selves, Making Subjects: Japanese American Women, Identity, and the Body.* Berkeley: University of California Press.

Zellen, Jody. 2002. "Paul Pfeiffer: UCLA Hammer Museum." *Art Press* 276: 72–73.

# INDEX

Abraham, Nicolas, 84

abstract expressionism, 164n.40

abstraction, xxiii, xxiv, xxv–xxvi, 163n.34, 164n.40; of beauty, 57; of Estrada, 128, 129; identity politics of, 129, 138–40, 141; inward or centripetal forces of, of American nineteenth-century imperialism, 65, 66; of Pfeiffer, 128, 129; political repressiveness of contemporary art theories of, 66; political violence enacted by, 67; relation to the real, xxv–xxvi; as strategy of indirection, 128–29

accent pun, 78, 79–81

acquisition, xv, xx, xxi, 64

activist art, 129–30, 139–40, 174n.6

Adiarte, Patrick, 122

Adobe Photoshop, 46, 53

aesthetic(s): of American imperialism, 45, 46, 65–66, 127–28; camp, 138; expansionist, 54–55, 64–67; hegemonic notion of, 139; minimalist, of Estrada, 128; politics of Pfeiffer's, 44, 45; return of (repressed), 62–67;

from the vantage of activist art, 139–40, 174n.6

African American slave narratives, 33

African American studies, 13, 149n.16

agency: Internet joke acts as agential, 76; masking and, 154n.19; rhetorical concealment of American imperial, xxi, 64; spatialized erasure of, 64; subjectivity and, 14, 34, 153n.17

aggression: aggressive language, 71, 166n.2; jokes and, 71, 76–78; social bonding and, 76, 79; stereotypes of Filipino men and, 88; unowned, 8

Aguinaldo, Emilio, 11, 173n.16

*Airport Music* (Ong and Hagedorn), xiii

Alejo, Albert, xiii

Ali, Muhammad, 159n.10

Alidio, Kimberly Ann, xxvii, 148n.12, 150n.2

alphabet, Filipino, 149n.15, 168n.14

Alumit, Noel, xiv

Amerasian children of American military servicemen and Filipinas, 92

Americanist studies of empire, xxviii–xxix

SARITA ECHAVEZ SEE is associate professor of Asian/Pacific Islander American studies at the University of Michigan, Ann Arbor.

All royalties earned from the sale of this book will be donated to the Filipino American Coalition for Environmental Solidarity, http://www.facessolidarity.org. FACES works in solidarity with communities in the United States and in the Philippines for transnational environmental justice through advocacy, education, service, and organizing.